A GODDESS IS A GIRL'S BEST FRIEND

A Divine Guide to Finding Love, Success, and Happiness

LAURIE SUE BROCKWAY

A Perigee Book

A Perigee Book
Published by The Berkley Publishing Group
A division of Penguin Putnam Inc.
375 Hudson Street
New York, New York 10014

First edition: December 2002

Visit our website at www.penguinputnam.com

Library of Congress Cataloging-in-Publication Data

Brockway, Laurie Sue.
A goddess is a girl's best friend : a divine guide to finding love, success,
and happiness/Laurie Sue Brockway.
p.   cm.
Includes bibliographical references and index.
ISBN 0-399-52826-1
1. Single women—Psychology—Miscellanea.   2. Single women—
Conduct of life.   3. Goddesses.   4. Mythology.   I. Title.

HQ800.2 .B756 2002
646.7'0086'52—dc21   2002017075

10   9   8   7   6   5   4   3

I dedicate this book to my mom, Shirley,
a feminine force to be reckoned with

and

to my beloved Avi,
my partner, consort and best friend.

CONTENTS

ACKNOWLEDGMENTS

I begin where it all began . . . with a thank-you to my dear friend and agent, Arielle Ford, who was there from the start and who helped me nurture a germ of an idea, and a deep sense of mission, into a book. And to her wonderful hubby and partner, Brian Hilliard, who has offered his wisdom, encouragement, love and warmth from the very start of our relationship.

This book was made real by the vision, courage and enthusiasm of my smart, savvy, thirty-something editor, Jennifer Repo, who recognized that this book could really help women in their twenties and thirties have more love, success and happiness and who encouraged me to craft it. Along with her dedication, terrific editing suggestions and support, I have been doubly blessed to have the support and the joy of knowing her twenty-something assistant, Christel Winkler, whose excitement and keen insights have helped shape this book. Both have made sure this book reflects the interests of their generation.

I have to thank some of those who have played a pivotal role on my path of the goddess:

Patricia Kennealy-Morrison, for reaching out a hand in the darkness and inviting me onto the goddess path years ago; Barbara Biziou, for being the Ritual Queen in our crowd, generously sharing her ritual work and encouraging me to create women's circles; Rabbi Joseph Gelberman and The New Seminary, for generously teaching me how to celebrate life through all religions and for opening my spiritual eyes to recognize the divine in all forms and by all names; Rev. Jeannie Weyrick of World Light Fellowship, for helping me trust that the goddesses are as real and alive as all the other spiritual masters whose energy we call upon for help and guidance; Connie Silver of The Crossroads Lyceum/Fellowship of Isis for helping me to see the goddess is part of all life, and for her gentle and loving encouragement; and to Amy Sophia Marashinsky and Hrana Janto, for their extraordinary creation, *The Goddess Oracle,* a collection of fifty-two goddesses in word and images that made a huge impact on me when I was in seminary school. Their loving portrayal of so many aspects of female divinity set me on a path to find out all I could about the divine feminine in all traditions.

To my book goddess girlfriends: I have learned so much from all of you, and I am so grateful for you all: Shelley Ackerman, Laura Day, Laura Norman and Judith Orloff, M.D. And to all those in the original Media Goddess group and those I came to serve afterward . . . you rock, goddess girlfriends!

There are many people whose work has touched me deeply and who've inspired my point of view. I would like to thank Dr. Rose McAloon, Dr. Patti Britton, Deepak Chopra, Barbara Glabman Cohen, Martin Cohen, Richard Cohn, Emmanuel, Robert Fritz, Theodore A. Hagg, Roberta Herzog, Daphne Rose Kingma, the late Carol Maracle, Charles and Caroline Muir and Pat Rodegast.

To my mother, Shirley Ruth Brockway, who *is* the great goddess and who instilled in me the notion that women are as powerful, capable and independent as they choose to be.

And to my sister Rikki Rosenberg, mother of eight, for being the ultimate loving and compassionate mother goddess. And my sister Nikki Fiske, my spiritual cohort, who has inspired me by her strength and courage.

To my son, Alexander Kent Garrett, a most loving and sensitive boy, who constantly inspires me with his heart, soul and courage. I am so lucky to have a son with such an awesome spirit!

To my beloved, Rev. Vic (Avi) Fuhrman, who is the temple gatekeeper of the goddesses, the hero I have always longed for and the partner I wished and prayed for for so long. His support of me on my mission to educate about the goddess cannot be measured in words or praise. I thank him for all he contributed to me, to Alex and to this book.

And I thank the Goddess, who always gives me what I need and often gives me what I want. The flame of the feminine divine has burned brightly within me, and I am grateful to have been privy to an amazing journey of discovering our heritage as daughters of the divine female.

And so it is. Thank you.

Young Girl Tells Her First Secret to Venus

EVERY GIRL NEEDS A GODDESS TO CALL HER OWN

"Women need images that validate their femininity, their sensu-ousness, and their mysterious magic, and that reveal the sacred dimension of their own gender. It's only natural that the goddess should have special significance for women, who long to know, too, that they are made in divine image."

—Jalaja Bonheim, *Goddess: A Celebration in Art and Literature*

In my twenties and thirties, I could so clearly see the divin-ity in men, yet had so much difficulty connecting to my own divine nature. Guys always seemed larger than life; more important, more powerful and more *connected* to the universe. It took me a long time to figure out I'd been trained by our culture to perceive divinity and power as exclusively male dominions; thus human men—even the worst ones!—seemed like Gods. *Who even knew there was a Goddess?* Di-vinity did not seem to be a chick thing.

As a little girl, when I asked the inevitable *Who is God?* question, my parents told me, "God is a man in the sky with a long beard." I seem to remember hearing something about Him looking down to keep an eye on us, and running our lives from "up there." Over time, that concept was confirmed to me by images of male divinity that pervade our culture. So it made sense that I grew up with the impression that Godli-ness was a *guy thing*, and that men were above me. As I got older, feistier, more self-possessed, I felt disconnected from religion and "God," because I felt excluded. I had the impression that the only route to a heavenly connection was if I believed in the "man in the sky with a long beard." Even though I craved some sort of spirituality in my life, I just could not relate to the idea that someone who looked like a grandfather was pulling all the strings and deciding my fate.

Since no one around my house ever suggested I connect with the "Goddess" or "Goddess within," I stumbled onto her (as many women do) when I began to search deeply for my own spiritual roots as a path to personal power, a sense of worth and self-expression. I never even realized that what I was searching for was an image of divinity that reflected back my own true power, worthiness and divine nature.

It wasn't until I attended a seminary, where I trained and was ordained as an interfaith minister, that I discovered how imbalanced my childhood image of God truly was. I was so happy—and relieved!—when I came to understand that in this universe dwells divine power that is both male and female in nature . . . that right along with God is God*dess* . . . that in reality, you can't have one without the other.

What I found along the way of both my personal and professional journey compels me now to make her more accessible to young women who are seeking their own unique path to success, happiness and peace in life. It is my belief that we can all use a bit of divine intervention and support in our lives, and that some of us will find our spirituality a bit more accessible if we can call upon divine beings of feminine form—with curves, and hips and even a touch of lipstick.

Youth is a time of searching for a stronger sense of self, a greater understanding and expression of our power and for our place in the world. Career, money, men, our mothers, our friends, our co-workers and our roommates are often on the front burner of our lives. We are hungry to meet the right people, get into the right places, find the right job, get the perfect place to live and meet the most amazing lovers. It is a time of evolution, and of struggling to birth our own true selves; a time of beginning to define our personal passions, dislikes and values. Many women come to these evolutionary years with a sense of confusion, disconnection and lack of direction—a need for a clearer sense of identity. There is a constant struggle between the new ideas we have about the way we want to live and the little voice in our head that plays messages that say we have no right to seek power in the world on our own terms. At this stage of life, a woman wants guidance, but she resents intrusion; she wants support, yet may not quite find the right role model or mentor.

Women have a natural, primal and ancestral connection to the Divine Feminine; knowing how to access that vital link can help us with just about anything. But many just don't realize it. Raised in a culture that easily gives goddess-like stature to women of astounding beauty and sexuality, those who do not fit the physical ideal are often left to feel unworthy. We grow up with uneven images of feminine divinity, or no concept of goddess at all—unlike men, who are raised with both religious and cultural role models for male divinity and power.

The road to *becoming a woman to be reckoned with* offers an extraordinary journey to those who dare . . . yet it requires us to tap into a deeper well of self-worth, strength and an internal power that many of us have barely glimpsed. Women who make their mark in this world share an important trait—they have learned how to access their own true power. While some women have gone about it the way men tackle the world, there are others who have mastered the art of tapping into the goddess within.

How do they do it? They live their lives from a state of entitlement akin to the consciousness of a goddess; it empowers them to feel worthy and destined for success, and hence, they create magnificent lives based on their personal, self-fulfilling prophecy of divine entitlement! Madonna . . . Julia Roberts . . . Jennifer Lopez . . . Venus Williams . . . Oprah . . . all in their own unique way, modern goddesses. Each seems to embody a different element of the feminine divine that calls forth her own true power, and gives her a clear sense of place in the world.

Many young women dream of creating lives of their own making and living them joyously and without apology. We all need role models and there are thousands of goddesses, from so many of the world's cultures, known by different names and images, which represented feminine aspects of divinity and also aspects of our humanity. They're wild and mild, powerful and soft, compassionate and passionate; they're virgins and queens, mothers and daughters, rulers of the universe who can transform the planet, nurse a baby and love their consorts simultaneously. Their images, energy and just the mere concept of female divinity can heal us, empower us, instruct us and help us find our way on life's rocky path. There are many awesome archetypes and mythic women who can be meaningful role models because that they look like us and have traits we want to emulate—and stories that we, as women, can relate to. They give us permission to be all we can be . . . and to be goddesses in our own right.

When I first began to get to know the goddess, I was afraid that I had to "worship" *only* a *She God* and practice a spirituality that excluded men. I soon enough discovered that this was untrue. Getting to know the goddess is an inside job and it does not require that you "worship her" per se or go to a temple to hang out with her. It doesn't mean you forfeit your religion of birth or ditch your beliefs about the male divine. And it is important to note that you don't even have to be "religious" to consider that the creative force in this universe that instills us all with spirit that includes both male and female energies. It simply requires that you open your mind to the awareness and inclusion of the divine feminine. For example: salt and pepper . . . soup and sandwich . . . god and goddess. You *can* have one without the other, but our lives and our world are more balanced with both!

Having been raised in a traditional religious culture, you may find it almost hard to believe that there were so many goddesses—not only in world mythology, but actively worshipped in the world's religions and traditions. Consider it this way: Picture a disco ball. The ball is The Big, Huge, All-Encompassing Spirit of Everything and the facets are the many aspects and faces of gods and goddesses by many names. We all come from one source—the big disco ball—but there are many aspects of that source to inspire, empower and reflect our divine nature right back to us.

Doesn't it make sense to consider that, if we are all created in the image of The Divine, that the Divine is created in many images? And that if divine nature is what gives us all life, and every breath we breathe, that divinity is also within us?

From Eve, the mother of us all, to Oya, the Yoruban goddess of change, this book explores thirty-one awesome archetypes who embody or represent abilities, traits and empowerment in various aspects of our lives—such as work, money, love, romance, play and family relationships.

Most of the divine females in this book are considered goddesses in one tradition or another, but some are included because they are revered as mythical heroines or saints who can help us identify and call forth our own true power. Each chapter describes a situation you may deal with, and the specific goddess who can help and why; it includes a "bio" of the goddess and insight into her history and mythology, as well as offers spiritual and practical ways to evoke the energy she represents—through ritual, meditations, prayers, blessings, wish lists, daydreaming, fun and creative exercises and activities. There are many suggestions on "how to invite her into your life." The variety is designed to give you many options to follow the guidance that feels most appropriate for you. In these pages we will explore:

+ The importance of divine role models for women

+ How to work with the essence and energy of the goddess in everyday life

+ How to boost confidence and self-esteem by embodying, emulating, embracing and harnessing the goddesses featured in the book

+ Etiquette for inviting a deity into your life

+ Learning how to celebrate the goddess not instead of, but in addition to, the god

+ Cosmic Correction: *God is a woman, too,* and within each woman lives a goddess

To get started, take the fun Goddess IQ Test to see how much you know about these divine figures. It's a simple quiz, and you might learn some great facts about the role goddesses have played in our history.

The female divine is a fabulous role model for women today. She's got powers in the world, and she is connected to all that is. She's got attitude, and she's got presence. The goddess rocks. She does things her way. She is the source of her own power; and in conjunction with the creative force in the universe that makes things happen, we are, too.

Blessings,
Rev. Laurie Sue Brockway
New York City

TEST YOUR GODDESS IQ

Goddesses are in our consciousness more than we realize. They are casually referred to and spoken of constantly in our contemporary culture; their images and stories have sunken into our brains. Before you turn the pages to meet the awesome archetypes of *A Goddess Is a Girl's Best Friend,* test your goddess IQ.

1. Cleopatra was the most famous Egyptian pharaoh, legendary for her love affairs with Julius Caesar and Marc Anthony and her attempt to rule the world via partnership with each. In ancient Egypt, all rulers identified themselves as gods and goddesses in human form. Which goddess was Cleopatra's guiding light?

A. *Nut*   C. *Isis*

B. *Hathor*   D. *Maat*

2. Who is the Greek goddess of war and wisdom who was born out of her father's head?

A. *Artemis*   C. *Athena*

B. *Hera*   D. *Hestia*

3. Which of these divine females were born, as fully formed women, from the womb of the sea?

A. *Lakshmi, Hindu goddess of fortune and beauty*
B. *Venus, Roman goddess of love and beauty*
C. *Aphrodite, Greek goddess of love and beauty*
D. *All of the above*

4. Who is the mother goddess who searches the earth for her beloved daughter, Persephone, who has been captured by the ultimate bad boy, Hades?

> A. *Gaia*   C. *Astarte*
> B. *Demeter*   D. *Tamuz*

5. Which goddess is friend to the Dalai Lama, Richard Gere and many other famous Buddhists who evoke her in Tibetan chants? She shares a name in common with a famous place in a classic movie.

> A. *Tara*   C. *Joy Luck*
> B. *Eve*   D. *Crouching Dragon*

6. Although the Jewish religion does not practice the personification of God, the tradition of mystical Judaism has long identified the feminine nature of God as an "indwelling presence." What is her name?

> A. *Sarah*   C. *Shekinah*
> B. *Sophia*   D. *Rebecca*

7. Jewish mysticism also believes that Adam had a first wife, before Eve, who huffed out of the Garden of Eden one day and was later demonized as a wicked *femme fatale*. Some consider her to be a powerful bitch goddess who owns her own life and takes charge! Female rockers named a huge music festival after her. Who is she?

> A. *Sarah*   C. *Ruth*
> B. *Beth Sheba*   D. *Lilith*

8. Many ancient cultures had temple priestesses who were considered "sacred prostitutes." It was their role to initiate men to the goddess through lovemaking. This was a fully accepted rite of passage. Who was the Sumerian goddess the sacred prostitutes prayed to?

> A. *Inanna*   C. *Venus*
> B. *Aphrodite*   D. *All of the above*

9. One of the earliest and most famous images of the goddess depicts her as a rotund and curvy female. Her pendulous breasts represent the hills and mountains; her big belly is the rich and fecund earth. What is the name of this goddess whose statue dates back about 20,000 to 30,000 years?

A. *Venus on a Half Shell* C. *Gaia*
B. *Mother Earth* D. *Venus of Willendorf*

10. Who is the most famous Hawaiian goddess? Her legend comes to life on Hawaii's Big Island, where it is said she lives in an active volcano.

A. *Haumea* C. *Maui*
B. *Laka* D. *Pele*

11. The first goddess of the Hindu Pantheon was birthed by the collective energy of the male gods to fight a mighty Buffalo Demon the guy gods could not destroy alone. She is pictured with eight arms, wielding weapons and one lotus flower, and she usually rides a tiger. What is her name?

A. *Lakshmi* C. *Parvati*
B. *Saraswati* D. *Durga*

12. Using tiny boats launched from the shores, Brazilian women make offerings of food and flowers to a beloved Yoruban ocean goddess who they credit with helping them heal their lives. By what name is she known?

A. *Oshun* C. *Oya*
B. *Seala* D. *Yemaya*

13. When searching for inspiration, the ancient Celts prayed to this red-haired triple goddess of poetry, blacksmithing and brides. She was later adapted as a Catholic saint.

A. *Dana* C. *Guinevere*
B. *Cerridwen* D. *Brigid*

14. What is the Greek name for the goddess whose image graces everything from courthouse reliefs to the business cards of lawyers? She is often seen delicately balancing the scales of justice.

  A. *Grace, goddess of justice*
  B. *Fortuna, goddess of justice*
  C. *Themis, goddess of justice*
  D. *Juno, goddess of justice*

15. Goddesses are showing up on T-shirts, lunch boxes and skirts. Which victory goddess has a successful line of sports apparel named after her?

  A. *Puma*   C. *Nike*
  B. *Adidas*   D. *Keds*

THE ANSWERS:

1. C. Isis
2. C. Athena
3. D. All of the above
4. B. Demeter
5. A. Tara
6. C. Shekinah
7. D. Lilith
8. A. Inanna
9. D. Venus of Willendorf
10. D. Pele
11. D. Durga
12. D. Yemaya
13. D. Brigid (a.k.a. St. Brigit)
14. C. Themis, goddess of justice
15. C. Nike

SCORING:

✛ If you got all 15 questions right, you are a "goddess expert."

✛ If you got up to 10 correct, you have a great "goddess awareness."

✛ If you got five or fewer questions correct, it's time to read on and expand your "goddess consciousness."

Part One

RECLAIMING EVE

RECLAIMING EVE

"The Bible began with a powerful acknowledgment of the dual nature of the Source of Being. But by chapter two of Genesis, Elohim was thought of as singular and male. When Eve did not obey 'Him,' she was cursed with male domination. And the divine feminine shared Eve's fate. Eve's story marked the end of the reign of the Queen of Heaven. . . ."

—Miki Raver, *Listen to Her Voice*

I'm no biblical scholar, but I think Eve got a bum rap. Or, as the popular T-shirt tells the story, "Eve was framed." Although she should be exalted and honored for her role as the first woman on earth, the Mother of Us All, she has been vilified for succumbing to temptation and looked upon as a role model for all that women *should not be;* making matters worse, she's been portrayed as poster girl for female subservience and *proof* that women are the lesser of men.

She is our first link to the Divine Feminine in human form, yet her tale is riddled with fear-based messages that have long made women afraid of their own curiosity, power and self-expression. Was she *really* such a *bad girl?* Or has she just been victim of some of the worst negative spin-doctoring in human history? I vote for the latter.

What's Eve Got to Do with Us?

The stern interpretation of Eve's role in Genesis tells us that women are servants, at best companions—not equal partners—to men, and that women who are curious and disobey male authority and ideology bring bad karma to their families. They wreak havoc on marriage, turn out dysfunctional children and are, in general, seductresses who cannot be trusted around men! As if messing up her own life isn't bad enough, Eve is blamed for the entire fall of the human race, thus, making the planet a living hell for the rest of us.

The version of Adam and Eve that has been droned into our brains since birth leaves most of us with the impression that something *very nasty* happened in the Garden of Eden, and it was all Eve's fault. That blame, shame and underlying fear of retribution has, unfortunately, become ingrained in us even if we rarely, if ever, give it a conscious thought. Whether we know it or not, women come into the world fulfilling an ancient, unconscious agreement that we are not as good as men, not as worthy and certainly not as divine. This cultural socialization impacts us all in some way, on some level. As the daughters of Eve, we carry on her legacy.

Low self-esteem is a malady of epic proportions among women today. It's not Eve's *fault*—but it's related. How is it that any of us can treat ourselves, or allow anyone else to treat us, unkindly? Although some women demand the world treat them as divine females, most of us are taking our cue from Eve: No matter how successful or together we are, we spend our lifetimes struggling with issues related to owning our power and trying to access and remember our true divinity. So many of us, consciously and unconsciously, suffer from the "Eve problem."

"The story of Adam and Eve is buried deeply in the Western psyche, and in many ways it continues to influence the ways in which we relate to one another," says Rabbi David A. Cooper, in *God Is a Verb: Kabbalah and the Practice of*

Mystical Judaism. "The literal reading of the story suggests that Adam and Eve were the first humans and that Eve was an easy object of seduction. She quickly succumbed to the wily serpent. Not only did she eat the forbidden fruit, but also she rushed off to get her partner to do the same. For this act of 'disobedience,' she had been reviled throughout the centuries."

On some level we have bought into the belief that our foremother was weak and unworthy—and, thus, so are we. This is a syndrome that is distinctly female, and not at all a guy thing. Most men have always had the image of male divine to relate their own divinity to, and, typically, they grow up empowered to hunt, chase, achieve, be powerful and make strides in life without asking permission. "Self-esteem, or the valuing of oneself, is based on beliefs," says Carolyn M. Ball in *Claiming Your Self-Esteem.* "What we think or believe about ourselves is what determines self-esteem. When there is low self-esteem, there is a belief that '*I'm not good enough.*' Typical feelings associated with thoughts of '*not being good enough*' are hurt, anxiety, frustration, anger, and most often, shame."

The "Eve problem" sets us up for a difficult internal struggle, that because Eve was bad and deserved to suffer, all women are supposedly bad and deserve to suffer: *How can we possibly feel good about ourselves if we all came from her? How can we possibly connect to the divinity within us if we have no model of a God who looks like us? How can we have the courage to follow our curiosity, passions and dreams after what happened to Eve?*

Some people believe that these kinds of beliefs are so imbedded in our collective conscious and personal psyche that they become as much a part of our makeup as our DNA, passed along as cellular memory. "Each of us carries a message from our ancestors in every cell of our body," writes scientist Brian Sykes in *The Seven Daughters of Eve.* "It is in our DNA, the genetic material that is handed down from generation to generation. Within our DNA is written not only our history as individuals but the whole history of the human race." Generations and generations of women have carried within them the belief that they are not good, worthy or powerful—a belief sculpted into our cellular memory by the ancient myth that the first woman was *no good*. By the same token, embedded within us is a different truth, a cellular memory perhaps, that Eve was not the evil, wicked, femme fatale who seduced her man and did us all in. If we can come to know Eve as the woman who was willing to go out on a limb to kick off the evolution of humanity and who initiated her man to knowledge (as women often do with their men), we can liberate ourselves from the story that the first woman was an embarrassment to humankind.

I believe we can reinterpret Eve and in doing so, reclaim the divine female that lives within us all. In this part, we will look at ways to de-vilify Eve, to redefine her and reinterpret her story in ways that empower women. For generations, women in general have been plagued by a small voice, an imaginary serpent that hisses in our ear: *"Who are you to be powerful, strong, capable, prosperous and successful?"* Time has come to put that hiss in its proper perspective, make the serpent recoil and transform its tune from negative self-talk to inspiration for success, spiritual development and personal evolution.

Reinterpreting the Story

In many ways, the story of Adam and Eve is a very romantic tale about soul mates. The idea of Eve being created from Adam's rib, from a part of him and being of one flesh with him, is the stuff of romantic fairy tales. She was given the chance every woman dreams of—to live in a heaven on earth with her honey and the protection of her father. And then, as our culture tells it, she *blew it* . . . because she disobeyed. Adam and Eve discovered that reality bites.

Eve is severely punished, and many other women in history follow in her footsteps. But what really was Eve's sin? She tried to seize a little knowledge beyond what was handed down to her as law by *her father* and she "initiated" *her husband.* Bucking authority is part of evolution. Stepping out of the box that people like to try to contain us in is how we grow. Pressing up against resistance and people who want to tell us who we are is how we find our power. Turning our men on to the new things we discover is part of being in a relationship. What Eve did was a natural part of human development.

In *Wrestling with Angels,* authors Naomi H. Rosenblatt and Joshua Horowitz point to the story of Adam and Eve as a metaphor for sexual awakening. They also suggest giving Eve a break for her role in initiating herself and her husband to the secrets of the forbidden fruit. They write, "Who can fault the woman for wanting to taste, to see, and to know good and evil? We all want to have our eyes opened to the unseen world, to know and understand what is hidden: *who's doing what with whom, why the sky is blue and our blood red, who will live and who will die?* Curiosity and imagination have kindled her hunger for knowledge."

Both the mystical schools of Islam (Sufism) and Judaism (Kabbalah) have a view of Adam and Eve that is useful for us all: The story of Adam and Eve is really a metaphor for the time for children to leave their father's house and go out into the real world. The human world has to expand, evolve and grow. It is a process of unfolding and becoming; and curled in the bud of the flower within us is our true power. Eve initiated the beginning of history. Had she not dared to taste that apple, had she not prompted her man to share the discovery, none of us would be here.

Another aspect we may have forgotten to question is where Eve came from. The missing piece for most women is that the story about the first woman neglected to say that there was also a divine female who fashioned Eve in her own image. *We all come from mothers;* doesn't it make sense that the first human female did, too? But how was the divine mother obliterated from the thousands of pages of scripture that follow Genesis 26 and 27?

Rabbi Joseph Gelberman, founder of The New Seminary and The New Synagogue in New York, says in *Kabbalah as I See It* that the Kabbalistic point of view tells us that when Adam and Eve left the garden, the feminine divine went with them, to comfort them and keep them company. "The creator was divided by an inner conflict about how to deal with Adam and Eve. God's children had disobeyed his only commandment: *Do not eat of the tree of knowledge or taste of good and evil.* One part of the divine insisted on punishing Adam and Eve. The other part of the divine, the Shekinah (who expresses the feminine qualities of God), suggested they should not be punished because they were merely innocent, curious children and this was their first transgression. The quarrel continued for a while. The part of God that insisted on punishment—exile from the Garden of Eden—did not waver. When the Shekinah insisted just as firmly that the punishment was too great for innocent children, the part that sought punishment said to the Shekinah, "In that case, you go with them."

The story of Adam and Eve can, and has been, interpreted in many ways. The wonderful thing about interpretation of any religious, spiritual or mythological concept is that we can all choose to interpret it through our own spiritual eyes. Reclaiming Eve's story from a woman-friendly point of view creates an opportunity for women to reinterpret our personal history, feel more connected to our female ancestors and exercise more choices about our connection to the divine. It helps us to feel we can help shape destiny, rather than be dragged along by it. As Rabbi David Cooper puts it, in *God Is a Verb,* "Obviously, a new perception of the Western creation story not only would dramatically affect our images of

Adam, Eve, and the Serpent, but also would permeate our collective consciousness in a way that could profoundly impact how we view ourselves as human beings, how we relate to one another, and how we relate to God."

Reclaiming Eve Exercise

Clearly, Eve needs a rewrite, or at least some revision and reinterpretation for modern times. In order to fulfill our destinies as powerful women, we have to go back to the Garden of Eden, as we know it, to reclaim Eve. When we look at the pleasant and unpleasant, dark and the light sides of her story and then come to our own personal interpretation, we reclaim our power by shifting our consciousness to include the wonderful divine aspect of the feminine. We also embrace and perhaps say good-bye to the little serpent who lives on our shoulders and hisses: *"You are not good enough, smart enough, powerful enough"* and *"who are **you** to be doing **this**, anyway?"* It is possible to be a scribe and to see, know and experience Eve in a different light, through spiritual eyes. We can all take a proactive approach to fixing the Eve problem, no matter how it manifests in us. Just get a special notebook or set up a special Eve file on your computer and begin doing the following exercises. You can pursue each step at your own pace, over a period of time, or do them all at once.

1) EVE MAPPING

The best way to start to heal any wounds you have experienced as a result of the Eve problem is to shine a light on the hidden thoughts and images that have helped formulate your belief system. Mind mapping is a way to understand what Eve means to you and what she has meant in your life. At the top of a piece of paper write *Eve,* and under her name, list anything and everything that comes to mind. This is for your eyes only, so be honest. Your list can have anything on it, for example, words that come to mind such as *apple, sin, naked, seductress, snake* or *fig leaf.* Think about some of the things you believe about women, men and creation. Some common concepts may include, "God is a male, women are appendages of men, Eve ruined it for all of us." Whatever concepts pop out of your mind, write them down. Write things that represent both negative and positive traits; try to let it flow without making judgments as you write or by self-editing. Make the list as long as you desire. Use words, sentences, doodles, etc.

2) LIST WHAT YOU LOVE ABOUT THE STORY
Culling ideas from your Eve map, and adding in whatever else comes to you, what parts of Eve's story do you *love*? Look deeply into her legacy, and consider the interpretations you know of and the ideas we've discussed in this chapter. Write down your favorite parts. This can include *anything* that turns you on.

3) IDENTIFY AND LIST WHAT UPSETS YOU ABOUT THE STORY
Whether you have strong opinions and dislikes or simply feel confused and baffled by certain aspects of Eve and her story, write down any part of it that concerns you or upsets you. For instance, perhaps it makes you fearful that *God gets so angry at Adam and Eve;* maybe it reminds you of your own growing-up years. Maybe it makes you angry that her punishment is so severe, or that she doesn't seem to have a divine mother to protect her. Maybe the way she was treated and the story about how her action impacts the world makes you feel very frightened to express your power or curiosity.

4) READ GENESIS
If you want to revisit her story or look a bit more deeply at how it reads, pick up a Bible and reread Genesis. See what other things come to mind about the story of Eve. You may pick up other nuances or ideas. Remember, many scholars,

religious leaders and artists have come up with interpretations over time; you can read and view theirs as well as having your own take on it.

5) GO TO A GARDEN

Make plans to visit a beautiful garden, a park, your backyard—any place that puts you in touch with nature in an environment that at least evokes the sense of Eden. Many states have real apple orchards where you can pay a few dollars and pick all varieties of apples from the trees and take them home, and also enjoy the beauty of the groves. Being around real apple trees with fresh fruit on them would be ideal because you can smell the sweet scent of the apples. Take your book of lists with you to the outdoor area you choose (or some paper to take notes if your Eve file is on your computer). In this beautiful place, you can begin to contemplate Eve and get in touch with how you view her deep within. And you can begin to redefine her in an empowering way in your own mind.

6) IMAGINE YOURSELF IN THE GARDEN OF EDEN

Find a comfortable spot, a place you can spend an undisturbed fifteen or twenty minutes, for some quiet time, reflection and meditation. Sitting with your back against a tree would be ideal, so you can feel the energy of mother earth coming into you, connecting you with the energy of the Tree of Knowledge. (If not, sit in a chair, on a bench or on a couch, indoors or out, and use your imagination to place yourself, energetically, in the Garden.)

Try this guided exercise as a meditation or a quiet time of reflection to enjoy a few moments with Eve:

Imagine the Garden of Eden. You are there as an observer of one of the most powerful moments in time, the moment that is said to have altered human history, when Adam and Eve tasted of the Tree of Knowledge. See this Garden as you believe it must have looked, replete with splendid surroundings, animals and beauty—*elements* of the story that are familiar to you, and those images that come to you now. Even though this is *the* Garden of Eden, it is a garden of your own creation. Be as inventive as you would like. Include the aspects of the Garden that you love, and try to include some of the aspects that are upsetting. See if they fit in your vision, or if your mind wants to replace them with other ideas and images. Notice what parts of the story find a place in your vision and what parts seem to want to delete themselves.

Follow your creative heart and your imagination to see Eve, along with Adam, and try to get a sense of what they are really like. Bring them alive, breathe life into those two-dimensional images of faceless male and female. See their faces, their flesh, their hair and their relationship to one another. Let them live in your mind's eye and observe the scene of the serpent inviting Eve to taste of the fruit. What is her body language? How does she act? What happens next? What was Adam's behavior? Did either of them seem bad, or ill behaved, or motivated by darkness? Notice if you see any negativity or ill will on the part of Eve. Or was she innocent, exploring, tasting of a new fruit that is part of their life's evolution and our evolution? Allow yourself to be there with her, watching, knowing and seeing who she really is.

As an observer, find your favorite spot in the Garden and feel the energy of the environment permeating your being. Sit there, rest, without judgment, and observe the moment when Adam and Eve eat the apple and God discovers them. Tune in to the crisis at hand and how Adam and Eve handle it. Are they frightened? Do they feel guilty? Are they arguing with God or defending themselves? How are they responding? What does Eve's response tell you about her? From what you are seeing in your vision, is this a malicious act of sin?

From your favorite spot in the Garden, your point of observation, ask this question: "The apple is sweet *and* it is tart, but it is delicious and wholesome . . . could eating this be so bad? Or has my mind deceived me from understanding the truth about Eve? What is the truth I need to know about Eve?"

Now, see if you receive a message. Just listen for any thoughts or ideas or small, still voices that whisper in your ear. Keep your eyes closed. Stay still for a while. If nothing comes to you, that's fine. (You can repeat this exercise more than once if you like.) Now, say good-bye to the Garden and any messengers you met along the way. Take a deep breath. Open your notebook to a fresh sheet, and make notes of what came to you in your vision. Write down any messages you received. Or jot down your thoughts when you get back to your computer. Prepare yourself to write a new, or at least newer, personal interpretation of Eve.

7) WRITE DOWN YOUR REDEFINITION OF EVE

Combining the elements you love about the story of the Garden of Eden, the vision you had of Adam and Eve in the Garden and the new thoughts about this ancient tale that are beginning to gel and emerge from you, redefine Eve. Write a brief statement about how you see her now, for example, *Eve was a curious woman who wanted to know more about life but who was oppressed by her father* . . . or *Eve was bold, and she never got credit for her chutzpah.* Write down whatever is a true belief for you now, personally. If you have not created a new belief yet, write down the concept you would most like to adopt.

In a separate paragraph, add one more element to this exercise: Consider a Garden of Eden that's empowered by both feminine and masculine aspects of the divine. Imagine that Eve has a mother she can turn to, a female role model to consult. What might that relationship be like? How do they commune with one another? Does her divine mother jump to her defense when her divine father punishes her and her husband Adam? How would a mother respond to her daughter being sent away from home? Would she turn her back and leave her on her own without contact? Or would she follow her and help her decorate her new tent? What role might you see for the divine feminine in reference to the first woman, Eve?

8) CELEBRATE EVE . . . AND HER APPLE

Let us honor Eve and her apple—long a symbol of her downfall—so we can reclaim the power of the feminine that lies within its sweet fruit. For the most part, the apple symbolizes fertility, love, joyousness, sweetness, knowledge and wisdom in many of the world's religions and mythologies. For example, offering an apple is often seen as a symbol of love. The Greek goddess of love, Aphrodite, and her Roman counterpart, Venus, were known to woo with golden apples that evoked love and desire. Apple blossoms are affiliated with the bridal day and are Chinese symbols of peace and beauty. As a fruit found in the garden of Norse goddess Freya, the apple symbolized immortality. On Rosh Hashanah, the Jewish New Year, it is a special blessing to eat apples dipped in honey, meaning, "May you be inscribed for a good, sweet year." The apple is also a sacred symbol of the divine feminine. Cutting open an apple we see, at the core, it is shaped like a vagina; we also see the natural design of the five-pointed star that is affiliated with earth religions that honor the goddess. In addition to all this, they taste yummy and sweet. And even if you bite into an apple that has a bitter edge, it still gives a sweet taste—sort of symbolic of life. Here's a suggested ceremony to help you celebrate and reclaim Eve.

+ Invite a few girlfriends over for a Celebration of Eve night.

+ Prepare a tray of delicious apples and apple juice. Slice one apple in half and rest it on the tray as a centerpiece, with its inner core turned upward. Pick a facilitator for the evening, a friend who is good at leading group activities, or let everyone share in the chores.

✦ Gather everyone in a circle. You can open with this prayer:

> *Mother, father, God, Goddess, all there is . . .*
> *Please fill this place with your sacred presence . . .*
> *Please open us to your love, light and wisdom . . .*
> *Please reunite us with our divine selves,*
> *And prepare us to reunite with*
> *our first human mother, Eve.*
> *Empower us to heal her . . . that we may heal ourselves.*
> *Amen. And so it is.*

✦ Speak the intention for the ceremony.

We now celebrate and affirm our communion and positive connection to the divine feminine and to the human mother of us all, Eve, through the sharing of apple juice and apples. The apple represents the feminine, as it held the key that opened the door to knowledge and wisdom; wisdom, in all scriptures, is always referenced as being feminine in nature.

✦ Ask everyone to wave a hand over the food in a gesture of offering a blessing and bless the apples together.

> *We bless this apple juice and these apples.*
> *We ask goddess to instill them with her divine energies.*
> *We ask God to instill them with balancing qualities of*
> *the divine male.*

✦ Offer participants the tray and let them take some juice and an apple.

✦ Offer this prayer as they ingest the sweet fruits:

May this apple symbolize wisdom, courage and living our personal truth. And may it symbolize our permission to bite into life, with passion. TAKE A BITE!"

May this apple juice symbolize the nectar of feminine power, and may it connect us more fully to the Goddess, and especially, to the goddess within. TAKE A SIP!

+ Afterward, sit in quiet communion. Play a soft, stirring piece of instrumental music.

+ Then, bring the sacred ceremony to a close with this blessing:

May the light of God, Goddess, all there is please guide us to reconciliation with the story of Eve that has wounded women. May our hearts replace untruth with truth. May our experiences and opportunities in life empower us to grow. May we all be the powerful and empowered women Eve was not allowed to become . . .

May the light of God, Goddess, all there is sustain and empower us . . . and lead us to personal truth and evolution. Amen. And so it is.

Part Two

GODDESSES
OF
SELF

1

SEE HOW BEAUTIFUL YOU TRULY ARE WITH HATHOR

"I feel pretty . . . oh so pretty!"

—From the movie *West Side Story*

There are a handful of supermodels in this world and then there are the rest of us. We live in a culture that is big on making us believe that beauty is only external, and we are often bombarded with unrealistic images and ideas of beauty from an early age. Madison Avenue has been hypnotizing us for decades, trying to make us believe that being tall, rail-thin, well-dressed in designer clothing and made up with pouty lips is what makes us beautiful and lovable. But beauty, however cliché it may sound, comes from within. It is a sad fact that girls in our society begin to have beauty expectations by the time they are nine, worrying about the way they look, dress and carry themselves around the time they hit fourth grade!

Our culture tends to assign goddesslike stature to women of astounding beauty and sexuality, yet women who do not fit the physical ideal of perfection are often left to feel unworthy. And we also end up working very hard to feel beautiful, instead of simply *accessing* the great reserves of beauty within. Despite anything you have been led to believe, now you must believe this: You are a beautiful woman! And it's time to honor this despite how you feel about your physical looks.

Hathor is a girl's best friend when it comes to owning your inner beauty and inventing a personal style and regime that helps you live it. She helps you see your truest beauty and also helps you use the realm of fashion and self-care to empower yourself; at the same time she opens your spiritual eyes to the gorgeous soul that exists beyond physicality and fashion. She represents inner beauty and self-admiration.

Who Is Hathor?

"The beauty of your face glitters when you rise,
O come in peace.
One is drunk at your beautiful face, O Gold, Hathor."
—Inscription from a tomb in Thebes

Egyptian goddess Hathor was goddess of love, beauty and pleasure and a guardian of women. A multifaceted divine female who represented many things to ancient Egyptians, she manifested in many forms. She is a fiery solar deity and close consort to Re-Harakhty, a lover who is a combination of the sun god Ra and the god Horus. She was a favorite among common folk and was also embraced by Hatsheput, one of the few female pharaohs, whose rule encouraged the cult of Hathor. Her religion was considered joyful. Her main place of worship was in Dendera, a city that thrived on ongoing celebration. As one of Egypt's most ancient goddesses, she's been blended with many popular deities. She is sometimes indistinguishable, in look and role, from Isis; she is also said to be the sister, or the milder aspect, of lion goddess Sekhmet. Hathor's first form was as a cow goddess, a mother deity who empowers and feeds devotees with her rich milk. Hathor was believed to materialize during childbirth to help women through it; she was a special guardian spirit of women and female animals. She was often depicted holding a mirror and, thus, the mirror represents the ritual reminder of the goddesses energy. The Greeks were fond of her, too, and equated her with their own goddess of beauty and love, Aphrodite. Hathor is usually seen as a slim Egyptian woman with dark eyes highlighted by coal and dark hair. She wears a wide and jeweled neckpiece, and her headpiece is that of cows' horns with a solar disk atop.

How to Invite Her into Your Life

The women of the Egyptian culture Hathor hails from were big on beauty treatments, cosmetics, essential oils, wigs and personal adornment. Women rich and poor would partake in rituals of beauty and self-care to feel better, protect themselves from the elements and enjoy their own expression of beauty. Hathor encourages the enjoyment of femininity, without stress. To look at Hathor's image is to see a woman who looks like *most* Egyptian women—an attractive figure, but not necessarily a ravishing beauty. Yet she decrees that all women are beautiful and evokes her own special charm. Devotees were often said to be overwhelmed and intoxicated by Hathor's glittering appearance. You, too, can evoke the beauty of the goddess within when you begin to see yourself through a new set of eyes and through a looking glass that offers a more soul-inspired vision of your true loveliness.

Almost every woman in ancient Egypt owned a mirror. Women were encouraged to admire themselves in the looking glass of the goddess. Each morning, they would sip milk, the drink of the cow goddess, to replenish their *ka* (spirit) and admire themselves in the mirror. It was a way to start the day feeling connected to her power. You can tap into Hathor's power by enjoying a few moments of self-admiration in a mirror. At the very least, you can turn your morning experience of putting on makeup into more of a self-love fest, connecting to Hathor as you put on lipstick and blush. Hathor's warmth is considered life itself and can help you see your true beauty. The way to access your inner beauty is to connect with and honor the goddess within. Hathor's mirror can help you look deeply into your own eyes and love who you see.

1. **Identify your special mirror.** Select a mirror you look into often, such as your morning makeup mirror or the mirror you dress in. Or purchase a special mirror that you can keep on your vanity, in the bathroom or anyplace you use frequently.

2. **Find an image of Hathor.** Purchase, download or copy a small picture of Hathor that really appeals to you. If you are not yet familiar or connected to her image or energy, she will understand if you would prefer one of her more familiar Roman or Greek counterparts—Venus or Aphrodite. Select any image, artwork or holy art that inspires you and connects you to what you deem to be the true beauty of the goddess.

3. **Attach the picture to the mirror.** Attach it to a handheld mirror (off to the side of the mirror) or tape it to a full-length or bathroom mirror. Be creative in how you place it; just make sure it is big enough for you to see clearly, it does not block your ability to see yourself in the mirror, and that it is placed off to the side, just where you can catch sight of it easily with a slight movement of your eyes or with your peripheral vision.

4. **Try a few eye exercises to meld with the goddess.** Keep your head in one place, but let your eyes take you on a journey. Look at yourself in the mirror, then look at the goddess. Look at yourself and, again, look at the goddess. Don't worry, you are not being narcissistic. This is a simple way to blend your beauties so that you can come

to see there is no separation between you and the goddess. This will bring you closer to knowing that she truly lives inside you.

5. Connect to your own beautiful essence. As you look back and forth, at yourself and then at the goddess, you may feel slightly "dazed," but it is actually a beauty trance of the goddess in which you become more open to receiving her love. Think of it this way: Madison Avenue has been hypnotizing you for years to believe in *their* version of beauty, and now, you are hypnotizing yourself to see and know the beauty of your own soul. Allow yourself to feel her true beauty. This is a connection to the Hathor/Venus that exists in us all. It cannot be bought in a bottle or worn on your body. It is a pure essence that comes from within. Don't be afraid to love that part of you. It is from that glorious dimension that your true beauty pours forth into the world and permeates all of your life.

6. Try these modern mantras. As you get used to the idea of truly seeing yourself as a goddess, you will know you can access anything. It is helpful to support the visual exercise with language. Whether you feel this way or not, whether you feel it sometimes and struggle with it at other times, treat these statements as facts that are completely and absolutely true. When you are ready, look at the goddess and look at yourself and affirm:

> I AM *divine*
> I AM *beauty*
> I AM *love*
> I AM *a magnificent being*
> I AM *a goddess.*

7. Plant these messages into your heart and mind. Say this mantra as often as possible. Make it your personal mantra if you like. Do this exercise as much as you choose and as often as you can. You might even want to put a sign near the picture of the goddess that says: I AM divine; I AM beauty; I AM love; I AM a magnificent being; I AM a goddess.

8. Love being a girl. Hathor showed the women of Egypt how to really love their beauty and personal adornment as an activity of self-pleasuring. Forget about trying to look exactly like the models in the magazines. It is so much work that it is painful! Somehow, the clothes, hair and makeup are never as perfect when translated from the slick magazine pages to us. Trying to be the models we see will instill us with a feeling of hopelessness that becomes a wound deep within. Don't go there. Instead, get some cute ideas and find things that are right for your personal look and utilize the models for ideas—rather than ideals.

9. Create your own style. Hathor was known for wearing a *menat* neckpiece, a beautiful, wide, beaded necklace of many strands that fit across her chest, and she always wore a form-fitting dress. She had a personal style, and you do, too. You never have to be a slave to fashion. Select the kinds of clothes you love, feel comfortable in and feel good in. Go for personal style over trends, and always trust your first choice in outfits. We spend hours preparing for dates, and we try on everything in the closet before heading out to a social occasion. We almost always end up with the first choice. If you learn to trust the first instinct and go for it, it will save a lot of time rehanging and refolding everything when you come home.

How to Keep Hathor with You

Treat yourself well, regularly. Have manicures, pedicures and facials that are empowering and beautifying because they relax you, give you some downtime in which to connect with your own beauty and help you feel good about yourself.

Enjoy reflexology. An ancient Egyptian healing practice of massage to target areas of the feet that effect the whole body, a reflexology session will relax, rejuvenate and enhance feelings of well-being and inner beauty. It stimulates your natural tendency to feel good. *Feet First*, by Laura Norman, will teach you how to do reflexology on yourself.

Install more mirrors in your home. Learn to love looking at yourself and connecting to your own eyes.

Own a mirror of Hathor. You can purchase a replica of the mirror of Hathor through the Brooklyn Museum and stores that sell Egyptian collections. They are about sixty dollars.

HATHOR AFFIRMATION:

*"I see my true beauty,
inside and out."*

2

DISCOVER YOUR DARK AND WILD SIDE WITH LILITH

"You're either a goddess . . . or a doormat."

—Pablo Picasso

Being nice is not *always* a virtue. Playing the "good girl" and acting "sweet" does not always get us what we want in life. Women who are living the lives of their dreams do not necessarily get there by being dainty and darling. They get there by being wild, daring, provocative and hungry. They demand what they want into existence and do what it takes to make it happen. It could mean breaking a few rules, breaking a few hearts and breaking a few habits along the way, especially the habit of constantly apologizing for who you are and what you think, say or do in the world.

If you, like so many women, were trained to mind your manners and act like a lady, it may be painfully difficult for you to break out of the mold—or it may be painfully difficult not to! If you are suppressing yourself because you're afraid of your own dark side, you might as well recognize the wild woman bitch goddess within before she bites you on the butt in an attempt to get your attention.

Sometimes we've got to access our internal power through external connections and role models until we manifest it into being. Just like children—who learn to *become* by pretending *they are*—you may have to fake it until you make it. Think of all the fun you can have pretending to be a fierce female, tough chick and a force to be reckoned with and evoking those energies from within. Consider it an exercise in seizing personal power.

Lilith is a girl's best friend when you're ready to unleash the wild woman within and take the lid off your self-expression. She may seem nasty, but she is simply an exaggerated metaphor for rising above meekness and doing whatever the hell you want to do—regardless of what people think, say or how they react. She represents freeing the wild woman within, exerting personal power and living without apology.

Who Is Lilith?

"He then created a woman for Adam, from the earth, as He had created Adam himself, and called her Lilith. Adam and Lilith began to fight. She said, 'I will not lie below,' and he said, 'I will not lie beneath you, but only on top. For you are fit only to be in the bottom position, while I am to be in the superior one.'"

—*The Alphabet of Ben Sira,* between the eighth and tenth centuries, C.E.

Lilith (*lil-ith*) is a Hebrew goddess known to possess great personal power and sexual appetite. In goddess spirituality and Jewish feminism, she is revered as fierce, potent and wild. According to mystical Judaism, she is considered Adam's first wife, while Eve is seen as God's more malleable, second try (although some believe Lilith represents an aspect of Eve's fuller power). Legend says Lilith was created in exactly the same way as Adam and at the same time, but that Adam refused to treat her as an equal partner; he tried to push the male domination routine and insisted on male-on-top, missionary-style sex. Lilith was *completely unwilling* to put up with his attitude. She *refused* to be beneath him and bolted. The Garden was too restrictive, and she wanted no man to be the boss of her. She opted for a romp by the Red Sea with a bevy of fallen angels. Lilith was not only branded a femme fatale and a bitch, she went down in history as an evil she-devil bad girl who birthed hundreds of mini-demons a day and populated the earth with negative beings. But she never looked back, and she never apologized. Although she lives in demon mythology as a succubus who kills children and takes sexual possession of men while they sleep, she's been reclaimed as a role model for female power and top female rockers even named a major concert event after her. She's often depicted with female face and serpent body; sometimes seen slithering about. She's often thought of as the snake who tempted Eve to taste from the Tree of Knowledge.

How to Invite Her into Your Life

Few of us crave the kind of heartless powers that are attributed to Lilith, but just a bit of her can go a long way in teaching us to stand up for our rights. Getting what we want sometimes requires us to "come out of ourselves" and be a little wild. One of Lilith's most coveted attributes is her ability to seek fulfillment of her goals without concern about other people's beliefs and judgments about her. If you're too nice, too meek, too wishy-washy or too much of a doormat, just a whiff of her stance on life might help you find a pathway to expressing more personal power. She can help reveal the wild woman within you at your own pace and comfort level. Lilith revels in the energy of living in her prowess. She may tend to be a dark goddess, yet she is willing to explore that part of herself and admit to it. Lilith is all about freedom of choice. Good or bad, dark or light—she makes the rules. She owns her shadow self, and all the dark desires that filter up from within. She does not oppress or distress herself over anything—ever. She may use the metaphor of sexual dominance to rule her universe, but it goes way beyond sex. She will not be told what to do or how to act—by anyone! She does not exist in this world to appease others. You should not, either!

1. Rent movies that celebrate "Lilith energy." She's a little nasty, but she's got attitude! She knows what she wants—and gets it. She's the woman most people refer to as a bitch, because she knows how to get what she wants—and they're jealous! Rent classic and modern movies that feature women characters who express their wild side, such as: *Body Heat,* starring Kathleen Turner; *Fatal Attraction,* starring Glenn Close; and *Three Faces of Eve,* starring Bette Davis; and *The Last Seduction,* the 1994 *film noir,* featuring Linda Fiorentino as a bitch goddess, love queen with amazing stamina for self-preservation

2. Practice being fierce. Lilith fosters a sense of anticipatory fear. There's something scary about her. Like a dominatrix or a "dangerous woman," she seems armed, but hers is an unseen power. Just as people don't argue or mess with an armed woman, they do not mess with a female who radiates an inner fierceness. You can opt for one of the most fun ways to evoke inner fierceness—clothing. Go shopping in a very cool store that has femme fatale clothing—maybe even a costume shop. Try on clothes and play around with "a look" that makes you *feel* fierce: black, wide-brimmed hat with veil, a bustier, miniskirt, leather pants, long evening gloves—whatever helps bring out your wild side. You don't have to buy anything or even wear it outside, but if it would be a breakthrough for you to don something devastating and wear it into your world, do it.

3. Take charge by speaking clearly and giving directives. Instead of molding yourself to the way things are, *mold your life to the way you are*. Essentially, there are those people in life who like to be in control and those who like to *give over* control. Lilith is one who calls the shots. Don't resist your own desire to take charge. People around you are just waiting for you to tell them what to do. Communication with a bit of an edge is often just the thing to inspire people to get things done. Most people respond to a clear directive—*do this by such and such a time*—that also has an imbedded message about consequences. This is not being harsh; it is just a way to keep life flowing with a sense of certainty. Notice the kind of language and ways of speaking that get the results, and practice these in everyday life, out in the world.

4. Develop an attitude that lets people know what you stand for. Lilith takes a queen-like stance as if to say, "Worship me." Anything less is unacceptable. To carve out the life you choose, you sometimes have to train people around you through actions, words and subtle threats—in the same way you would train a puppy. But it first has to come from within. Look at yourself in the mirror and practice saying, over and over, "I am a goddess . . . worship me" until you begin to get that you are worthy of reverence. Then, look deeply into your own eyes and blow yourself a kiss. You may feel funny, stupid or out of your element, but see if you can get into the groove. This will enhance your sense of self-reverence and help you magnetize what you want. When you're willing to own your goddess nature, people will want to serve your needs.

5. Stay firm in your choices, without apology. If you give someone an ultimatum or tell them how it's going to be, stick with it or you will lose power. Don't second-guess yourself or wimp out of the right decisions. When Lilith left the Garden, God sent three angels to fetch her, at Adam's behest, and she wouldn't even bend to the will of the divine. Whether she made a good choice or not, she still made a clear choice. No one can argue with that. Practice making decisions that are in your best interest and impenetrable by others. If you chronically apologize every time you set forth a decision others may not like, you'll negate yourself. Did Lilith say sorry to Adam for not wanting him on top of her? No. She said *ta-ta*. One day, take notes on how many times you say "I'm sorry." The next day, think twice about it and assess if an apology is truly called for. By the third day, you should find that you have less to say than you ever imagined because you are filling up too much time with apologizing for nothing!

6. Never use another person as an excuse to not have what you want in life. Lilith ditches whatever and whoever does not empower her. If a man will not honor her choices, or if an environment does not support who she is, she is outta there. You, too, always have a choice. Choose what and who in life is worth your continued effort and attention. Then take right action. If you are giving your power away, take it back! Try being a little bit stern—especially if you are someone who is generally passed over, ignored, not taken seriously or is always giving in to others. There is no need for you to become dark and disturbing, but it's important that you follow your authentic urges to seize your power, make your own choices and shape your own reality. Lilith encourages you to own your wilder side and express it when called for, to help you claim the rights and privileges that are yours.

How to Keep Lilith with You

Allow for your dark desires. The number one rule when it comes to expressing our power in the world is that it be legal, moral and that it not cause injury to self or others. You may not want to go down to the Red Sea and date fallen angels—but maybe you will. Certainly a dark thought or two may pass through your head. Allow the thoughts to surface and do not judge them.

Distinguish between fantasy and true desire. Just because you fantasize about doing something dark and disturbing doesn't mean you will do it. Most schools of psychology tell us that giving ourselves permission to explore the darker side of our nature is sometimes enough to help us accept our true selves and let ourselves off the hook for not being perfect angels.

Get your own bitch goddess T-shirt or tank top. Lilith, obviously naked, was able to get her point across—but you can declare your attitude on a T-shirt. Invent a slogan or get the official "Bitch Goddess" T-shirt to help you preside as queen of your own domain (available from Fineline's *Out There Wear*).

LILITH AFFIRMATION:

"Treat me like the goddess I am."

3

WELCOME THE WINDS OF CHANGE WITH OYA

"Finally, all we can do is let the days instruct us . . .
There is no holding on in this world."

—From the movie *I Dreamed of Africa*

Change is not always easy to accomplish or accept, even when it's for the best. While common sense tells us certain things must be changed in order to grow, there is a part of us that resists like crazy. Even great, wonderful, blissful change can be a fright because, while we may sometimes know our starting point, we usually don't have any idea where we will land. Even when a change is desperately needed, a part of our personalities wants to hold on and cling to that which is familiar and comfortable. For better or worse, it is what we know. But the truth is, creating change means taking risks, and risk-taking is a common denominator with successful and happy people.

Change can seem painful and scary, yet our fears about change are often more exhausting than change itself. Some of us approach a major life change like a jail sentence, and we go kicking and screaming. The truth is, the thing that we refuse to change is what keeps us locked in a prison of our own making! Life will be much happier and balanced when we learn to surrender gracefully to the winds of change and work with them to create the life we choose. When we have the choice to change, we should take it because the universe has a way of changing things for us when we can't find the wherewithal or courage to do it ourselves.

Oya is a girl's best friend when it comes to making changes in your life. She will not tolerate any hanging onto the shreds of a dead relationship, job or lifestyle. She forces you to do all the things you *said* you wanted to and to fulfill as many dreams as you dare. She represents sudden change, surrender of the old and radical rebirth.

Who Is Oya?

"Great Oya, yes
Whirlwind Maquerader, awakening
courageously takes up her saber."
—Judith Gleason, *Oya: In Praise of the Goddess*

Oya (*oy-yah*) is the goddess of change and female power who hails from the Yoruban and Macumban traditions of Africa and Brazil. She's a warrior goddess whose domain is major weather changes, such as hurricanes, tornadoes, earthquakes and storms of all kinds. As the Mother of Chaos, she is the Orisha (spirit) who propels and rides on the whirlwinds that wildly bring about great change and sometimes devastation that forces people to reevaluate and rebuild. Her name means "tearer." Like pulling a bad tooth, she yanks up what no longer serves you, by the root. Her consort/husband is Shango, the powerful thunder god; together they are *fierce*. She is sometimes called "The Mother of Nine" because nine is her sacred number, and it is said to represent the birth of her nine children, who were born out of a sacred rainbow cloth. The cloth is sometimes called Grant-That-I-May-Live-Long. Closely associated with the cemetery, she is believed to be a special spirit link and representative of the ancestors and the greeting committee when you cross over; she lives between the worlds. She is also guardian of the marketplace and is considered a shrewd businesswoman. She is sometimes seen as an Amazon, who rides the winds wielding a beaded horsetail and a saber. She is also thought of as a tall and stately African woman.

How to Invite Her into Your Life

Change or be changed—that's Oya's general theme. She is not the goddess relished by slowpokes and procrastinators because she is aggressive, wild and unpredictable. Sometimes the best you can do is surrender to her powers and work with her as gracefully as possible. She is more than willing to let you catch a ride on the air she breathes, but she will blow you away if you disrespect the powerful forces she brings to bear.

Oya's saber is considered a sword of truth and wisdom, a weapon that helps cut away stagnation. If we work with Oya's energy to *create change,* we are better equipped to handle it and have more resilience, when it comes. In order to grow, we must stretch and go beyond where we are, into the unknown. Each time we take responsibility to change our lives for the highest good, we gain confidence and trust in our ability to let go of whatever holds us back. We learn to allow a part of us to die or dissolve—we learn that is okay and part of life—and then allow ourselves to be reborn, transformed and anew.

Oya has a way of correcting imbalances that we refuse to address. Resist and she creates a whirlwind around you to bring your attention to the places you are due for a change. If you resist, she persists, urging you to take a second look at what you truly want in life. It works something like this: If you stay in a job, relationship, friendship, home, addiction or habit longer than it takes to get the lesson or move on, Oya takes initiative and begins to move you on.

1. **Journal your way to change.** Get a special "Time to Change Notebook." Make it a loose-leaf notebook that can be easily added to and changed. On the very first page, dedicate it to Oya: "*Mother Oya, my changes and awareness are my offerings to you. I surrender what no longer serves me and ask you to help me manage the winds of change by showing me how to ride them honestly and gracefully.*"

+ **Write what is good.** Jot down things you appreciate, like and value in yourself. This can include physical attributes, abilities, talents, attitudes, spiritual awareness, the way you are with others or things you've achieved.

+ **Write what is not so good.** Next, make a list of people, places and things in your life that you know are holding you back, keeping you down or keeping you stuck. The idea is not to judge yourself, or them, but to clarify the aspects of your life that need your attention. For example, if you know that a particular job, friend, lover, family member, lifestyle, living arrangement, neighborhood, attitude, is wreaking havoc or standing in the way of your growth, jot it down. Be honest. Look at all the things that jam up the process of living and create stress and things that are cluttering your life or draining your energy. Acknowledge dark or dysfunctional aspects of your life; it's challenging but worth it.

+ **Eliminate.** Go through the list of things that keep you stuck and prioritize which need your attention first. Rewrite them into positive goals written in current tense. For example, "I hate my weight" is transformed and translated as the positive, affirming, present-tense statement: "I am slimmer, healthier and feel better about myself."

+ **Delete the old.** After you have rewritten all the affirming statements, get rid of the "not so good list." As a symbolic gesture of the change you are willing to make, tear it into tiny pieces and flush it down the toilet, or shred it, burn it in the fireplace or outdoor barbecue pit, bury it near a tree, or roll it into a tiny ball and feed it to the garbage truck.

+ **Give yourself a fresh start.** Once you have processed the lists and feelings that come up around places you are stuck, make a list for a new life. What and who will be in it? Create your new reality on paper so you have a place to head for as Oya helps you disengage from places you have been stuck.

+ **Say a little prayer.** Always ask Oya to make life's changes as gentle as possible. *Oya, guide me to make changes at an appropriate pace and in a way that harms no one—including me!* Let her know that if she can do anything to soften the experience, you would appreciate it greatly. Tell her you want to make your life great and that you want to learn how to work with her gracefully.

+ **Make an offering in her honor.** Oya is sometimes worshipped with animal sacrifices. It may sound gross, but for millennia people have been making such offerings to the gods and goddesses to appease them and win favors. Your offering can be something very personal that will make Oya just as pleased: Sacrifice one negative behavior, something that is causing you pain or keeping you stuck—whether it's an addiction to buying shoes or to smoking cigarettes—and make the change on your own. Every time you think of it, want it or crave it, give the craving over to Oya as an offering. This will let her know you mean business and that you do want to work with her, not against her, to change your life!

2. Use cowrie shells for small changes. Not ready for a major change? Work your way toward it with small changes. Take one issue at a time—like finding a new doctor, updating your résumé, doing your taxes—and handle it step by step until it's completed. Then take the next thing, then the next until you get the momentum to work through your physical, emotional and spiritual space, to clean up your life and make room for the new. Cowrie shells are sacred to Yoruban goddesses and gods. Porcelain-like shells that were originally home to sea snails, they are considered the mouth of the Orishas. Cowries are also called money shells, as they were used as currency in Africa. They are found in the Indo-Pacific region and can be easily and affordably purchased by the dozens from online shell stores.

+ **A cowrie a day keeps Oya's storms away.** There's an ancient proverb that says, "The woman who removes a mountain does so one stone at a time." In this case, you move one shell at a time! Get eighty-one cowrie shells. This is Oya's sacred number times itself—nine times nine. (Or get some combination of nine, such as twenty-seven, which is three times nine.) Put them in a big jar called "My Change." Get a separate big empty jar and label it "Done."

+ **Small changes add up.** Identify each smaller subject— i.e., "finding a new doctor"—and identify every small step toward it. Move a cowrie shell every time you complete a related task. For example, if you unearthed your insurance carrier's directory out of the closet, that's one cowrie; if you flipped through it, that's another. If you call to make an appointment, that's another. Each small task equals a cowrie. It is like a tick sheet, or an abacus. As you watch the original "My Change" jar empty and the "Done" jar fill up, a sense of accomplishment and pride will come over you. Your subconscious mind, and Oya, will get the message you are someone who takes care of business.

+ **Start again.** When all the shells have been named and transferred to "Done," soak them in sea salt to clean the energy, dry them and start again, filling the "My Change" jar. Go through the small task acknowledgment process again. Do this until you've developed a good sense of how to move energy and create change by acknowledging each small step.

3. Know what changes teaches us: Change is an ongoing process. Every day of our lives we shed a little of our old skin and new skin is regenerated. In the course of a lifetime we may undergo a million tiny deaths and the passing of phases. Everything must eventually change. Work on accepting these statements:

+ **Change in small increments is best.** Making small changes at a slower pace helps you to adjust to a new reality, rather than suddenly feeling shocked by it. Weight loss is a good example. It may be a change you crave, yet if it happens rapidly, you have no time to process the emotional changes; it can make you feel vulnerable when you are used to that "padding." Slow weight loss is healthier and gives you time to adjust to the new you. Whenever you can, choose change at a lower pace.

+ **You can cope with a sudden change.** If a big, sudden change comes your way, you will find the strength to handle it. When Oya blows into your life like a tornado or a hurricane, it's almost impossible to accept that there's anything good about it. However, in the darkest night of the soul, we somehow come to understand that whatever the loss, there is a reason. From the depths of our pain, we can find a way to process the confusion and not just survive, but also thrive and find our true power.

+ **Crisis can be a path to evolution.** If you find yourself in the winds of sudden, scary change—a job loss, a health scare, an unexpected breakup—trust it is all in divine order. It is a way of creating a breakdown that opens the way for something new. It is a way to bring the lies we live to consciousness and give us an opportunity to change them.

+ **You will rise from the ashes.** Oya shows us the true impermanence of life. She teaches us that, like the phoenix, we must let go and surrender to each moment, trusting our ability to let go of whatever holds us back. She teaches us that we must allow a part of us to die or dissolve and then allow ourselves to be born anew.

+ **You are not a victim.** You may feel like one at times and may have a "victim consciousness." But if you choose to be queen of your own destiny, you must begin to see that you sometimes unconsciously draw Oya's dramas and disasters to you to precipitate change.

+ **It's healthy to keep tossing out the old.** Take a big black garbage bag—or ten!—and dump things. Let go of anything that ties you inappropriately to the past. Allow Oya to move you through the process like a wild woman in heat, blood pumping as you surrender your unused, unneeded and unhealthy stuff! Give anything you don't need anymore to the garbage goddess or to charity.

How to Keep Oya with You

Keep on keeping on. When you can't figure out your next step, when intellect does not apply and when you just don't know what to do, surrender it to Oya. Go with the flow. Release yourself into the hands of the divine and let her figure it out.

Get an Oya candle. The temptress of change is evoked in an Oya candle available from Illuminations that urges you to gaze at her flame and gather strength to take on personal transformation. Her scent includes essence of patchouli, clove, cocoa and amber.

Listen to her drumbeat. The famed African drummer Babatunde Olatunji offers a passionate ode to her in "Oya" (Primitive Fire) on his *Drums of Passion* CD.

For practical insight. Consider reading *A Year to Live,* by Stephen Levine. He describes a process of how to engage more fully in life by operating on the assumption you have only one year to live. The book explores many engaging questions, including: *If you had so little time, would you waste it on resisting growth and change?*

OYA AFFIRMATION:

*"I am willing to change my life
for the better, now."*

4

CLAIM YOUR VICTORIES IN LIFE WITH NIKE

"Just do it!"

—Nike commercial

On your mark . . . get set . . . go! At a certain age in life, some of us start to sweat, thinking: *If I am already twenty-five or thirty or thirty-five and haven't yet achieved a certain success and status, it may never come.* Even if you don't see yourself as a go-getter, there comes a moment when you realize it is time to go after bigger, brighter and better dreams and goals; a time to step to the fore so you can let your light shine for all to see. There's nothing wrong with wanting it all! The ultimate success in life is to achieve true balance and to have greatness and success in all areas. Like so many powerful women before you, when you are ready to uplift yourself in all ways and create the life you choose, it's time to put aside all childish ways and old hurts from the past, put on your running shoes and just do it!

Some of us are born with the desire to win; we're up and running, right out of the cradle, ready to compete and always aiming for victory. Some of us crave the kind of success that will make us stars and bring public recognition. Others just want to be able to make things happen and manifest everyday dreams into reality. Success, winning, victory—these all have different meanings for different women. Regardless the ultimate goal, when you feel it's time to make your mark on the world, it's time to pick up the pace on making dreams come true.

Nike is a girl's best friend when it comes to focusing on and achieving success at the highest levels and attaining victories of all kinds. She brings a focused, edgy and active approach to tasks at work, home and in your personal life, and ensures success at the outset because she inspires you to find the wherewithal to reach the finish line. She represents success on all levels, personal greatness and winning at the game of life.

Who Is Nike?

"The statue of Athena is upright with a tunic reaching to her feet . . . she holds a statue of Nike about four cubits high, and in the other hand is a spear."
—Pausians

Nike (Greeks pronounced it *nee-kay* and we tend to say *ny-key*) is the Greek goddess of victory. The daughter of the giant Pallas and the river Styx, she is a fierce and focused, winged river goddess, known for her ability to sprint, get to the finish and celebrate victory. She is famous for success in war and battle, but was said to deliver victory in all forms of competition and accomplishment. Considered the divine messenger who brings the coveted laurel wreath to victors, she is the goddess to whom the ancients prayed when they competed in any forum. She came to be recognized as a mediator of success between gods and humans, in all sorts of human undertakings, such as culture and athletics; she was an important deity at the Olympics. Although she was at one time inseparable from Pallas Athena, also a dispenser of victory who will not put up with defeat, she became known independently, yet is still considered a cheerleader and support to the goddess of war. There is very little written about Nike, yet she abounds in ancient images. Both Zeus and Athena are often seen carrying small figures of Nike, indicating she is an important aspect of their success. Some believe she is Athena with wings, yet they have evolved as two separate deities. When depicted alone, Nike is a young, winged goddess in flowing tunic, barefoot. She often carries a palm branch, wreath or shield of victory; she is sometimes seen carrying a cup, jug and incense burner. In the famous *Nike* (Victory) *of Samothrace* in the Louvre, she is headless yet fluid.

How to Invite Her into Your Life

As a divine harbinger of success, Nike can inspire your winning spirit by motivating you with enthusiasm and the desire to win. The ancient Greeks would chime in to Nike with a prayer before any major endeavor, asking her to bring victory and success. Nike travels with you on the path, from start to finish, on your adventures toward success. She is a cosmic mover and shaker who sees to it that you stay on track to fulfill your destiny and dreams. Petitioning Nike with very specific requests is the key to gaining her attention and assistance. She thrives on your clarity.

1. **Build a victory altar.** Because of her close association with war goddess Athena, Nike is especially fierce and powerful when it comes to getting things done, but she also operates with a cool head and calm demeanor. There is a small temple on the Acropolis of Athens that was dedicated to Athena Nike, which honored Athena as goddess of victory in military encounters and political intrigues and Nike as the wind beneath her wings. Athena brings

deeper insight, calm baring and extraordinary powers of strategy to the mix. The two together bring a double whammy of winning.

+ **Keep images of Nike with Athena.** Replicas of statues of Athena and Nike are easy to get in statuette form. Athena is dressed in armor, looking kind of macho. Nike is more feminine, usually in a flowing gown with wings. They are the balance of masculine and feminine energies. There are images of them together, with Nike in Athena's hand. You can also find classic pieces of art of each you can frame and put on an altar. While Nike is the primary deity to call upon for victories, Athena offers a steady hand to the process.

+ **Keep a dream box on your altar.** It will be the keeper of all your desires, filled with requests you leave at the feet of the goddesses. Consider it a temple for your dreams. Buy a beautiful Greek-style box or a metallic or wood box; or, if you are creative, fashion your own out of a shoe box that you paste and cover with images of famous sites in Greece as well as emblems and images of Athena and Nike.

+ **Have a bowl of laurel bay leaves.** You can find them in your kitchen or local supermarket. They symbolize protection and manifestation of the gifts of victory brought by Nike. The laurel wreath was always placed upon the head of Olympic winners and was associated with the crowning of poets and scholars (that's were poet Laureate and Baccalaureate come from). It was the crowning glory of Nike's domain.

2. **Do a victory ritual:**

+ **Celebrate success.** The way to create more success is to celebrate all that you have already have achieved. Appreciate life's little victories; they are the precursor to bigger dreams. Never judge your station in life, just seek to change it when you are ready for bigger things. Before any new endeavor, list or run down in your mind your recent achievements. Thank Nike for all her help getting you to where you already are.

+ **Clarify goals.** Take a few moments to think of what is next for you. You may have some pressing goals, or perhaps you have some overall goals or need to revise your goals because you have attained the last batch. Have a felt-tip pen handy so you can write down some of your dreams.

+ **Write on laurel bay leaves.** Use Nike's symbol of victory to create more victory for yourself. Go through your bowl of bay leaves and find the smoothest, most well formed in the bunch. Just the act of selecting the best will be a symbolic gesture that you now choose the best in all areas of your life. On a hard surface, begin to write your goals: *Annual salary of $100,000, beautiful new home, great love affair, respect of my peers, fame, delirious joy, travel to exotic locales, great adventure . . .* or whatever you seek. Just write short sentences that will fit on the leaves.

+ **Pray and ask for divine assistance.** Place the bay leaves with your goals in your dream box. Hold the box in your hands and pray to Nike to please come to you and help you make all these dreams so. Then pray to Athena to please bring the power of wisdom and strategy:

To Nike:
With fleet foot and wings, please bring your grace to the manifestation of these goals. Bring me strength, stamina and passionate desire to make it to the finish line and claim my prize.

To Athena:

With the power of knowing all that is, please connect me to the inner wisdom to know what I must do and when to make my dreams come true, and bless me with the gift of strategy so I can follow right action and good timing to bring my goals to victory.

To Nike and Athena, thank you both. And so it is.

+ **Give your dreams over to the victory altar.** With your intensions placed into the leaves by your own hand and your goals now empowered with prayers and petitions for divine help, place the dream box back on the altar and promise to make your success an offering to the goddesses.

+ **Make offerings.** Legend has it that Nike would spend her mornings studying the victories of men and women to consider to whom she would offer help. She would review them as she took her meal of ambrosia and nectar, the drink of immortality of the gods. It was said that if you prepare an altar that highlights her bright flame she will fly down and pour a libation on the altar as a sign of victory to come. Sometimes she would carry incense to the site of victory so the victor could be cleansed. You can reach out to her by lighting incense for your own purification, lighting a candle in honor of her victorious spirit and placing a small glass of nectar (mango or pear juice) nearby for her pleasure. For Athena, leave a small owl statue or image to honor her wisdom and powers of strategy.

+ **Commune daily.** The trick to winning is to *assume* victory. Go forward with the notion that you will win and you will make your dreams come true. Nurture this notion by communing with the goddesses daily. Just sit by the altar and talk to them. Tell them what you've accomplished so far and where you are in your journey. Ask for help along the way. Do not be afraid to speak up and trust you will be heard.

3. Take responsibility for your life. Decide what you want in life at every stage, on all levels, and go for it. Support your goals spiritually as you pursue the practical and active aspects. Take inspiration from the action-oriented approach of success sports stars, musical stars and actresses who inspire you. Live the advertising slogan that has made Nike sportswear a symbol of victory and *just do it!*

4. Be impeccable in all you do. Be elegant, not arrogant. Be appreciative, not abrasive. Be a diva, not a brat. Create what you want in life by calling upon the grace and refined skills of Nike. Pursue your goals with strong intensions, but don't let them consume you. Be someone who is a pleasure to work with, to know and to love.

5. Include financial power in your plan. Part of success is the financial ability to pursue dreams and the promise of greater things to come. Don't shy away from taking responsibility for finances—making money, managing it, saving and spending it, paying bills, taking care of debts, signing contracts, making major purchases and commitments, having investments and using finances wisely.

6. Face challenges head-on. Success in life does not always equal comfort. Nike knows the last few yards before the finish line are the toughest, the place where many women give up and discount their dreams. It can be a lot of work to set up an extraordinary life, but if you take on and face life's challenges along the way, you are halfway there. Nike always helps the devoted to the finish.

7. Tune out naysayers. The mark of all great athletes and stars of every field is their willingness to follow their own hearts and surround themselves with people who empower their *perceptions* of what success is. Everyone will have opinions, but it is not your job to take them inside yourself. Your polite answer to anyone with advice on how to run your life should be a smile and, "Thank you for sharing."

8. Choose battles wisely. On the track to success, there will be bumps, and there may be people who try to block you so they can get to the finish line first. Focus only on the things that will move your goals forward. If you come up against little skirmishes or jealousies along the way, avoid engaging in petty battles. These things can be draining and overwhelming. Save your energy for the important stuff.

9. Take charge of your own destiny. Believe in your dreams. Live your life fully, every moment, and seize all the good moments to empower your spirit; use all the difficult times to build character and fortitude. Set forth a vision for your future and follow it like a religion. Never, never give up. If you fall down, pick yourself up and get back in the game. See the laurel wreath that awaits at the other end of every goal in progress and know that Nike will help you draw closer to victory as she draws victory closer to you.

How To Keep Nike with You

Wear her on your body. Since Nike is a goddess who is especially famous as the inspiration for Nike sneakers and clothing, purchase a pair of Nike sneakers. There is an entire line of NIKEgoddess sports clothes to choose from as well.

Run or exercise. Claim your power through physical exertion and expression.

Watch birds in flight. As a winged goddess, Nike is associated with victory just as flight is associated with victory over death. Even watching birds in flight gives a sense of freedom and possibility. Seeing how they scale the heights so naturally and elegantly is a skill that can be translated into a smoothness and grace in everyday life.

NIKE AFFIRMATION:

"I am victorious in all things."

Part Three

GODDESSES
OF
STRENGTH

5

CONNECT TO YOUR HEALING POWER WITH MARY

"In joy and woe, in good and ill,
Goddess, Mother, be with me still."

—Edgar Allan Poe

No matter how old we are, whenever we feel sick, exhausted or bullied by life, it's nice to be able to run home to Mommy. The comfort and warmth of a mother's touch has long seemed like an anecdote to many ills. Even if we don't have a great relationship with our own moms, most of us have the need for motherly love—a kind of unconditional and soothing comfort. Whether we run to Mom, or seek the support of a friend, sister or therapist, it always makes us feel better knowing there is someone to go to for healing and a hug.

Sometimes we conjure challenges much greater than the healing capacity of our own mothers—or friends, therapists or health-care providers, for that matter. If illness, injury or emotional distress comes our way, we do not have to bear our burdens alone—even if family and friends can't seem to help or if it is them we are trying to help. It is in those times that we can seek healing of the highest order and use every health and wellness challenge as an exercise in calling forth our own healing abilities and powers.

Mary is a girl's best friend when it comes to healing. She is the mother whose arms await you when you need a shoulder to cry on. She's the witness to your sadness and the warm heart to let you know everything will be okay. With love and understanding, she makes you feel better as she shows you how to be your own healer. She represents the all-encompassing energy of the healing mother and the power to heal that lives within.

Who Is Mary?

"I salute you glorious virgin, star more brilliant than the sun, redder than the freshest rose, whiter than any lily, higher in heaven than any of the saints. The whole earth reveres you, accept my praise and come to my aid."
—Ancient Prayer of Protection, translated by Andrew Harvey

Mary of Nazareth is an icon of the Catholic Church, yet she is a spiritual mother to all women. She is the virgin called upon by Archangel Gabriel to carry God's only begotten son . . . the Jewish mother to the rabbi prophet whose birth, death and resurrection are the foundation of Christianity . . . the holy spirit who balances out the triad of the Father and the Son. She holds a sacred place in the heart of Catholics as the mother of Christ and conduit between the earth plane and heaven. While her church has not titled her a goddess, she clearly possesses the clout, divine connections and magical healing powers of a goddess and is afforded the worship, reverence and prayer of a divine female. It is through her high placement in the Catholic Church that the feminine principle has been represented most prominently in traditional religion for more than 2,000 years. Yet she represents even more. She is the virgin maiden. She is the great mother. She is the queen of heaven.

And she is the wise woman. She is it! She continues to be worshipped and adored around the world as "Mother Mary," "the Blessed Virgin," "Our Lady of Immaculate Conception," "Our Lady of Lourdes," "Our Lady of Guadalupe," "Stella Maris, Star of the Sea," etc. In many parts of the world, such as Mexico, her adoration equals that of her son's. One of the most painted and portrayed women in history, her image is widely known around the world.

How to Invite Her into Your Life

Mary has long been a widely adored, accepted and accessible Spiritual mother. Because of her extraordinary popularity and iconic presence, Mary cuts across religious boundaries. She is respected for raising her son to be strong, loving and a true believer in the power of a kind heart and a proponent of social equality. Like all moms, she's got influence! A major intercessor between her son and those who seek his healing, she is the one to whom devotees run with all manner of broken parts and hearts—and she is a healing hand and wholesome energy unto herself. While those raised in the Catholic faith may have an established relationship with her, she is, in many ways, the adopted spiritual mother of all women, and people of many faiths embrace her as a universal mother. She is there for all of us, always, at any time, and accessing her energy is quite easy.

1. **Go into any church, at any time, to commune with her.** She is so visible and so easy to be with. There are more Catholic churches named after her than her son. When you are hurting, suffering, dealing with illness or coping with a loved one's illness and trying to help them heal, you can find her almost anywhere in the world. No matter what your religion, you can always sit in the quietude and sanctity of a church and be in the presence of her grace. Many churches offer a way to kneel before an icon

of Mother Mary, light a candle and petition for help. As a thank-you, you can leave a financial offering to the church.

2. Perform a solo healing ritual. You can ask Mary into your life, into your home, into your very being. Many people who swear to have sighted or experienced her tell of miraculous spontaneous healings and ongoing heavenly help.

+ **Get Mary art or an icon you love.** You can find her image everywhere and anywhere. She is depicted holding baby Jesus standing with arms outstretched in a protective blessing or revealing her sacred heart. Find the image that connects you to her healing grace. Keep it in a sacred place in your home and visit her anytime you are hurting. Ask her to take your pain away.

+ **Meditate with Mary.** Close your eyes. Imagine she is in you. Not outside, not above, not separate. If you are sitting in a chair, see her in the same chair, sitting the same way. In your mind's eye, with your spiritual sight, know that you and she occupy the same space at the same time and that you can call upon her healing powers as if they are your own.

+ **Identify and name your pain.** Tune in to the part of you that is hurting. If you are ill or in physical pain, identify or pinpoint the source of your suffering if you can. If you are suffering emotionally, give your suffering a name (sadness over a loss, fear about medical tests, devastation over drastic life changes, deep despair over financial or work situations, for example). Allow yourself to feel Mary's presence with you. She holds your head gently in her hands, calming your emotional upsets with the soothing light of heaven. She places her hand on whatever hurts and fills that place with love. And she helps you illumine your aching heart, opening it to goodness and protecting it with her own sacred heart. Feel her healing energies within you as if they are your own.

✦ **Carry her inside you.** Many Catholic mystics acknowledge that Mary is the Holy Spirit, the aspect of Christ that enters us, heals us and makes us whole. Few devotees will dispute her magnificence and her healing ways. While many believe that she brings the cure, she might argue that she delivers healing light at the exact moment you are ready to receive it and, hence, your own inner healing ability is awakened. Pray that she fill you with her healing spirit. Catholics have always evoked her gracefully and easily by repetitions of this invocation:

> *Hail Mary Full of Grace,*
> *The Lord is with you.*
> *Blessed are you among women,*
> *And blessed is the fruit of your womb, Jesus*

3. **Call upon her with healing waters.** Millions of people make the pilgrimage to see her Shrine at Lourdes, in France. They follow in the footsteps of young Bernadette, who saw Our Lady of Lourdes at the opening of the grotto and received a message about the miracles of the body and soul that would be performed at Lourdes. Mary appeared with a rosary in her hand and yellow roses at her feet. Bernadette received a series of messages over time and would go into ecstatic trances of communion. Through Mary, Bernadette's healing powers opened. One day, she scraped away some soil from the side of the grotto and a spring suddenly appeared. Water trickled out, and

then poured, and provided 27,000 gallons of fresh water that, to this day, replenishes daily.

+ **Anoint yourself and loved ones.** The healing water is available in small bottles that can be ordered from The Lourdes Center in Boston, Massachusetts. While the water is not considered "holy water" or "magic," it is believed to have healing qualities and many people say the Blessed Mother has granted healing favors in conjunction with its use.

+ **Apply the water to where it hurts.** While it is always best to seek a physician's approval for use of anything not prescribed by your doctor, many people use Lourdes water as an adjunct to medical care; they often apply it to affected areas of the body or drink it. People at Lourdes bathe in it without ill effect. When you apply it, imagine with all your might that the hand of the mother is touching you and healing you and making you whole, as she activates the healing powers of your own touch. You can also anoint loved ones, with their permission.

+ **Pray to her.** Holding the intention for healing is powerful, but it is always nice to commune with her in prayer. This prayer from the Novena to Our Lady of Lourdes is perfect. You can adapt it if you are praying on behalf of a loved one.

Mother of Mercy, Health of the Sick, Comforter of the Afflicted,
You already know my sufferings and my needs; look on me with mercy.
At Lourdes you have given us a sign of your compassion and your love.
Many sufferers have already found healing through your intercession.

I come before you with confidence in your motherly
  care.
I ask that you listen to my requests and grant my peti-
  tions.
In gratitude, I will try to imitate your life so that
I may have some share in the glory of the kingdom.
O Mary, conceived without sin,
Pray for us who have recourse to you. Amen.

4. Recognize that illness can be a gift. Illness and crisis are usually our body's way of telling us to slow down, take time out and nurture ourselves. Whether it's a cold or cancer, all illness finds its genesis in disease of our bodies, minds or souls. Because we are forced to search for solutions and ways to get better, we often find a fuller power emerging in our lives as we participate in self-healing. Great healers, such as medicine women and shamans, come into their own being by healing themselves of grave illnesses. Each breakdown of the physical, emotional, mental or spiritual system is an opportunity for discovering a way to rebuild, renew, reemerge and grow.

5. Help loved ones. Mary shows us how the power to heal can surge through us and from us. From the dawn of time women have been healers—the unlicensed doctors, the counselors and family ministers of health. Women of the ancient worlds offered health care to their family and villages via herbs, homemade medicines and the power of their touch. They were so connected to the cycles and rhythms of nature and the natural healing capacity of the body they did what came naturally. Mary brought her baby into the world by immaculate conception and birthed him in a manger to a wonderful welcome, but she could not save him from his death, and she wasn't meant to. The hardest work of a healer is to know when we can help and when it is simply not in our hands; no one's ultimate health or fate is ours to decide. Sometimes the best healing we can bring is love, and that love is like medicine from heaven.

How to Keep Mary with You

Choose a rosary. No matter what religion you practice, the rosary brings Mary to you, along with her blessed son. She resides in each bead; hold it in your hand and call to her.

Wear a Mary medallion. Buy a small Mary medal that will allow you to keep her with you, by your heart, wherever you go. These can be purchased for less than one dollar in any Catholic shop or church store.

Seek her out in a pilgrimage. Mary appears in visions to mystics and civilians alike and has reportedly been cited in visitations around the world. It's said that many of Mary's shrines, cathedrals, sacred springs and "appearances" are at old goddess sites. Check with local church groups. For additional information, see *Goddess Sites: Europe,* by Annel S. Rufus and Kristan Lawson.

MARY AFFIRMATION:

"I feel the healing power in me."

6

LEARN TO TRUST YOUR INTUITION WITH SOPHIA

*"From ancient times intuition has been
equated with the feminine."*

—Judith Orloff, M.D.

In the hustle and bustle of our overly busy lives, we sometimes forget that we possess something that can be handier than a cell phone and more constructive than a board meeting—a sixth sense that has often been referred to as "women's intuition." Many of us check in with all our best friends, business associates, assorted experts and a psychic here or there to try to divine the best way to handle big decisions before we even think of trusting our own gut. Ultimately, we end up more confused than when we started, with too much input and opinion from others.

Women's intuition is our pipeline to divine messages and wisdom, and we all have the ability to receive inner guidance. The big challenge is hearing all the great advice that is channeled through us and trusting it. We have to learn to have faith in the quiet times, and to live inside the silences, without getting so antsy. Through the silences come great messages of wisdom that can guide us in everyday life and even help people we care about.

It is easier than you may think to learn to trust your own inner knowing and access it at any time. Intuition is demonstrated in small ways every day of our lives: You think of someone and out of the blue they call; you have a feeling you should go to a certain event and it turns out you meet someone who leads you to your next great job or boyfriend; you go out for a run or walk and suddenly your mind clears and all these great ideas pop into your head. Intuition also manifests as signs and sensations, such as a headache, dizziness, nausea or a general "bad vibe" about someone. How many times have you had a sense that someone was trouble only to later have it confirmed? The trick is to go with your intuition even when you don't have immediate "evidence" that it is "right."

Sophia is a girl's best friend when it comes to hearing the still, small voice within you that whispers the wisdom of the feminine. She is the essence of female intuition, in that she *knows*. She is a source of infinite wisdom and a divine counselor. She represents wisdom, inner knowing, self-trust and truth of the highest order.

Who Is Sophia?

"I was sent forth from the power,
and I have come to those who reflect upon me,
and I have been found among those who seek after me.
Look upon me, you who reflect upon me,
and you hearers, hear me.
You, who are waiting for me, take me to yourselves."
—Sophia speaks, from *The Thunder, Perfect Mind*

Sophia (*So-fee-a*, or *So-phi-a*) is the goddess of wisdom, personified in the Gnostic Christian tradition and referred to in the Judaic holy writings. She is called the Mother of the Universe, Mother of the Creator God (Yahweh) and Bride of God in the Gnostic Gospels. In the Hebrew texts Proverbs, Sirach, and the Wisdom of Solomon, "Wisdom" is a woman who has relationships with both humans and divine. Sophia is her Greek name; her full name in Greek, Hagia Sophia, means "holy female wisdom." She is known as Chohkma in Hebrew and Sapienta in Latin. Many feminist theologians also call her the Holy Spirit. She was embraced as God's equal partner in the early Judeo-Christian tradition, when her wisdom balanced his force. One of the first references to Wisdom as a feminine entity unto herself was in the Old Testament Book of Proverbs, which depicts her as a loving partner or consort, a co-creator. She also plays a prominent role in the Apocrypha (the body of works that came after the Old Testament and preceded the birth of Jesus by two centuries). Although they contained elements that were eliminated from the "official" Jewish and Protestant Bible, they survive to this day as an appendix to the Old Testament in the Catholic Bible. *The Book of Ben Sirach* contains sonnets and poems to, and attributed to, Sophia; the Wisdom of Solomon is like a love poem to her. In the Gnostic Gospels, Sophia is also referred to as the "Wisdom of Christ" and the consort of the divine male who created the universe. It is said that she was hidden, stashed in those texts since the fourth century B.C.E., as part of the Christian movement to remove anything that did not completely espouse Christianity from the popular Roman perspective. The Gnostic Gospels are part of the *Nag Hammadi scrolls* unearthed by an Egyptian farmer in 1945. Sophia is depicted in Eastern Orthodox Icons, with stars around her head and her feet standing on the moon. In Michelangelo's *Creation of Adam* on the ceiling of the Sistine Chapel in the Vatican, God is pictured as reaching out with a finger from his extended right hand and touching Adam's finger. In the same fresco, his left arm is wrapped around a classically beautiful blonde woman with wide eyes who many say is Sophia, God's consort and partner in creation.

How to Invite Her into Your Life

Although we all love to get really great advice, or insight, there is nothing like being able to trust your own wisdom and hear your own truth without an intermediary. When communing with Sophia, you are communing with your soul, the highest aspect of yourself. Her divine thoughts become your thoughts. Her divine wisdom becomes your wisdom. If you have ever had a problem you were trying to work through and then suddenly the answer came to you in a moment of silence, you might already know Sophia's handiwork! Now you can learn to seek her out. It's been said that prayer is when you speak to the divine and meditation is when the divine speaks to you.

Tap into her cosmic wisdom. Learning to spend time alone to seek out and listen to that sacred voice within will teach you how to become a natural receptor of divine wisdom. Meditation, or a meditative state of relaxation, is the most powerful way to connect with her. It reduces stress, puts you in a relaxed state and helps you open your "channels of communication" to the divine.

1. **Meditate:**

+ **Get quiet.** Meditating will give you the ultimate sacred connection to her. Make sure you have a comfortable, quiet place where you won't be disturbed for twenty minutes. Draw the shades; light a candle if you like; play a suitable piece of relaxing music. Sit comfortably with your legs uncrossed and your feet gently but firmly touching the ground. Keep your back as straight as possible without too much effort, and allow your hands to rest gently on your lap with your palms turned up. If you possibly can, record the meditation on a cassette so you can easily pop it in a tape player and use it as a guide.

+ **Open with a reading.** Begin by evoking her with an ancient reading on wisdom. There are many. The Wisdom of Solomon, in the Hebrew Scriptures, offers tribute and worship to wisdom. Many believe that Solomon, considered the wisest Hebrew king, took his lead from the bride of God. Reading from ancient holy writings helps you validate her presence and access her wisdom. The following is from the King James Bible, Wisdom of Solomon (Apocrypha 6:12–17), with the language slightly modified for modern times. Speak it out loud.

Wisdom is glorious and never fades away:
She is easily recognized by those who love her,
and she is found by those who seek her.
She hastens to make herself known to those who
       desire her,
Those who seek her shall have no great travail;
Rather, she will be found sitting at your door.
To think therefore upon her is perfection of wisdom,
and who watch for her shall quickly be without care.
Go about seeking her and make yourself worthy of her,
And she will show herself favorably,
And meet you in every thought.

+ **Identify the issue you need help with.** Name it, formulate a question and hold it in your mind as something you will address to Sophia. If you have a short memory, write it down before going into meditation. Keep pen and paper handy to write down any insights Sophia offers. Before the end of the meditation you will have a chance to be a scribe and channel the answers you need.

+ **Become the daughter of wisdom.** In the Hebrew tradition, a female is described by her Hebrew name and as daughter of her mother; *daughter of* is described with the word *beth,* e.g., "I am Gavriela Shoshanna *beth* Sura Rachel." When you begin your meditation, bring your complete awareness to the experience by saying your name (doesn't have to be Hebrew), the name of your mother and the name of wisdom. For example, "I am Gavriela Shoshanna *beth* Sura Rachel *beth* Sophia."

+ **The meditation:** Now close your eyes and take a deep breath and hold it for three counts. One . . . two . . . three, and exhale slowly all the way out with a big sigh. Again, inhale deeply and hold it for one, two and three, and exhale slowly. One more time, inhale and hold for one, two and three, and slowly exhale completely. Allow your breath to return to its normal pace and start focusing on it. Get into the experience of breathing and revel in how good it feels to breathe. Each cycle of inhalation and exhalation renews you, relaxes you and makes you feel so good. As you relax, begin to let go of tension you may have about whatever challenge you are dealing with. Give yourself the gift of being in this perfect moment, your moment to unwind, release and enjoy the simple pleasure of just breathing . . . inhaling and exhaling . . . relaxing and healing . . . letting go. If an occasional thought crosses your mind and takes you away for the moment, don't fight it. Think of it as a cloud passing by in a beautiful blue sky. Acknowledge it, see it pass and let it go. Continue to be aware of your breath. Now imagine that you are in a beautiful place that is spiritual and joyous. You could be in a temple, on a ranch in Montana gazing up at a sky full of stars or floating on a cloud in a place that feels like heaven. In this place, you feel totally at ease and connected to all that is. Although you can see distinct forms and images that are outside of you, get the feeling they are actually part of you. Keep breathing and

allow your comfort to increase. Know you are in total
security, balance and comfort. See yourself there, enjoying the essence of this perfect place, whatever it is to
you. Feel the winds of heaven blow gently against your
soul. Sense a presence that is larger than yours, yet the
same as you; an energy that is dynamic to you here on
earth yet natural and part of you in this heavenly place.
Hang out there and keep breathing . . . becoming more
a part of all that is with every breath.

Continue to breathe appropriately and to stay in touch
with the sensations of this glorious place and its nuances—a
breeze that caresses your skin, a sight, a scent. As soon as she
gives you the go-ahead, ask Sophia your question. Dwell in
the question for a few moments and then open your eyes and
start writing her answers. (If taped, pause the tape for a moment.) If you hear her voice, enjoy the intonation and communication, but keep writing down what she says. Don't edit,
or think, or even read it. Just write whatever comes. When
you are done, when you feel all that must be written has
come through, return to the meditative state. Pay attention
again to your breathing and renew the sense of surroundings.
This is your special place, where Sophia and the wisdom of
the feminine dwells. She is a part of your soul, and you are a
part of her. Know that this special place is yours to return to
whenever you choose and whenever you seek wisdom and
guidance. Ask for a sign, a special emblem or sensation, so
you can always connect with Sophia through your special signal (it could be a dove flying, a breeze, a cloud floating, a
sound, a sense somewhere in your body). Then gently bid it
farewell, feeling gratitude for the time of quiet and guidance.
Slowly make the journey back to the present place and
time . . . slowly coming back as you deepen your breathing
and ever so gently begin to move your fingers and toes . . .
your hands and arms, your neck gently from side to side . . .
and, keeping your eyes closed, take three more deep, cleans-

ing breaths . . . one for the body . . . (pause) . . . one for the mind . . . (pause) . . . and one for the spirit (pause). Allow your breath to return to normal, and when you are ready, open your eyes. Thank Sophia and ask her to stay close. May the spirit of wisdom always be with you!

Keeping Sophia with You

Meditate regularly. Just ten minutes of meditation daily can help you develop intuition, awareness and wisdom. These regular quiet times allow you to "check in" with Sophia to get her impressions and insights, but also help establish an ongoing channel of communication that you can easily tune into at any time.

Sign of the dove. The dove is a symbol of peace and an emblem of Sophia. Keep a picture, image or small statue of a dove to remind you of her.

Stay connected to her ancient presence. Anytime you doubt the wisdom of the feminine, remember she was there long before history wrote her out. Repeat her words in holy texts. Here she speaks in the Old Testament, Book of Proverbs, 28:27,30: *When he prepared the heaven, I was present with him . . . I was by him, suiting myself to him, I was that wherein he took delight; and daily I rejoiced in his presence continually.*

See her special home. One of the most magnificent examples of Byzantine architecture is the Hagia Sophia or Cathedral of Divine Wisdom in Istanbul, Turkey. You can still visit her cathedral to this day or get a photo to keep with you. Connecting to that energy will help you develop intuition, awareness and wisdom.

SOPHIA AFFIRMATION:

"I am guided by my
feminine wisdom."

7

HAVE COMPASSION FOR YOURSELF AND OTHERS WITH KUAN YIN

"You've got to be your own merciful mother."

—Barbara Glabman-Cohen, psychotherapist and teacher

Some of us are haunted by an internal battle that puts us in direct opposition with . . . ourselves. We fret, regret and feel remorse for the tiniest things and continuously beat ourselves up. We can't forgive ourselves for indiscretions of the past or something dumb we said a minute ago. If someone else were beating up on us the way we do ourselves, we'd have to fight back in self-defense.

We often have a very hard time giving ourselves the love and compassion we deserve. We judge, hold grudges and never let ourselves off the hook. We are unforgiving of ourselves. Sometimes we take on the blame for things that others inflict upon us—the mean teacher, boss or supervisor, the emotionally abusive parent or partner—and turn it against ourselves. Depression is anger that is really meant for another. It's anger turned inward, upon ourselves, because we are afraid to express what we really feel. Women who tend to be very sensitive are like sponges, soaking in other people's "stuff."

By the same token, when we cannot give to ourselves all that we deserve, it is impossible to give it to others. We can "pretend to care" and "act nice" toward others, and we can be very accommodating and even border on being co-dependent, but when we do not love and give to ourselves, we cannot authentically offer it to others. When we lock ourselves into unforgiving attitudes, they act like chains on our hearts.

Healing the pain within that robs us of self-love takes time. But the only way to start to heal and balance the ill will we might have toward ourselves is with compassion—a compassion born of understanding, full acceptance and recognition of true inner feelings without judgment. When we give this to ourselves we can make it available to others and offer a helping hand to those in need.

Kuan Yin is a girl's best friend when it comes to forgiving yourself and finding the deep well of compassion that lives within you. As the embodiment of compassion and loving kindness, she brings a wonderful presence to any difficult moment and offers a cosmic shoulder to cry on. She also enables you to reach a hand out to help others. She represents compassion, mercy and unconditional love.

Who Is Kuan Yin?

"Many women coming from Asia to live in the United States bring with them stories of Kwan Yin. They learned to revere her as little children, taught by their mothers or grandmothers at the family altar, encouraged to offer flowers and fruit and incense to this powerful goddess."

—Sandy Boucher, *Discovering Kwan Yin,*
Buddhist Goddess of Compassion

Kuan Yin (*kwan-yin*) is the Chinese Buddhist goddess of compassion, mercy and healing. She is the "Compassionate Savioress" worshiped for centuries throughout China, Japan,

Korea and Southeast Asia. Known also as Quan Yin, Kwan Yin, and Guan Shih Yin, she is the patron and protector of women, children, sailors and artisans and those who are imprisoned. She is as popular as the Virgin Mary is in Western culture. She's frequently called upon by women having difficulty conceiving and is seen as a great source of fertility and feminine vitality. Statues of her divine form bless every Buddhist temple in Asia, and, in addition to many public displays, almost every Chinese home is adorned with Kuan Yin artwork. Her name is translated as the being *who hears the cries of the world*. She is a Bodhisattva, which in Buddhism is a human being who has completed all karma and reached enlightenment. Although her Bodhisattva status entitled her to enter the paradise of Nirvana, Kuan Yin decided to remain on earth until all suffering was ended. Each culture has a different tale of Kuan Yin's beginnings, from suggesting she began life as a male to the story of Sainted Chinese Princess Miao Shan, who was sentenced to death by her own father because she refused to obey him and marry and insisted on living in a nunnery. Kuan Yin is often depicted as a classic Chinese beauty wearing a flowing white gown with her hair pulled up in a headdress. She's seen seated on a lotus or majestically riding on the back of a dragon. Sometimes she's pictured with many arms, as the Thousand-Armed Kuan Yin. She's seen carrying many special emblems, such as a willow branch that she uses to dispense flower essences and ambrosia; a porcelain vase, which carries these pure sweet and healing unguents or tears; scrolls or books of Buddhist prayers and wisdom; and a crystal rosary used for meditation.

How to Invite Her into Your Life

It is said she never turns anyone in pain away. Kuan Yin can be your bodhisattva; your personal savioress. If you are too tough on yourself and others, or if you are struggling to open your heart to compassion, she will be right there with you, helping you cast out self-criticism and negative judgment. When she hears the cries of humanity, she manifests in any form needed to help—perhaps as a helpful passerby, an angel who can help in a crisis or even as a friend who shows up just when you need them.

1. Chant to her any time. Her powers and gifts can be invoked by calling her name or chanting the famous "Mani":

> *Om Mani Padme Hum*
> (Oh-m mah'-nee pahd'-may hoom)

This mantra celebrates and honors her altruism and selflessness and acknowledges her as the "jewel in the lotus." Chinese custom often suggests that everything be done in threes or nines, as those are auspicious numbers, so always chant at least three times . . . or nine times, when you especially need to connect.

2. Perform a healing ritual. You can give your sorrows to Kuan Yin because she has compassion enough to embrace all the tears of the world. You can pour your tears into hers, release your pain and open to her compassion. This is a ritual that is suggested only if you have sufficient emotional support in your life to help you process emotions that may be stirred up. If you are in therapy, check with your therapist prior to (or schedule an appointment soon after) doing this work. Make sure you have an undisturbed hour or so, and put all the ingredients together before beginning this ritual:

+ **Supplies and setup.** Select a big bowl. Fill it with water and a half cup sea salt. Get a dozen white carnations (you will use nine and hold on to three). Have two small vases or glasses with water for the flowers handy; do not put the flowers in there yet. Have a CD player nearby and select soulful and sad music that stirs your heart and helps you maintain a reflective state to begin the ritual and select music that is uplifting to close the ritual (the instrumental pieces from the *Message in a Bottle* motion picture soundtrack are great). Place the bowl of water on the floor or a table (where it will be comfortable for you to sit for a while) with a big towel beneath it to catch any splashes. Make sure the music and the CD player are handy. Set up a small altar with incense, the vases, an image of Kuan Yin if you like and a picture of yourself.

+ **Begin with the Mani, incense and music.** Call to her with her chant of invocation nine times. Light a stick of incense to honor her and also send healing prayers up to the heavens on the smoke. Play the soulful, sad music.

+ **Feel the sadness within.** Take three deep breaths and center yourself. Bow your head in reverence to Kuan Yin and also in acknowledgment of your pain. Go into a state of sorrow and reflection, and look within at all the unhealed parts of you that need *your* love—the places where you lack compassion for yourself, where you are mean and unforgiving to yourself, where you feel guilt or where you feel like a bad person. Also tune into those places where you hold yourself accountable for other people's problems or hold the blame for things others have done. Allow yourself to know and feel the depth of the pain in your heart. It hurts, and it has been getting in the way of your happiness. Let all painful feelings surface so you can shine Kuan Yin's light of love upon them. This ritual is designed to take the pain out of you and give it over to Kuan Yin, for she can handle all your pain and more as she shows you how to increase your own ability for self-compassion and healing and how to forgive yourself.

✦ **Put your pain into the flowers and the flowers into the water.** The white carnations are a substitute for the white lotus Kuan Yin sits upon. They are as pure and untouched as she is and as willing to take on your pain as she is. Hold nine carnations on your lap or rest them on the table near your hands (save three for later). Having evoked the sadness within, begin to name all those things that get in the way of your compassion for yourself and, ultimately, others. For each pain you name, using one carnation at a time, pull off a petal from the carnation and throw it into the bowl of salty water. For each feeling that comes up, let it go into the flower, then let the flower petal go into Kuan Yin's healing waters. Surrender your sorrow to her. She will bear witness to your sorrow and take it from you. Cry, express yourself, scream, release—verbally express whatever is there. Throw as many flower parts into the water as you feel moved to, and as you wrap up this part of the ritual, make sure all designated nine flowers—stems and all—eventually end up in the water.

✦ **Bring your sorrow to a close.** Once you have completed the release process, sit and reflect. Relax and begin to feel the sense of relief come upon you. The act of tossing flowers into the water helps you make a physical statement, and you might even feel a physical release, as if a weight has been lifted. Once you feel you are done with that, change the music to the more uplifting, instrumental music. Take the remaining three intact carnations and hold them close to your heart. Ask Kuan Yin to fill you with compassion and the self-love you need to live a loving, compassionate life. Meditate on that for a moment as you feel you heart opening, no longer shut down by your pain.

✦ **Offer the three whole carnations to Kuan Yin and you.** Place one in a vase next to the image of Kuan Yin, one next to the picture of you and one on your pillow to inspire loving compassion as you sleep. Let the flowers symbolize a healing that helps you feel loved and loving.

+ **Final release of pain.** Before the end of the day, take the bowl of water with the torn up flowers to a body of cold salt water if you possibly can—a nearby river, ocean or stream. You can transfer it into a bucket or place the flowers in a leak-proof plastic bag to transport them. It is a strong symbolic gesture of release if you can return the flowers, filled with your pain, to the source—the salty waters of the mother. But if you can't, do not despair. Flush them, a bit at a time, down the toilet and say your good-byes.

+ **Before you go to sleep.** Look at the flower near the image of Kuan Yin and thank her. Look at the flower near your picture and thank yourself. When you lay down your head, let the carnation rest nearby. May it bring the sweet smell of healing and loving compassion to your sleep and your waking the next day. A new possibility has begun.

3. Practice connecting to others. It is a long-time Buddhist and Hindu tradition to greet fellow and sister travelers with the Sanskrit salutation "Namastè." The spoken term (pronounced *nom-a-stay*) is accompanied by a hand gesture that looks like praying—two hands together, in the prayer position, right in front of your chest. This is done simultaneously with a slight bow of the head. It is a gracious and very cool way to acknowledge others. It means: *The divine in me honors the divine in you.* When we take the time to greet people with a spiritual salute, it gives us a chance to transcend the pettiness of life and rise above our egos; from that perspective we have more compassion for the suffering of others.

4. **Volunteer to help others.** The ultimate offering to Kuan Yin is to help her with her work in the world. Once we have healed our own hearts with self-compassion, we are fuller beings with more to offer others. Find a cause that you can get behind, a group that is doing something you believe in or a charity that is helping people in a way you support, and volunteer. Give of yourself, and of your time, and watch your capacity for compassion begin to develop.

5. **Continue to embrace your own human nature.** There will be times that you have thoughts that contradict your compassion for self and others. Don't beat yourself up if you hear the voices of prejudice or criticism rise up from within, and don't try to suppress them. That gives them more power. Let them come up . . . and disappear like puffs of smoke. The more you practice compassionate action, the less your mind will oppose you!

How to Keep Kuan Yin with You

Savor her energy in tea. Royal Kuan Yin Tea is a premium oolong tea—like the kind you get in Chinese restaurants—that is gentle and decaffeinated—like her! You can also conjure her divine essence in Lotus Decaffeinated Green Tea from Tazo, a tea said to promote inner radiance and the essence of the lotus flower. It is soothing and calming and helps you feel like a goddess. It smells sweet and pure the way you imagine a Goddess would.

Wear pearls. Kuan Yin is often pictured with pearls (or a rosary) around her neck, and her purity is said to live in the beautiful and precious white jem. She wears a necklace of pearls; you can, too, allowing it to hang right over your heart. Pearls also connect you to the energy of the moon, which is symbolic of compassion, love and an open heart.

Bow to her. Prostration, also known as deep bowing, is an ancient Asian and Buddhist custom. It is believed to purify and humble us as well as offer homage to the divine and to one another. Practice bowing deeply to Kuan Yin—an image or to her perceived energy—and you will connect more deeply to your compassionate self.

KUAN YIN
AFFIRMATION:

"I forgive myself for any ways in which I have disappointed myself or others. And I forgive others for disappointing me."

8

FEEL SAFE AND PROTECTED WITH GREEN TARA

"Adversity is the diamond dust heaven polishes its jewels with."

—Robert Leighton

Few of us leave the house in the morning in search of bad news and trauma. However, some of us may find ourselves faced with one of life's terrifying moments or crossing paths with a crisis that we can't control. Even if you are one of those people who believe things happen in this world for a reason, bad news can hit with stunning force. It hurts to hear you've been fired, that someone you love is very ill or has been injured, that the person you love is leaving you or that the money you were counting on is not coming through. If the bad news were that you are in the middle of a traumatic event—an accident, fire or crime—no one would blame you for freaking out. When your world is being rocked by a crisis, it may not be easy to "be spiritual" about it.

That's why it is so important to strengthen ourselves on a daily basis, not just when emergencies happen. It can help us to remain calm and centered in the face of fear and stress. The first response many of us have to very difficult news and traumatic events is denial—*no, this can't be happening*—and then real life will set in. Hopefully, down the line, we will find ourselves on the path of somehow accepting and reckoning with the truth, and perhaps even searching for and finding a deeper meaning or hidden lesson in the pain that was endured. But when it is happening, it is terrifying and confusing. Our greatest power is the willingness to stay present in the moment of truth and pain, lean into the forces of the universe that are there to love and protect us in our darkest hours and trust that throughout whatever is happening to us, we are enfolded in divine arms.

Green Tara is a girl's best friend when it comes to handling bad news and very high-stress situations that may involve perceived danger or threat to your physical or emotional well-being. She is the all-embracing, all-knowing mother savior who takes us in her arms at our hour of greatest need and feeds our souls with manna from heaven to help us cope and get through the physical and emotional reality of a crisis. She represents the ultimate protection and grace of the cosmic mother into whose spiritual arms we can run and rest.

Who Is Tara?

"The worship of Goddess Tara is one of the most widespread of Tibetan cults, undifferentiated by sect, education, class, or position; from the highest to the lowest, the Tibetans find with this goddess a personal and enduring relationship unmatched by any other single deity."
—Stephen Beyer, The Cult of Tara

Tara (*ta-ra*) is the much-loved Tibetan Buddhist mother goddess. Considered a female Buddha, monks and devotees around the world chant and evoke her energies daily, calling upon her for everything from world peace to peace and protection from within. She represents *all that is,* and her energy can permeate all things. Tara is worshiped in both mild and wild forms and exists in a rainbow of colors based on various attributes. The Green and White Tara of the Tibetan Tantric tradition are the most popular forms, with Green Tara seen as her fiercer, most dynamic form. As Green Tara, she is a goddess of action, great strength and special protective powers who wards off evil and shields you from spiritual harm. The mythic tale of her origins is that she was born from the tears shed by Avalokiteshvara, the Buddha of compassion, as a gift to end the suffering of all creation. The tears trickling down the left side of the Buddha's face formed the motherly and mature "White Tara," and the salty drops on the right birthed the fearless and youthful "Green Tara." Some believe, however, that she was a human princess who lived a life of total service, compassion and the highest spiritual aspiration, dedicated to serving the Buddhist monks. Because of her path, she earned the right to be reborn in male form and teach the ways of the Buddha. She told the monks that since the concepts of male and female were only illusion, she would remain in female form until all of humanity was liberated from illusion and reached enlightenment. She is often depicted as a slender, Asian woman with jade-green skin and adornments, sitting on a lotus with one leg folded in front of her in the traditional meditation pose and the other leg extended and ready to jump to protection.

How to Invite Her into Your Life

Tara is a protector who offers us her body and wisdom to shield us from danger. The ancient texts say, when called upon, she protected people from the "eight calamities," which are described as Lions and Pride, Wild Elephants and Delusions, Fires and Hatred, Snakes and Envy, Robbers and Zealots, Prisons and Greed, Floods and Lust and Demons and Doubts. She is often the deity evoked by Tibetan nuns and monks who have miraculously survived arrest and torture in their native land; people in trouble pray to her for deliverance. Because she represents compassion in action, she becomes the bridge from fear and suffering to happiness and good tiding. Devotees trust that with Tara in their corner, even in the worst of situations, they will somehow be all right.

DAILY RITUALS:

1. **Chant her mantra.** The root of Tara's name is the sound *tri* meaning, "to cross." When we call upon Tara, she immediately comes to our defense and helps us cross from danger to safety. It's believed that Tara's protection and favors are granted instantly just by calling her name or chanting her mantra:

"Om Tare Tuttare Ture Soha,"
(Ah-um Tah-ray Too-tah-ray Too-ray So-hah)

It translates to: "Hail Tara . . . her enlightenment and compassion protects me and liberates me from external fears and internal delusion . . . may I honor this in myself!"

2. **Meditate with Tara.** To develop resilience and spiritual preparedness for life as it occurs—with all its twists, turns and surprises—connect with Tara every day. Meditating or connecting with her in your own way in peace and quiet can help you in overcoming long-term fears, phobias and self-doubt and can also bring clarity and strength that enables you to feel more potent in your daily life.

+ **Preparation.** Buddhist practitioners will often set up a small meditation altar and comfortable meditation pillow so they have a special "place" set for Tara in their home. You can set up a very simple altar with the following items:

- Two green candles.

- A bowl of salt water for purification.

- Incense (Green Tara Incense is available in Tibetan stores and on eBay).

- A small icon, or postcard-size image, of Tara.

- Tibetan *tingsha,* which are two brass cymbals that are clanged three times to begin and to end a meditation. The distinct sound clears the negative energy of the room at the start and restores you to normal consciousness at the end.

- At some point you can add a "bell and dorje," the sacred symbols of Tibetan worship that represent both the feminine (bell) and masculine (dorje) principles.

+ **Light up.** The candles represent healing and compassion. The incense is an offering to the goddess.

+ **Sit before the altar in a comfortable position.** Have the tingsha in hand. Begin by taking a few deep-cleansing breaths. Close your eyes. Breathe deeply . . . and release. (Chime the *tingsha.*) Feel your heart open. Breathe deeply, again, and release. (Chime.) Feel your mind open to new possibilities. Take another breath and release it with a sigh. (Chime.) Feel your spirit open to your own highest knowing.

+ **Chant.** The traditional mantra for calling in Tara's presence is all you need:

"Om Tare Tuttare Ture Soha."
(Ah-Um Tah-ray Too-tah-ray Too-ray Soh-hah)

Repeat this chant at least three times and, if comfortable for you, thirty-three times. (Metaphysical experts believe in doing Tara's chant in repetitions of eleven, and they believe it is especially powerful to do them in sets of eleven times three, because thirty-three is a powerful number. If you need some inspiration and company, there is a wonderful version of His Holiness The Dalai Lama leading a seven-minute meditation with the "Green Tara Mantra" on *Prayer: A Multicultural Journey of Spirit*. On the same CD is the enchanting "Praise to Tara" with beautiful vocals by Nada Shakti.)

+ **Let Tara come to you.** Inhale as deeply and comfortably as you can, and exhale as you chant. With each repetition, the energy of Tara will come through stronger and stronger. When finished with the mantra, allow your breath to return to a normal rhythm. Visualize Tara sitting behind the altar across from you in her traditional pose. Admire her beauty and strength. Look at her third eye and imagine a beam of pure white light connecting her third eye to yours. Sense this light as a conduit of her wisdom, courage and enlightenment, and become one with her in this energy. Realize that all these gifts have always been with you and that Tara has come as a mentor to assist you in self-realization. Dwell in this energy and release any doubts or negativity into the bowl of water to be cleansed, purified and returned to the universe.

+ **Close with a clang and a vow.** When you are ready to end the meditation, open your heart to Tara and thank her for her sistership and love. Make a promise to nurture an internal image of her and hold her in the inner temple of your heart. Vow to call her when you need her help and be open to her power when she comes. Begin to take a series of deep grounding and centering breaths, and when you are ready, open your eyes and end the ritual by chanting: *"Om Tara . . . Om Tara . . .*

Om Tara . . . Om." Clang the tingsha three times as you say her name.

For Emergency Protection: This quick meditation and prayer can be used for protection anytime or anywhere you feel danger (or perceive danger), anxiety or stress and to bring the energy of Green Tara around you to ground you and help you feel more secure.

1. Call Tara's name. Out loud or to yourself three times, *"Tara . . . Tara . . . Tara!"*

2. Visualize her immediately appearing in front of you. She is youthful, strong and beautiful yet fiercely determined to protect and defend. Tell her the source of your upset and ask for protection from those things in the material world. Tell her that you also desire clarity and understanding of those things that are welling up inside of you.

3. Ask her for immediate instructions. Trust whatever insight comes to you immediately—the first thing—and combine it with your inner wisdom and instincts.

+ Action may be key. If it is, Tara will enable you to act quickly and wisely. Keep in mind that action may be something simple, such as "leave the room" or it may be more intense, such as "call the police." Honor whatever comes through to you, and put aside any feeling that you may be overreacting, or any fears you have about offending or embarrassing anyone else.

+ She may even guide you to stand fast, remain calm and center yourself as the best defense, especially in stressful, non-threatening situations. As always, express your gratitude to her for her assistance.

How to Keep Tara with You

Always carry a bottle of rescue remedy. This Bach flower classic offers a calm-down to humans and animals alike. If you feel nervous, just a few squirts under your tongue or on your skin will help. It's a natural flower remedy that is like Green Tara in a bottle.

Wear green. Let her color embrace you, hug your skin and protect your heart.

Serve the goddess. Tara's love is best served when we live our lives in service to others, with nonattachment to the way things are and an ongoing quest for enlightenment. As budding bodhisattvas, we can develop strength enough to help others so that if a crisis or bad news comes, the focus is larger than your own fear.

TARA AFFIRMATION:

*"I am safe and sound
in the arms of the mother."*

9

CREATE PEACE
WITH WHITE BUFFALO CALF
WOMAN

"In the Native American culture, it is woman who is held in high regard. Women are considered the peace seekers in time of great disasters."

—Don Evans, Ojibwa descendant

Now, more than any time in history, we need the energy of the sacred feminine to balance our lives and balance our world. We must be spiritual warriors, and this means culling the profound and important aspects of the power of feminine wisdom and directing them toward peace within, as without, and utilizing the energies of the goddess and all mythical women and spiritual heroines to help direct the course of history. It is the absence of feminine energy that kicks off a cycle of destruction. It is the restoration of the feminine that will help heal this imbalance. Creating peace is a chick thing! We can all partake in creating a more peaceful world.

White Buffalo Calf Woman is a girl's best friend when it comes to activating your ability to build peaceful community and spread peace. She helps you see the distinction between the masculine and feminine approach and honors that both can exist side by side: While men, historically, fight and defend, females seek to draw peaceful resolve to any situation. The important thing is to have both and a chance for balance—in women *and* men! She represents the balance, and the peace, we all crave.

Who Is White Buffalo Calf Woman?

"It was told next time there is chaos and disparity, she would return again. She said she would return as a White Buffalo Calf. Some believe she already has."
—Lakota Chief Arvol Looking Horse,
modern-day keeper of the sacred pipe

White Buffalo Calf Woman is a Native American spirit woman considered a holy woman-savior who came here to give instructions for living the sacred life to "the People." In Native American culture, she's on the "A list" of awesome women, a role model for teaching men how it will be and for inspiring women to take their rightful place as leaders and facilitators. She is credited with helping the Lakota and Sioux establish rituals and a sacred social life that would bring them closer to Great Spirit, the Great Mother and one another, as well as teaching them how to perpetuate peace and honesty in their world. As legend has it, many moons ago, amidst a great famine, two Lakota scouts went out in search of buffalo and instead came across a haze of smoke through which a beautiful woman suddenly appeared. She was, to their eyes, quite alluring and magical. One of the scouts was overly lustful and tried to make a play for the maiden; the other was respectful. The woman invited the lustier of the two to approach her; then both scouts disappeared in a puff of smoke. When the smoke cleared, the respectful scout stood there and the lusty one was reduced to a pile of bones. The scout who honored the woman was given the task of taking her word to his nation. She told him to tell his people to "build a teepee" and prepare for her arrival. Soon she arrived and taught them the Sacred Pipe Ceremony, along with the Seven Sacraments, which are the tenets of Native American spirituality. She is often pictured as a beautiful young woman standing near a white buffalo. She always has long, flowing hair and a sacred pipe in her hand.

How to Invite Her into Your Life

Many of the Native American traditions handed down by White Buffalo Calf Woman are still practiced today at certain special events, reenactments and ceremonies that are held in urban areas and on actual Native American reservations. Although not as accessible as Sunday Mass, there are many places in the United States where you can attend and participate in an authentic Native American experience as well as learn more about her culture.

1. **Observe a sacred pipe ceremony.** Smoking of the sacred pipe is a traditional Native American way to get in touch with her healing energy and peaceful ways. Over time, it has been referred to as smoking the "peace pipe." The ceremony is conducted in a circle, with others of like mind, who hold the same intention for the ceremony. Ojibwa descendant Don Evans explains that in a state of prayer, the pipe is smoked and passed around. It contains strong ceremonial tobacco or the bark of a red willow tree. No one inhales—they just take a toke and release, and as smoke releases, so does your prayer, and it travels to the Great Spirit on plumes of smoke. The ceremony represents the truth being spoken. The pipe is considered a religious artifact—the bowl represents the feminine and the stem represents the masculine—and it's used in a sacred manner.

2. Host your own Native American–style healing ceremony.
As an alternative to a sacred pipe ceremony, you can gather
some friends of like mind and create a sacred healing circle dedicated to personal and planetary peace. Instead of
passing around a pipe, pass a sacred object such as a
branch you find in nature or a store-bought crystal that
can be viewed as a "talking piece." Each person who
holds it has her chance to speak her truth, while the rest
of the people in the circle bear witness. This is how it
would typically be organized:

+ **Set an intention for the sacred circle.** Make sure everyone knows they are attending a sacred ceremony and
  why they are there. Tell them, "We are gathering in the
  name of peace" and that the theme of the evening is
  sharing how we feel about peace in our world today,
  sharing individual ideas for creating a more peaceful
  life and praying together for peace (add whatever else
  you choose).

+ **Spiritually cleanse the ceremony room and participants.**
  In all Native American ceremonies, there is a spiritual
  cleansing of participants and the creation of a sacred
  space. First, white sage is lit, because it is believed to
  absorb and clear negative energies. Using an abalone
  shell in which to burn the sage and a feather with
  which to gently fan it onto each participant, someone
  brings the smoking sage around to each person in the
  circle to ritually clear negative energies. This is called
  "smudging." The person doing the smudging can also
  walk around the circle clockwise three times, creating
  a circle of sage smoke and ensuring a purified area for
  the ceremony.

+ **Open with a special invocation.** The Native American
  tradition adheres to the belief that ancestors, spirit

guides and divine beings guide us. They exist in all dimensions and from all directions. The first invocation calls in the four directions (North, East, South and West); then the directions of Above (Father Sky), Below (Mother Earth) and Within (Great Spirit) are acknowledged and evoked. You can ask several people to participate by giving them each a direction to call in. To add a special touch, get a shaman's rattle and shake it after each direction is called.

Caller 1: We call to spirits of the North. We honor Mother Earth and her abundance. May we stand steady on her ground. May this dear planet and all her children grow stronger every day.

Caller 2: We call to the spirits of the East. We honor wind and ask that new opportunities for peace fill the air and that the white dove of peace flies freely in all nations.

Caller 3: We call to the spirits of the South. We honor fire and ask that we be infused with warmth, enthusiasm and passion for the mission of creating peace on earth.

Caller 4: We call to the spirits of the West. We honor water and ask that it cleanse the hearts and souls of all women and men and soothe our angers and wounds so that we may never again thirst for war.

Caller 5: We call to the spirits of above, below and within. We ask to be united with Father Sky, Mother Earth and with God, Goddess and Great Spirit of all that is. With all the forces of the universe, we pray for harmony in our world.

+ **Light a candle.** The fire symbolically represents the sacred smoke of the pipe and brings the warmth and glow of White Buffalo Calf Woman into the circle. You can say: *We light a candle to White Buffalo Calf Woman and ask her to teach us and to guide us in this circle of peace.*

+ **The ceremony.** The "talking piece"—which must be selected before beginning the ceremony—is passed around the circle and held by each person in turn.

  • Each takes a moment to reflect and speak her truth.

  • Because many people have personal concerns about peace, you might suggest that everyone pick an "issue" to share and one "solution." For example, issues may be *"I feel fear in my heart, and it is stressful"* or *"I am afraid of what is happening in our world today."* Spiritual solutions may include *"I promise I will pray every morning for peace"* or *"I will do volunteer work toward healing our planet."*

  • Request that people keep their issues and solutions brief.

  • Each person who holds the talking stick should be given full attention and respect while speaking.

  • There should not be commentary or back and forth discussion while someone is speaking. Reverent silence and bearing witness to people's issues and their solutions is what this is about. However, after every individual has completed speaking, it is tradition for everyone in the circle to proclaim *"Ho"* or *"Aho."* This is a Native American symbol of completion and agreement, and something of a prayer that says, "And so it is."

+ **Closing the circle.** After everyone has spoken, you can all stand and hold hands for a final prayer and offer thanks to all energies that attended and guided the sacred circle. (In general, it should always be initiated and summarized with a prayer related to personal and planetary healing and peace.) To close, we say: *Thank you God, Goddess, Great Spirit of all that is, for filling our gathering with your presence and grace. Thank you to the directions—south, west, north, east, above, below and within—for guiding us in your ways. Thank you White Buffalo Calf Woman, for your healing and compassion. May anything expressed that needs healing be healed; may all dreams and declarations be made real. May we all leave here with peace in our hearts. Aho!*

How to Keep White Buffalo Calf Woman with You

Focus on peace, every day. Go to sleep with peaceful thoughts, and you will wake with the same. Consider trading in the eleven o'clock news for a peace meditation or even a few moments of silence, a peaceful book or warm relaxing bath or a loving experience with your mate, roommate or child. Going to sleep after absorbing visual and verbal stimulus about the day's tragedies brings those elements into your dreamtime. Let bedtime be peacetime.

Take time out. During the course of your day, if you feel symptoms of stress, fear or panic overload, take time out. In the spirit of the sacred pipe and the sacred circle, tell yourself the truth of the moment—*I am stressed, I am scared, I feel panicked*—and seek to balance the imbalance by allowing feelings of peacefulness to flood through you. Even if you have to walk out of a business meeting and sit in a ladies' room stall for five minutes, do it. Don't give unpeaceful feelings a chance to take hold. Peace within is always the first step to peace in the external world.

Try a Native American peace prayer. Take a "peace break" in lieu of a coffee break, and softly or silently chant *Peace to my right. Peace to my left. Peace in front of me. Peace in back of me. Peace above me. Peace below me. Peace within me. Peace all about. Peace abounds. Peace is mine.*

See a miracle with your own eyes. The prophecy is that White Buffalo Calf Woman will return to help establish a new world that unites all races. Several years ago, a white buffalo calf was born on a farm owned by a couple in Janesville, Wisconsin. It was named Miracle, and many believe she is White Buffalo Calf Woman, returning to bring peace to our world. Anyone can visit her, and each year there are festivals honoring her birth.

WHITE BUFFALO CALF WOMAN AFFIRMATION:

"I radiate peace everywhere I go."

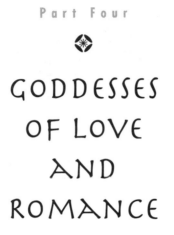

Part Four

GODDESSES OF LOVE AND ROMANCE

10

BE THE ULTIMATE SELF-LOVE GODDESS WITH VENUS

"To fall in love with yourself is the first secret to happiness."

—Robert Morely

Most of us want love, passion and delicious romance in our lives. We want to feel the tingly excitement of going out on a hot date, the sheer joy of knowing someone really cares, the security of having a relationship we can depend on and the dream come true of marrying "the one." There is nothing in the world that beats the feeling of falling in love with someone *so* fabulous that it makes your heart sing with joy!

However, we often put so much focus on finding love "out there" that we never get a chance to develop it within ourselves. If we seek love from others in order to feel happy and complete, we end up placing too much expectation and burden upon that person. The healthiest way for two people to come together is for mutual sharing and support—not to fill a hole that exists within. We constantly draw to us people who mirror our internal feelings; if we do not give love to ourselves 100 percent, the person who stands before us isn't likely to either.

It's so important to learn to love ourselves before trying to build a relationship with another. It is not narcissistic or stuck-up to care about oneself as much—or even more than—you would care for another. It is, in fact, a prerequisite to mature and lasting love. Once we have nurtured ourselves along, we have greater ability to experiment with making our relationships work. Without self-love, we're like bottomless baskets: There is no foundation to uphold love; someone can love you with more heart than you ever imagined, but where will it go if you have no internal mechanism for recognizing pure love?

You deserve to have an amazing man . . . the perfect mate . . . the ideal husband . . . the soulful partner . . . whoever your heart longs for. But your first love has to be you. If you are willing to give to yourself all that you wish to be given by a partner, you are making yourself ready for his love. It is a universal principle that likes attract likes: Give to yourself, and others will want to give to you. Believe in your own worth, and it will cast an alluring aura all around you that radiates wonderful vibes that say *I am loveable. I am hot. I am a female love force to be reckoned with. I am a love goddess.*

Venus is a girl's best friend when it comes to self-love and self-appreciation. She is all that's divinely feminine, the essence of loving to be a girl. She loves her life, her men, her universe and having it her way. She relishes gazing at her own reflection, admiring how beautiful and stunning she is. Venus helps us open our hearts to ourselves and our eyes to our own value. She represents self-love, self-esteem and a woman's divine worth.

Who Is Venus?

"With her, beauty comes. The winds flee before her and the storm clouds; sweet flowers embroider the earth; the waves of the sea laugh; she moves in radiant light. Without her there is no joy or loveliness anywhere."
—Edith Hamilton, *Mythology*

Venus, the Roman goddess of love, beauty and sexuality, is one of the most famous goddesses on the planet and also has her own planet—Venus, planet of poetry, music, pleasure and love. Her name is synonymous with all that is feminine and with love and passion. She is reputed for her sizzling sexuality, her thorough enjoyment of her own exploits and for a complete and utter appreciation of self. Well aware of her own stunning beauty and status, she cherishes her power and, when expressing her dark side, will squash all annoying competition. She has her generous side, helping mortals manifest their own great love stories. She represents the divinely independent female. Her love affairs with the hottest men of mythology are legendary. Volatile Mars and gorgeous Adonis are among her great paramours, but you won't see her waiting by the phone for her hunky god to call. She is more likely to go out and find a replacement to suit her every whim or be happy left to her own devices. Venus possesses a magic girdle—crafted with love by her husband, Vulcan—and when she wears it, anyone around her will fall under her spell. She is often pictured naked, rising from the sea on her shell, covered only by her hands and hair.

How to Invite Venus into Your Life

Venus does not feel she must fawn all over men or find her nourishment from them alone, nor should you! You honor her just by making sure you nourish your own needs. Venus was born of water, and it is to the water she returns for purification and rejuvenation. In ancient Rome, the women would take down the statue of Venus and ritually bathe her in honor of female sexuality and sensuality each April 1. It was a day for all women to celebrate the powers of the goddess. Later women would gather and do rituals in the temples. Some would bathe in the famous Roman baths in honor of the goddess, and it was said she would take their blemishes away. At the baths, attendants would scrub then scrape away dirt and remove unwanted hair; scented oil was used to rub them down. You can bring elements of this ancient ritual home by creating your own special self-love bath.

VENUS ROMAN BATH:

Practice self-love by being a goddess for a day. This act of self-love will bring you closer to receiving such pampering from another. Unconsciously, it gives the mind an impression that you are someone who deserves divine treatment and who is willing to be nurtured like a goddess.

1. Pick an auspicious day. Friday is typically the day of celebrating Venus and doing love rituals in her name. Astrologically speaking, Friday is governed by her planet and is said to help us access more of the feelings of love and joy that can help raise self-esteem. But any day that feels right should be your day! Just make sure you have enough time to really relax into the experience.

2. Surround yourself with roses. The rose is known as "the Flower of Venus." The scent generates her essence because it is associated with love and self-love. Get as many roses as you desire—and can reasonably afford—because they will be used in vases as well as for their petals. Red roses represent love and passion—the goddess herself. White are for purity. Pink for appreciation (of self). Yellow is for joy. These are all qualities you want to evoke, so include as many colors as possible. Get a little basket for the rose petals. Also make sure you have rose water (for a lighter scent) or essential rose oil (for a heavier scent) as well as a small handheld mirror. Venus loves looking at her own reflection; you can, too.

3. Prepare the atmosphere. Replace the light in the room with a few candles to give a nice glow. Set roses in a vase or two around the bathroom. Take the petals off the remaining roses and fill your small basket. Draw a delicious warm bath. Put a half cup of rose petals in the bath so you can enjoy the scented luxury of bathing like a goddess. Also add a little rose water to enhance the scent or a dab of rose oil if you want it stronger. Save some of the petals (you will need them right before the bath).

4. Change into a flowing robe. Once the room is ready, prepare yourself by taking off your "civilian" clothes and putting on a pretty robe or flowing nightgown, white if possible. Or wrap yourself in a white sheet, like a toga.

5. Play music that opens your heart. Select romantic instrumental music, classic music or a recording of the sounds of the ocean to take you back to the source of Venus. With the help of the music, put yourself in the mind-set that you are about to love and be loved as you never have been before.

6. Walk down the aisle to your altar of self-love. In a wedding ceremony, the flower girl usually goes right before the bride, sprinkling flowers in her path to signify purity and a new life. Whether your walk to the bathroom is long or short, take your basket of petals and be your own flower girl, sprinkling a trail of rose petals, as if you're a bride on your wedding day. Sprinkle any remaining petals into the tub. Step in and speak out loud, as if making an offering to the goddess:

Venus, goddess of love, I come to you pure of heart, mind and spirit. Let me bask in your loving embrace and know what it is to evoke the great love from the goddess who dwells within.

7. **Sit back, sink in and relax.** Daydream and relish the feeling of the warm water on your skin. Let the goddess wash over you with scents, sounds and feelings, and let her spirit move you. Contemplate what it would really mean in your life to treat yourself as a goddess and be treated as one. What would you need to give to yourself in order to heal anything now in the way of self-loving? What would you need to agree to do for yourself to make sure that your needs are always met?

8. **Take a vow of self-love.** Begin with a prayer: *Dear Venus, hear me please. I offer my vows to you for safe-keeping and for assistance in setting them forth and honoring them always.* Take the handheld mirror, and as you look at yourself, know you are looking at someone divine and deserving. Let your thoughts flow freely and try to express them as vows, for example: *I promise to treat myself well and offer the same kindness, love and compassion to myself as I do others; I will live my life in a manner that allows me to always nurture and love myself; I will embrace my sexuality and express my passion. I will always honor and cherish myself.* Whatever comes to mind, say it out loud as if speaking to Venus directly.

9. **Recessional of the roses.** When you are done with your bath and walk back out through the rose petals, imagine the goddess is walking with you toward a fresh start, to a new beginning, where you appreciate yourself, nurture yourself and come to love yourself more and more each day.

Self-nurture on a regular basis. A date with yourself is a powerful metaphor for self-nourishment. A bath is just one way to take a sacred moment of self-honoring. You can also light a candle and incense and take fifteen minutes to relax in a favorite chair or take yourself to a movie, out to dinner, or to a museum exhibit you've been meaning to see. Many of us take time out for ourselves just *once in a while,* and we neglect to create the foundation for ongoing revitalization. Carve out time and put things in order so you can access these experiences regularly. This may mean keeping your favorite bath oil and candles on hand at all times, or ensuring that you have several hours a week alone, to yourself. Think of it this way: If you were dating, wouldn't you go out of your way to make time to see the person you are going out with and focus attention on the relationship? Do it for yourself first, treat yourself like a goddess and be loving with yourself. This will set the groundwork for someone to come into your life and treat you in the same, loving way.

How to Keep Venus with You

Write a love letter to yourself. Put pen to paper and say all the things you would want to hear from a beloved. Go for it—be mushy, romantic, loving, generous with praise, comforting, adoring, wild, passionate. Evoke the energy of the love you want to experience in your life. Be generous in commenting about your own beauty and grace. Mail it to yourself, and when you read it, allow your heart to open even more.

Re-read the letter. Any time you feel a little beat up by the world or just don't seem to feel connected to the love within you, read it and smile.

Get your own personal girdle of Venus. It was magical because she felt magical in it. Find a garment that makes you feel like a goddess and wear it to evoke the energies of Venus in your own heart and feel good inside your own skin.

Shave like a goddess in a Roman bath. Enhance your experience of self-adoration with a smooth shave with a Venus razor, from Gillette for women. Named after the goddess, this super feminine shaving system helps you feel like a goddess, too.

VENUS AFFIRMATION:

"I am worthy of love."

BRING OUT YOUR SENSUALITY WITH OSHUN

"I wanted to heal myself, come out and play, have fun."

—Charlotte Rose, from *The Doctor Is In*

Many of us wish we could be completely comfortable in our own skin and feel liberated in our own bodies. We long to feel good about ourselves, no matter what we *think* we look like, regardless of those areas we always think we can improve. Maybe some of us want to be able to express that raw, unedited female passion. Perhaps we dream of dancing on tabletops, skinny-dipping in the moonlight at the drop of a hat and doing a slow, sensual striptease for an excited audience of one. Maybe it is just a sense of personal freedom, confidence and pleasure we seek. Whatever the motivation, sensual expression is healthy and good for the soul.

While we may feel we want to express our sensual side more, many women fear they can't "pull it off." We tend to believe that sensual self-expression is reserved for the kind of sexy babes and stars we see in movies and the airbrushed models in magazines. However, in *real* life, women have *real* bodies, faces and attitudes, and we all have the potential for sensual expression. It's so important to recognize that sensuality is an inner glow and fire—an authentic femininity brought to life in our very being.

When we stifle our sensuality or limit ourselves from expressing it fully, it's as if a part of us is being hidden and denied. We have to reach into ourselves to find it and be willing to bring out its essence. The effects can be wonderful—it can enhance self-esteem, improve our love lives and help us feel youthful and beautiful.

Oshun is a girl's best friend when you are ready to take the lid off your sensual self-expression and be completely natural with yourself, your lovers or your mate. The ultimate wild woman, she helps you bring out raw and primal sensuality. She represents self-appreciation and giving oneself permission to have sensual pleasure.

Who Is Oshun?

". . . Oshun loves bathing in cool waters, pampering herself with fragrant soaps and oils and wearing and changing her elegant clothing several times a day."
—Diedre Badejo, *Oshun, the Elegant Deity of Wealth, Power and Femininity*

Oshun (*o-shun*) is the Yoruban goddess of rivers and an Orisha (spirit) that sustains life. She is seen as proprietress of sweet, flowing waters. Her worship is widespread, including the United States, Cuba, Africa, Haiti and beyond. A primary deity of the African Oshogbo religion, she is also revered in the religions of Santeria and Brazilian Macumba. Believers say that she honors them, in certain ceremonies, by coming into their bodies. She is the youngest Orisha to be hailed as "Iyalode," meaning Great Queen; she's also called "Lady of Secrets," "Lady of Love" and "Lady of Gold." She's a major love goddess who is prayed to for real and lasting love, good marriages, peaceful home life and healthy babies; she governs diplomacy, and brings support to the community as well. She also rules beauty and flirtation and evokes the essence of in-your-face sensuality. She is said to protect the abdominal area and teach pleasure and happiness to her devotees. She is depicted as a sensual woman, usually with light brown skin and full hips, wearing jewels and holding a mirror and a fan.

How to Evoke Her

The pathway to sensual liberation is feeling comfortable in your own skin, comfortable enough to express and access power through your physical form, comfortable enough with your own nakedness. Oshun revels in the feel of her body. She is fluid, like the water; she loves to swim, dance, writhe naked and bathe naked. She's fond of finer things and nice jewelry and loves the feeling of jewelry jangling on her body. She gets turned on by her own image and loves to gaze at herself in the mirror. It is said she wears a mirror on her belt so she can admire herself! If you are daring enough to explore your own body with the intention to love and appreciate it, try this sensual beauty ritual for one. Let Oshun be your guide.

1. **Dance, dance, dance.** Pick a time when you know you will have quiet time alone. Put on some fabulous music and dance. Whether you think you can dance or not, start moving your body to the beat of music that turns you on and makes you feel excited. Dance like you used to dance when you were a little girl—without inhibitions. Jump around, jump on beds, wave your arms all about, go wild and get lost in the music. This will raise your energy as it helps you rise above shyness and hesitation. In Nigeria, Oshun is honored with the Ibo-Osun festival, where the women dance in honor of the goddess, hoping to be her favorite. It's said that when the goddess enters a

woman, the woman dances wildly yet fluidly as if she's swimming; she jangles her bracelets and jewelry and experiences a strong desire to look at herself in the mirror.

2. Create a safe, sensual environment. After you've had some fun dancing, turn down the music or pick a slow, sensual tune (or beating drums and heated congas) and create an environment in which you continue to feel loose and at ease. Dim all the lights and light a candle. Have a sip of wine if it will help you relax a bit.

3. Look at your body without judgment. Strip off all your clothes and stand in front of a full-length mirror. Try not to criticize yourself! Notice your curves, your coloring, your breasts, your butt and all the areas you don't normally look at: armpits, knees, toes and fingertips. If your eyes begin to focus on parts of you that you tend to judge harshly, find another place to focus. The more you can begin to focus on seeing your most beautiful self, the more beautiful you will become, right before your very eyes. Beauty, as they say, is in the eyes of the beholder. If you are someone who has been critical of your own looks, it's time you recognize that what you are being critical of is a distorted image of yourself based on old beliefs about what is beautiful and sensual and what is not.

4. Look into your eyes. After you have surveyed the skin you are in, let your eyes catch those of the woman in the mirror. See the sparkle in those eyes . . . and then look beyond it. Try to connect to the sensual goddess within you. She is beyond your body, beyond the sparkle and way beyond the critical beliefs you may have about your looks—and yet, right there. She comes from a place where there is no such thing as flat-chested, fat, too skinny or ugly. She is pure and untouched by the world that has tried to make her believe she is not pretty or sexy or shapely enough. Look into your own eyes and see if you can find her there. Greet her with love and a smile.

5. Give yourself a new name. In the African Ibo-Shun festival, women selected by the goddess are given new names and a new sense of identity and responsibility in the community. You can give yourself a new name that represents your newfound sensual identity or who you hope to become. For example, if you feel connected to Oshun, you can borrow one of the monikers already attributed to her; or invent one of your own, such as "Queen of Sensuality," "Princess of Passion," "Mistress of Self-Expression," or "Sexy-and-Loving-It-Woman." Use your imagination!

6. Practice makes perfect. Do this sensual beauty ritual as often as you like. (It can be at home, or in a hotel room when you are traveling, which may be even more relaxing.) The more you move your body and get to know your own physical form and appreciate it, the more comfort you will have in your own body. It will become easier to unleash your sensuality in life—on a hot date, in your steady relationship or just for the heck of it. As you go deeper into the process of unfolding sensuality, you can give yourself a new name according to your own evolutions.

How to Keep Oshun with You

Experience her in all of life's waters. When you bathe, shower, swim, wash your face or even wash laundry or dishes, think of Oshun and her sweet waters. Let her expressions of self-love flow into you with each drop of H_2O.

Have a sensual breakthrough in the rain. Run into a rainstorm naked at least once in your life. Don't do it in the middle of rush hour or in the midst of a dangerous thunderstorm, but when the moment comes that you are somewhere private and the rain beckons you to let it kiss your skin . . . say yes.

Wear her emblem on your body. Women honor Oshun by wearing a brass bracelet. It is said that Oshun herself owns five. On occasions when you especially want her with you, wear five brass bracelets that jangle a sensual tune with every movement of your arm.

OSHUN AFFIRMATION:

"I am a beautiful, sensual goddess."

1 2

BE A MAN MAGNET
WITH FREYA

"Remember, there are only two things without limits—
Femininity, and the means to explore it."

—From the movie *La Femme Nikita*

Although many women prefer a softer, more romantic approach to dating and relationships, there are those who'd love to experiment with being a sexual enchantress—the kind of woman for whom it is second nature to allure and charm any man. Even if we're content with who we are and with the men we meet (and even if in a relationship already), we may just wish to be a little more daring, bold and expressive when it comes to interacting with guys. Some girls just want to have fun.

The art of magnetizing men is not just a sex thing; it is enhanced by our talents, brains and personality. It's a combination of sharing all of who we are in an honest and open way and raising our sexual energy. Instead of viewing sexuality as something in the vicinity of underwear, experience it as a life force that flows through you—something that stimulates you and feels like good energy pulsing through your whole body. When a woman organically transmits that to a man, just through her being, it is extremely alluring, charming and stimulating. Men love being around women who are truly in touch with their sexual prowess.

There is nothing slutty about becoming skillful with feminine power, but it is important to never manipulate men or make an intentional energetic sexual connection with someone you are not truly interested in. If we explore sexuality with great consciousness (and, it goes without saying, safety), we can very responsibly awaken to our own allure. It also teaches us how to truly enjoy the natural sexual sizzle between men and women and be playful and easy-going with men in a way that makes life more interesting—it's enlivening and empowering for all involved. Instead of feeling you have to "get a guy to notice you," you live in the world as a woman who enjoys her own energy, enjoys men and, therefore, attracts men—very naturally.

Freya is a girl's best friend when it comes to owning your sexual prowess and integrating it with your true personality. She helps you express your sexual power in the world in a responsible way, and she also encourages you to draw the man—or men—of your choice because she is the mistress of pure sexual essence and inspires women to live their sexuality. She represents sexual self-expression and giving you permission to have pleasure and fun with men.

Who Is Freya?

"Utterly promiscuous, she took all the gods as lovers."
—Patricia Monaghan, *The New Book of Goddesses and Heroines*

Freya (*fray'-ah*) is the Norse goddess of love and fertility and hailed from the family of deities known as Vanir. She is the leader of the Valkyries, the goddesses who chose which warriors die in battle and then escort them to the other side. Considered one of the most beautiful, fortunate and powerful female deities in the Norse pantheon, she is a divine female of raw sensuality and vigorous passions—a vixen who is not shy about expressing herself. She is identified strongly with sexual freedom. Her residence is a beautiful palace called Folkvang ("field of folk"), a place that love songs were always heard playing. Her passions include music, spring, flowers and fairie folk. Her hall (in modern language, "crib") is considered a cool hangout, where women also go to gather. She hails from a culture that accepted infidelity as a standard operating mode, rather than a deception, because she is affiliated with numerous partners and yet also loved her consort husband. Although he was not her exclusive lover, when her husband, Od, went missing it's said the goddess cried tears of gold. She wore a precious necklace that was a magical and prized possession; when she wore it, her allure intensified and people fell under her spell. It is said she obtained the magical piece of jewelry by sleeping with four dwarves. Some say she also wore a rainbow around her neck. She also possessed a cloak (or skin) of bird feathers, which allowed its wearer to change into a falcon. She is often pictured as naked, or clothed and in a sensual pose, on one of her favorite modes of transportation—a chariot pulled by two cats or her "battle boar," who some say is her human lover in disguise. She often wears a Viking-style helmet.

How to Invite Her into Your Life

Freya can show us that when it comes to the expression of female power, sexuality is a metaphor for life. Given that we are all hormonally driven creatures, given to sexual urges and needs, it's healthy to desire pleasure, a decent selection of men to choose from, exposure to activities that enhance your sexual self-esteem and even a little nookie if the right person comes along. When you feel sexually empowered, you are more likely to take risks in other parts of your life. It can be invigorating and can boost your confidence.

1. **Create sex goddess runes.** Ancient Viking, Germanic and Anglo-Saxon peoples used "runes," an oracle based on the Viking alphabet. Used to shed light on situations related to the present moment and the future, people still consult them today. The Norse culture treated the runes and many other symbols that appeared on stone and rocks as sacred inscriptions from the gods. They had specific ways of deciphering and interpreting them. The rune symbolizes what you are experiencing in life and what you could learn from it. You can create your own set of "sex goddess runes" so Freya can speak to you through them daily and lead you, day by day, to greater liberation.

+ **Collect some stones.** Go to a lake, beach, pebble-strewn park or any place that has a nice supply of smooth, round rocks or stones—preferably the same color. Always ask the goddess for permission to remove stones from a public place or natural area first. Make the process of collecting them a passionate pursuit as you search for the most beautiful stones, appreciating their texture, running a finger over their tops to make sure they are smooth. Collect at least thirty-one and a couple extra. Wash them at home and let them dry.

+ **Buy thin, felt-tip markers that will write on stones.** Seek out the perfect writing utensil, one that will not "bleed" on the rock or be too light to read. You may have to take your rocks to the store to test out felt-tip pens.

+ **Create your sex goddess stones.** Take out your stones and pen, and get into man magnet mode (even if you have to watch a movie or think of a friend or an actress who exemplifies that energy to you for inspiration). Choose at least thirty-one qualities related to sexual expressiveness that you would LOVE to experience. Be as daring as you are willing, and also include very practical aspects. You can include some of the following, or make up your own: *hot, sexy, alluring, passionate, enticing, sensual, alive, queen, goddess, attractive, temptress, bewitching, beguiling, beautiful, fulfilled, charming, enticing, mesmerizing, desirable, wild, popular, sought-after, beloved, confident, joyous, liberated, powerful, appreciated, ecstatic, pleasure, energetic, honored, satisfied, pure, open-hearted, tingling, erotic, poetic, romantic.*

+ **Write them down and speak them out.** Write one of your thirty-one qualities on each rock (one for each day of the month). As you do, call it out: *I am desirable . . . I am appreciated . . . I am tingling . . .* etc.

+ **Give them a home.** Find a pretty container to keep your stones. Keep them in a sacred location—on an altar or by your bed.

+ **Pick one.** Use them as a divination tool, your communication with the goddess. There are enough stones for an entire month so, for at least one month, pick a stone each day. Take a moment to visualize yourself surrounded by white, brilliant light. Close your eyes, dig a hand into the container and choose one stone. See what it says—that is your quality for the day! Take a moment to hold the stone in your hand and tune in to the quality written on the stone. Think about what the quality means to you, and let it begin to permeate your being. If the stone says "mesmerizing," then begin to feel like a woman who mesmerizes. Whichever stone you pick is Freya's advice to you for the day. You may carry the stones with you or leave them on your altar. It is okay if you end up getting the same stone more than once or many times—it just means the goddess wants you to practice!

+ **Go about your business.** The messages on the sex goddess stones will give you a chance each day to practice *being in a state* of raised sexual energy and attention. On high alert, you might say. Let the qualities of the day percolate within you as you go about your business *as if* you are . . . sexy, alluring, popular . . . or whichever is the quality of the day. You may find that just by having the quality in your consciousness that things occur that validate that you are indeed sending out specific vibes. Eventually, all thirty-one qualities become a part of who you are. Imagine it this way: Just the way a radio tower broadcasts a radio signal and you hear music that makes you want to dance, you can broadcast "an invitation" to inspire a man to want to get to know you. Working with these runes can help you develop subtle energetic communication skills that will help you take charge of your own romantic destiny.

2. Invoke the sex goddess within. Freya lives in some of the classic tools of verbal and nonverbal sexual communication. Once you have begun to percolate your sexual energy using the sex goddess runes, here are some ways to practice being aware, alluring and authentic in interactions with men.

+ **Show you are open and interested.** You have to let a guy know you want to meet him; even if you get a little nervous, don't shut down and pretend you are not *really* interested. What draws a man is a woman who sends clear signals and is open to his approach. Be real. Let your body language show you are relaxed and open. Smile.

+ **Be yourself.** Posturing and putting on airs defeats the purpose and sets up a dynamic you may not be able to live up to. When getting to know a guy, share whatever is real for you. Are you feeling sexy and turned on? Let him know. Are you smart, savvy, successful, funny, enthusiastic, passionate and fun? Share it. You don't have to tell everything, but let him see there is more to you than your sexuality.

+ **Give him** *that* **look.** Your soul, your desires and your intensions all come through your eyes. If you like a man, look right at him and engage him with your look. Try not to turn your eyes away, even if you get nervous. Stay present, stay with him. The longer you can keep his gaze, the more intense the connection.

+ **Repel unwanted attention.** Learn to fine-tune your "man antenna" (i.e., put out the right vibes for the right men, as opposed to drawing every male in the vicinity). Sometimes being a man magnet can translate as a great, authentic feeling of confidence that glows within and generates more of the same. If you find yourself getting hit on by people you want nothing to do with, imagine your sexual energy is like electricity that powers the lights. Flip the switch to "off" until you can get out of the situation.

How to Keep Freya with You

Always have a signature. A favorite perfume can help cast a spell on a man. It has to be a fabulous, perfect scent that makes *you* feel like a goddess. At home, spray it in the air and walk through the mist so that it goes everywhere. Make sure it is a scent that makes you feel powerful and that it is strong enough to leave a *slight* scent trail as you walk. A man never forgets the scent of a goddess.

Try pheromones. Life is a pheromone fest. Like animals, we sniff the subtle scent of sex on each other and want to get closer. If you want to up the ante on the Freya experience, try some of nature's little helpers. Athena Pheromone 10:13 from the Athena Institute, mixed with your favorite perfume, enhances your natural charms and signals. It generates good feelings within, promoting a sense of attraction to your own energy, which energetically translates to others. Studies have shown that it has a direct effect on people in your immediate area.

FREYA AFFIRMATION:

"I magnetize men through the natural expression of my feminine energy."

LIBERATE YOURSELF FROM BAD RELATIONSHIPS WITH PERSEPHONE

"A woman has got to love a bad man once or twice in her life, to be thankful for a good one."

—Marjorie Kinnan Rawlings, from the book *The Yearling*

Few of us will escape the universal experience of sister-hood that initiates us into the sacred fraternity of being a woman: the bad relationship. While you hopefully will never find yourself in the grips of an abusive partner, you may stumble into a union with someone who steals your heart only to abduct you into "relationship underworld." Once there, you may find you're on a journey through relationship hell as you recognize that the man you believed to be Mr. Right is the lover you must leave.

His infractions may be relatively minor—he's cheap, un-appreciative, unconscious or just so unmotivated that it is im-possible to build a relationship. Worse, he could be a cheater, liar, con artist, big-time emotional withholder or someone who continually acts in a manner that is demeaning or mean or makes you cry a lot. It might seem like a no-brainer that it is time to flee, but some of us stay . . . and stay . . . and become casualties of love. There is some invisible glue that holds us or forbidden fruit that tempts us.

A relationship that contributes to you feeling bad about yourself or that brings about symptoms of depression, despair and rage (because you are *not* getting what you need) requires introspection and, eventually, action. Although many women rationalize, at first, that they have to change themselves, none of us can fix a broken man who has no desire to change. If you find yourself sliding downward into your man's dysfunctional world because you can't elevate him or encourage him toward a fuller potential for your relationship, you have to stop and wonder if you are selling yourself out. No one has to settle for a bad relationship or make herself smaller in order to make a man happy. Abused women are often afraid to leave their abusers; to them, abuse equals love. It's all they've known. Many of us feel guilty setting a guy free in the world, as if we fear he will not make it on his own.

Mr. Wrong may just be a blip on the screen for a brief moment in time . . . or you may find that you are living with or married to him. You may be toying with the idea of separating, or you could be crawling out of your skin, itching to get away, afraid if you stay another moment you will be forever lost. Even if you experience a temporary power lapse—because you are not sure what to do, or how to do it, or because you're dependent on him in some way—you can *make yourself* stronger and deal effectively with difficult men and unhealthy unions. If you find you are exhausted and depressed from a relationship that takes too much work, ultimately, it may be time to learn your lessons, count your blessings and move on.

Persephone is a girl's best friend when it comes to freeing yourself from bad relationships. She gives us great insight on what it feels like to be trapped and out of control in a relationship, and on how to extricate ourselves from unhealthy unions. She helps us evoke sunshine, springtime and liberation. She represents balancing light and darkness in a relationship, recognizing dysfunction, breaking free and returning home to ourselves.

Who Is Persephone?

"He caught her up reluctant on his golden car and bared her away lamenting. Then she cried out shrilly with her voice, calling upon her father, who is most high and excellent. But no one, either of the deathless gods or of mortal men, heard her voice . . ."

—Homer, *The Iliad*

Persephone (*per-sef-oh-nee*), Greek goddess of harvest, vegetation and spring, was seen as the rich fertile earth, the seed that was planted in the earth so it could bloom. A virginal maiden who became a queen of darkness, she came to represent both the loss of innocence and a woman's occasional journey with a man to the dark side. She was at play in a field, gathering flowers, when she came across the beautiful narcissus flower. As she went to pick it, without warning, the earth suddenly opened and out came Hades, god of the shadowy underworld and ruler of the dead, in a chariot. It turned out to be her surprise wedding limo. Frightened, kicking and screaming, she is carried off to his home in hell. Her mother, Demeter, freaked and confronted Persephone's dad, Zeus. It turned out that he had given Hades *permission* to take Persephone's hand—and more. Demeter roamed the earth in search of Persephone and could not find her. Finally, she refused to let her grains and fruits grow until her daughter was returned; thus, a deadly winter fell upon the earth. Eventually, Zeus gave in and ordered Hades to let Persephone go. But before Hades relinquished her, he persuaded Persephone to eat from the pomegranate. Because she had tasted the food of the dead, Hades retained a claim on her. She ate six seeds so a deal was struck that she would spend six months of the year with Hades and six with her mom. The cycle continues that we have spring when Persephone is free from the underworld and winter when she leaves and her mother mourns.

How to Invite Her into Your Life

There is a jewel tucked into every relationship—even the bad ones—that can give us valuable insight into our own behavior (and help us move forward to a relationship that is more suited). Once we find that jewel and polish it, we must decide whether we are meant to remain in a relationship we know in our hearts is not really right for us. As Persephone knew all too well, there is also a sweet fruit that can tempt us to keep coming back for more. But if a relationship is dragging you down, holding you back from your power, bringing insanity to your life, there may come a time when you need to gather your strength and start again. The first thing to do is honestly assess your situation.

1. **Recognize denial.** When someone fulfills a need in us we may tend to overlook certain things, reasoning: *Maybe my bad boy is not so bad* or *My emotionally dysfunctional lover is not that dysfunctional.* Hades snatched Persephone, the very breath of springtime, and took her to hell. He insisted she come to his world because he could never raise himself up into hers. After spending so much time there, she began to forget who she was; some say that she co-conspired to eat the forbidden fruit so she could stay in Hades' world with him, yet this was not something she would admit.

2. **Healthy relationship checklist.** Love does not mean taking a hostage. The recovery movement has put forth a classic definition of a healthy partnership and healthy partners. Brenda Schaeffer outlines some of these quali-

ties in *Signs of Healthy Love*. See how many you can check off on the healthy relationship list:

+ Allows for individuality

+ Tolerates both oneness and separateness from each other

+ Brings out the best qualities in each partner

+ Accommodates change and exploration

+ Encourages growth in each partner

+ Establishes true intimacy

+ Has built in freedom and allows each partner to ask for what they want

+ Encourages each partner to experience giving *and* receiving

And a healthy individual, capable of a healthy union, would ideally:

+ Endure endings well

+ Be self-sufficient

+ Have the ability to accept the limitations of self and partner

+ Be up to handling commitment

+ Have high self-esteem

+ Enjoy some alone time

+ Express feelings spontaneously

+ Welcome closeness and be willing to take some risks

+ Treat themselves and their partner as equals

+ Would never think of trying to change or control the other.

3. Inventory your past relationships. The fruit that haunted Persephone could only be experienced in the underworld, with Hades. Sometimes, even though we *know* a man is killing our potential, we keep going back, because of the *one thing* we think we can get only from him. The more willing we are and the more skillful we become at identifying those things that we keep replaying in our relationships, the closer we will come to heading toward healthier, happier relationships. Make a list of all your major boyfriends and write down:

+ The significant problems and chronic issues.

+ Why you broke up, who left first and how it ended.

+ What you told yourself about men when the relationship ended (*they always leave, they never love me enough, they cheat,* etc.). See if you can identify a "belief" you may have that keeps manifesting in your life.

+ If you are in a relationship now, notice if there are similar issues and fears.

+ Take some time to explore whether you have a standard M.O. for the kind of men you select. Is there: A relationship pattern? A bad boy antenna? Do you seek out the wrong kind of men because they are exciting or because you feel needy for love? Be gentle with yourself as you try to shine a light on these issues.

4. Look at your relationship with Daddy. Recognizing the root relationship issues is the first step to healing them. Persephone was betrayed by her father. Many women have, or perceived they have, been betrayed by their fathers in some way. Even if that is not the issue, you can be sure there is some issue related to Dad that begs exploration. Whether he was mean, cold or simply a well-meaning man with flaws, to a little girl, he was a god. It's important to focus on gently illuminating and discovering how the relationship with Dad may have impacted, or even interferes, with your adult relationships with men. In quiet, alone time, explore these points:

+ **Acknowledge the influence of your father.** He's your first model for how men are in the world. We tend to draw men who are like our dads, for better or for worse. Look through some old photos of your dad and remember what it was like growing up with him. Think about things he taught you about relating to men, through words and his way of being. Then give some thought to how you maybe turn your boyfriends into your father—by wanting him to be responsible for you or by picking men who replicate some of your dad's least favorable traits, or even selecting classically "unavailable" men because your dad was, technically, unavailable.

+ **Healing the daddy wound.** This can be a lifetime project, but with every relationship we get better at understanding how we've been hurt and disappointed. Write a letter to your father, whether he's alive or has passed on; this is a letter you will never send. Its only purpose is to help you clarify some of your pain and begin to liberate yourself from its grip. When you have some quiet time—perhaps outdoors with nature, at a beach or somewhere healing—take pen and paper and hold the intention that you can be honest enough to write anything you need to say to Dad and strong enough to recognize anything you need to know about your relationship with him. Cry, laugh, feel whatever feelings that come up, and when you feel you have written all you need to share, fold the letter and put it somewhere sacred—a sacred book or a favorite keepsake box. Make the choice to heal anything that stands in the way of having a healthy relationship with a man who is mature, balanced and appropriately loving and attentive. Seek professional support for the tough parts.

5. Ritual to reclaim the right to a wonderful relationship: Persephone's legendary descent to the underworld six months a year brings us winter, and her ascent returns the spring and summer; the earth is reborn anew. You can rise up, liberate yourself and come back to a new life where you only invite in men who are truly worthy of your love. Perform the following rituals to reach for your highest relationship potential:

+ **Say good-bye to bad relationships by planting new seeds within you.** A striking work of art by Yuroz called *Seeds of Desire* suggests the pomegranate is a vehicle to help a woman judge the worthiness of a lover. It depicts a man lovingly feeding a woman the seeds of a pomegranate, one seed at a time—patiently, careful not to drop any. This is how she can gauge if he is truly a worthwhile lover. Rather than hold in our consciousness that the sweet fruit can be used to hold us captive in the relationship underworld, use the pomegranate to empower yourself to liberation.

+ **Buy a pomegranate and let it ripen.** The interior of the pomegranate is composed of many pink red sections of pulplike tissue, each with a tiny seed within it. The seeds usually taste juicy and sweet and sometimes have a slightly sour aftertaste. The pomegranate is basically the only fruit from which we eat only the seeds. Selecting each seed from the fruit, feeling the texture in your fingers, raising it to your mouth and taking it inside your mouth are very sensual and freeing. Pray for the lover who will someday feed the seeds to you with love and patience, but enact this by feeding them to yourself. You can declare your liberation from a bad relationship by asserting your dreams, hopes and aspirations for love.

+ **Eating the seeds as a sacred act.** You can do this exercise alone or with a friend (pick someone with similar relationship values, as you will each be evoking qualities you choose in a relationship with, and for, each other). Cut the pomegranate into two even pieces. Play some really fun and inspiring instrumental music to get you in the mood.

+ **Chant your way to liberation.** Take turns, or alternate back and forth, as you call out and declare a positive relationship trait that you seek in a man. Speak out: *He's sensitive, He adores me, He worships me in a healthy way, He's generous, He's spiritual, He is a nice person, My friends love him,* etc. Calling out what you want puts forth a thought form that is the first step to making it real in your world. As you swallow each seed after declaring a positive relationship trait, you embody the qualities you seek in a man. After doing this, you may find the man in your life becomes more of whom you want—or you may see clearly that he is nowhere near the ideal partner you deserve. Then, you can make a choice to move on. First, you have to create a new relationship model and make the pomegranate a tool to assist your ascension from the relationship underground.

How to Keep Persephone with You

Wash that man right out of your hair. Anytime you feel the pain of loss or a broken heart welling up within, wash your hair and declare that sadness is moving out of your body and down the drain. Say a prayer to Persephone to bring back spring.

Let the sun shine. When you don't know what to do with yourself and you feel antsy from pent-up emotions, step out into the sunlight—like Persephone retuning to bring forth the spring—and let the sunshine warm your heart.

Explore spirituality. Go deeper into who you are and what you are about. There is a tendency to focus on "him" and what he did and what he may be going through. Try pursuits that take you out of your head, *and out of his head*. If not a religious institution, go to a lecture or a class that is good for the body and spirit. Once you have been to the relationship underworld, the first glimmer of recovery is like the first burst of spring. Let Persephone help you come home and see the light.

PERSEPHONE
AFFIRMATION:

"I raise myself up."

MOVE TOWARD MARRIAGE WITH GAURI

*"You have become mine forever. Yes, we have become partners.
Hereafter, I cannot live without you. Do not live without me.
Let us share the joys."*

—From "The Seven Steps," a traditional Hindu wedding saying

Many of us spend our entire adult lives hoping to meet the man of our dreams, only to find that when the possibility for real love and a lasting intimate relationship shows up, we spin into a tizzy of confusion, fear and doubt. Some people say "they just knew," at the outset, that they were meant to marry their mates. And maybe they did. But for most of us, when we fall in love and get the urge to merge, there is a period when we may have many doubts; we wonder if we can actually handle being married, succeed at it and have what we want in life with the partner we've chosen. Even if you love someone dearly, relationships are risky, the divorce rate is high and many of us fear that marriage will snatch our freedom, when in truth, a good marriage liberates you even more.

Then there are those of us who have no commitment issues and who seem to be able to truly handle a serious kind of love, but our honey is a bit altar-shy. Maybe he's in love with you but not in love with the idea of marriage. Or perhaps he's crazy about you, yet he's afraid of not being good at being your husband or losing his freedom. You may begin to worry that you will never get to say "I do."

Most couples entertain the idea of marriage, but one or both usually have a lot of worries about taking the next step in the relationship. It's understandable. Stepping up to the plate to take those vows is a *whole other* ball game. However, there comes a time in a relationship when you reach a point of no return. You have invested a certain amount of time, energy and love into one special relationship and you want your boyfriend to become your husband or he is anxious for you to be his wife. Hopefully, you will both come to that decision simultaneously. But it doesn't always work that way.

With love, patience and good communication (and counseling when needed), you can begin to work on the issues that get in your way, and/or his and seek to resolve whatever stands between you two and "I do." Simultaneously, you can focus on the ultimate goal—to be married—and begin to live life as if you will soon be walking down the aisle. As you get ready for love, you have to be willing to make the internal changes that marriage requires. You can take a spiritual approach to moving yourself toward feeling ready for marriage and a prayerful approach to asking that the love of your life meet your halfway.

Gauri is a girl's best friend when it comes to selecting a wonderful, reliable mate and moving toward a solid and loving marriage. Gauri is the divine mother you can trust to guide you to marry a mate who is *really* right for you! She inspires you to make wise and wholesome choices and to develop the maturity needed for marriage. She represents working with your higher self to pave the way for true love and that walk down the aisle.

Who Is Gauri?

"After years of prayer to Gauri to bring her a 'groom like Shiva' on her wedding day the bride takes the groom to Gauri's abode in her family shrine to thank the goddess for answering her prayer . . . and to show the goddess the groom, the husband she is responsible for bringing."
—Department of Anthropology, California State University web site

Gauri (*gow·ree*) is a Hindu love goddess who is worshipped as the bestower of "virtuous husbands." She is the young, unmarried Parvati, who ultimately lands the great god Shiva as her beloved. She is considered the bride of Shiva—just before the honeymoon. They call her "the Golden One." While most marriages are "arranged," according to ancient customs of India, many women consult Gauri, local protector of relationships and cosmic matchmaker. They believe she will help magnetize the best mate possible for marriage, because she was, in fact, able to do that for herself; she is a role model of success, having won the heart of Shiva. It is also said that some of the most notable heroines in Hindu history prayed to Gauri for good men. Gauri is celebrated in the Gangur Festival in India, an event attended by married women, who beseech the goddess to bless their husbands and families, and singles, who pray for a suitable life partner. The festival is a *girls-only* event, featuring Gauri and the goddess Parvati. On the final day, a bedecked and bejeweled icon of Gauri is wheeled out into the streets. The women, balancing brass pitchers of water on their heads and wearing their finest saris, escort the icon to the temple of Gauri where the goddess is ritually bathed while her name is chanted in many forms. The close of the festival includes the arrival of an icon or depiction of Shiva, who comes to escort his bride home, along with horses and elephants. A divine wedding, to say the least! Pictured as a beautiful young sari-clad Indian woman, sometimes sitting on a throne and displaying four arms, she is the personification of purity and serious marital intent.

How to Invite Her into Your Life

It is Gauri's pleasure to bring soul mates together and help create circumstances in which honorable people can marry. She brings something to a union that many of us find elusive—a sense of security. Just before partaking in the marriage *samskara* (sacred rite), Hindu brides and their womenfolk will often pray to Gauri for a blessed union. But they also pray to her long before the wedding, for a wedding . . . to someone wonderful!

PARTAKE IN GAURI CUSTOMS:

1. **Create a marriage altar:** The Gangur Festival, which celebrates Gauri each spring and honors her marriage, gives women hope that they, too, will marry the perfect mate. You can honor Gauri in your own way in the privacy of your own home. If you want to have a symbol of Guari, select an object that represents her, such as a beautiful sari or a miniature throne. Or be creative, as many Hindu devotees are, and create an icon from a coconut with the mask of a female face on it. To keep it simple, you can just light a candle or use a traditional oil lamp (ghee or coconut oil with small string wicks that can be purchased on the Internet or in a local Indian goods store). To begin to imagine your own marriage, cut out a picture of a wedding gown that you love and put it in a standing frame on the altar. Let the altar be your focal point for prayers to the goddess that you, too, will have the opportunity to marry a wonderful man.

2. **Pick a wedding date.** It is the Hindu tradition to find out the most auspicious day for a wedding by consulting a

Vedic astrologer. Called *Jyotish,* this kind of Hindu predictive astrology is a little different than the astrology we know in the United States but it is considered highly accurate. Even if you've not heard a proposal—or proposed—yet, you can consult a Vedic astrologer about the most auspicious time for you to get married. You wouldn't want to get attached to an exact date, but there is certainly nothing wrong with *anticipating* a time frame. It can help you psyche yourself up for the possibility that the stars will conspire to bring you and your boyfriend closer together.

3. Try marriage paint. *Mehndi,* the Indian art of hand-painted design with henna, has become very hip. But in Gauri's culture, *Mehndi* has long been associated with marriage. Dry leaves of the henna plant are crushed into powder, made into a paste and applied to a woman's hands and feet in elaborate, intricate designs. It's almost always a sign that there is about to be a wedding! Prefabricated *Mehndi* kits are readily available, and you can also go into an Indian beauty parlor for one. If you treat the experience as a sacred adventure befitting of a bride-to-be, you may find that it is a nice symbolic intention that you, too, intend to marry—someday soon! It lasts about six weeks.

4. Getting ready for marriage ritual with Guari:
+ **Petition and pray to her with specific requests.** This simple, nondenominational ceremony will give you a chance to articulate your heart's desire, and "petition" the goddess to help you fulfill your marriage destiny. There's an important ground rule that must be followed when people in relationships pray for marriage: When praying and expressing your desire and plan to marry, never use the name of a specific person—unless there is already an engagement. Refer to him only as

your true love. This is a nonmanipulative approach that leaves it in the hands of the divine. You would never want to pray, "I want Jack to ask me to marry me"; instead you might say, "I choose to be emotionally ready to marry my true love." It is very important that you focus on moving yourself forward and not put any spiritual demands on your mate. Trust that when you are truly ready, he will be, too. If love is true and you are meant to be together, the natural energies of your love and intention will move him forward as well.

+ **Create a sacred space.** Use some uplifting sacred music or ring a bell three times to start your ceremony.

+ **Make an offering of fruits and sweets.** Put them in front of the altar (if you have one set up) or just leave them in a bowl to symbolize a gift you are giving to the goddess before asking for her help.

+ **Bring in light.** Light a pink candle (or an oil lamp) to symbolize the love that already exists in your heart and the heart of your beloved.

+ **Pray.** Use the following prayer (feel free to tweak this or write your own) to call out to your divine matchmaker Gauri and ask her to get you and your true love closer to the altar.

Dear divine matchmaker of all there is.
In the name and spirit of the goddess Gauri,
Please fill this place with your sacred presence.
My heart is pure; my intentions clear.
I ask for your guidance and your help.

In moving forward wisely and maturely to marry my true love,
The one who is my most perfect partner.
The partner who enhances me by his/her very being . . .

Who brings more love, joy, peace and prosperity to my life . . .
Who I can love fully and who can fully receive my love . . .
Who loves me fully and whose love I can fully receive . . .
Who loves, honors and cherishes me completely, and always.

✦ **Call out the qualities you will bring to marriage.** Now, contemplate the vows and commitments *you* are willing to make. If you choose, softly call them out, as if you are whispering to Gauri and describing a marital union that already exists. (You can write them down if your prefer.) As an example, you can choose from or add to any of the following:

- I trust his love implicitly.

- I seek to grow and grow up together.

- I am a true partner.

- I put him and our relationship first.

- I give up childish ways and offer mature love.

- I face my fears with him.

✦ **Close with this benediction:**

I have spoken truly from my heart.
Please grant my desires for love—of self and with my true love.
I trust you will bring this to me lovingly and gently,
At the exact right moment in time,
In a way that is completely right for my love and me.
I give thanks for your presence, your guidance and your love.
Amen. And so it is.

✦ **Take in sweetness.** In a typical Hindu worship service, which is called a puja, or pooja, the fruit and sweets that are offered to the deities before worship are shared with devotees after worship. It is called *prasad,* and taking it in allows you to take in the energy of Gauri. Eat a piece of fruit that has been blessed by your prayer.

✦ **Take Gauri's divine advice.** If you tell Gauri what you want, she will align that with what she knows is in your highest interest and lead you to the altar with your true love at the right time. Like a wise mother, she may not rush things. Be patient, have faith and continue to envision yourself moving toward marriage with a mate *who loves you dearly, who would devote his life to you and who is committed to common goals.*

How to Keep Gauri with You

Keep praying and honoring the goddess. Praying regularly keeps you connected and keeps the goals you have alive in your consciousness and activated in the world. Try this "Hindu Prayer to Mother Gauri": *Adorations to the goddess who is the auspiciousness of all that is auspicious, who is the consort of Lord Shiva, who is the bestower of every desire of one's heart. Adorations to you, o Devi, I have taken refuge in you.*

Read epic love poetry. Read poetry that stimulates your mind and your emotions and keeps the flame of your desire for love alive. Gauri lives in the epic poetry of India as Parvati with her consort, Shiva, and their relationship is hot and heavenly. Any poetry that enhances your yearning for love will help.

Daydream about your wedding. Think about what your marriage ceremony and celebration would be like. Who would you invite, what dress would you choose and where would it be and during what time of year? What kind of ceremony would you have? What type of vows would you speak? Allow your mind to run away with this fantasy and see yourself, at the altar, speaking your vows to your beloved.

GAURI AFFIRMATION:

"I choose to marry my true life partner."

15

RESCUE YOUR RELATIONSHIP
WITH ISIS

"Love doesn't just sit there, like a stone, it has to be made, like bread; re-made all the time, made new."

—Ursula K. LeGuin

While the idea of living "happily ever after" is what we all hope for, most of us will find that it takes some work and that there is no such thing as the "perfect partner" or the "perfect relationship." Our partners may be perfect for us, and we can even learn to see them *perfect just as they are,* but even the most soulful and loving couples will have to slay a few relationship dragons as they travel the trail of true love together. Eventually, as we put our energy toward striving to perfect our ability to love—instead of trying to fix our mates and ourselves—we will reap the rewards of a solid partnership. Our relationships will become our homes, and there will live *two against the world, instead of one,* and a foundation upon which we can build our lives.

A good relationship must be nurtured, created and built over time. In the process, it is guaranteed that the person you love the most will also challenge you, press your buttons, remind you of one or more parent, drive you nutty with the mirror he holds up in your face when you least want to look . . . and enfold you in arms that feel safer than any you have ever known before. A powerful way to keep your relationship sacred is to nip problems in the bud in a mature and loving fashion. Whether you are facing a major disagreement or an irksome miscommunication, it is important to make time for an immediate rescue, rather than wait until your relationship needs extraordinary measures and resuscitation.

Isis is a girl's best friend when it comes to demonstrating commitment to her partner and doing what it takes to make a relationship work. She helps us maintain extraordinary intimacy and divine relations while living in the real world. She represents commitment in the long haul, devotion and keeping relationships sacred.

Who Is Isis?

"She was the personification of the female creative power that conceived and brought forth every living creature and thing. She used power not only in creating new things but in restoring what was dead."
—Anthony S. Mercatante, *Who's Who in Egyptian Mythology*

Isis (*i·sis*) is one of the earliest and most important goddesses in ancient Egypt. Her worship, still active today in goddess religions, was a major part of Egyptian culture just over 2,000 years ago; from there it spread to Greece, Rome and elsewhere in the world, making her a universal goddess. Her image abounds on the walls of temples and tombs in Egypt and in museums around the world. Because her powers and skills are so vast and all-encompassing, she's referred to as goddess of 10,000 names. She was known as healer, physician, enchantress, magician, patron of women in childbirth, mother and devoted wife. Together with Thoth, scribe to gods, she taught mankind the secrets of medicine. She represents both a maternal spirit of nurturing and the ultimate magic of restoration and resurrection. One of the most striking aspects of her story is her eternal relationship with her beloved Osiris—her brother, husband, lover and co-ruler. Isis and Osiris shared the same soul. Along with siblings Set, Nepthys and Horus the elder, they were nurtured in the womb of their mother, Nut, until it was time for their birth. Isis and Osiris ruled the rich lands of Egypt and taught their people agriculture, arts and literacy. Their brother, Set, was jealous of Osiris and devised a plan to kill him—twice. Isis revived Osiris and brought him back; but the second time, he would never be the same man. Isis was able to get pregnant with their son, also named Horus, and raises him to seek vengeance for his father and claim his rightful place. Osiris became king of the underworld and Isis the queen of heaven, and together they ruled still. She is often seen a young mother suckling young Horus or as a very trim Egyptian woman with dark hair, wearing form-fitting gowns and elaborate jewelry. Her headdress is a throne or a solar disk with horns. She is sometimes seen with wings.

How to Invite Her into Your Life

Although we're not likely to come across the exact same circumstances, women can relate to the trials that Isis had to surmount to save her relationship. The first time Set killed Osiris, he tricked him into stepping into a coffin made especially for him and cast him upon the Nile. Isis was out of town delivering babies and came home to find her husband missing. She threw on raggedy clothes to disguise herself, and in emotional agony, she combed the earth for her beloved. She asked everyone she saw and tracked every lead she could. He was her partner, best friend and truest lover; she refused to let him go. She knew if she kept looking, somehow he'd hear her and he would come back. In *The First Love Stories,*

Diane Wolkstein eloquently relays the call of Isis to her beloved as she searches for him:

> *My tears flood the land.*
> *They burn my face.*
> *Do not forsake me, Osiris.*
> *Come to your sister.*
> *Take away the pain in my body.*
> *You who never found fault with me.*
> *Do not leave me.*
> *Heaven has fallen through to earth.*
> *I walk the roads searching for you.*
> *Fire burns in my heart.*
> *I grieve that you are alone.*
> *I stretch my arms out to greet you.*

Isis finds him. She turns herself into a winged goddess, flies up and flaps her wings above his body and fills his nose and mouth with air to revive him. It works. Relieved, she hides him. When Set learns this, he finds Osiris again, this time cutting him into fourteen pieces and tossing them all about. Isis is able to gather every part of him except for his penis, which she creates from wax and gold. She puts him back together and mounts him to produce his heir, Horus, who will claim his father's kingdom on earth. Isis and Osiris are together still, but Osiris is now in a different realm. Through his gates the dead must pass, if they are to be allowed into the afterlife. Isis becomes the guardian of Osiris and of their sacred relationship. She loves him dearly, though he has changed.

To the human consciousness it would appear Isis is separated from her beloved by the veil between the worlds. But in truth, he is just a shout away. They are, in many respects, a working couple—she the queen of heaven and he lord of the Dead and Ressurection—and they represent above as below. As a working couple, they each have separate responsibilities—just as you and your beloved get wrapped up in your jobs, your friends, your stress and your fears. Sometimes, when enough time goes by, even people who adore one another can become distant and feel disconnected, whether it is because of a fight, lack of communications or other problems. Having truly been disconnected from her beloved, Isis knows how important it is to reconnect as soon as possible. Here is a loving, conscious way to share some time, clear the air and reunite:

1. Isis and Osiris ritual of renewal for couples:

Before you do this ritual, say a prayer to Isis—with or without your partner present—and ask her to share with you her great gift of resurrection and rebirth so you may be empowered to do this ritual with your own beloved. As a thank-you, you can place incense, a loaf of bread and two glasses of wine or juice as an offering to Isis and Osiris. Leave it on the kitchen table. When the ritual is complete, you and your honey can have a snack on behalf of the god and goddess. (Or if your beloved is resistant to a heart-to-heart ritual of reconnection, make him a fabulous dinner and introduce the ritual as a fun idea that will hopefully end with an even more fun time "making up.")

If you find yourself in unhappily-ever-after land, assess the situation and bring healing to any rifts, distances or arguments. Whether you are rehashing an ongoing issue or you have both been working too much to spend time together, find a quiet time and create a setting that will allow you both to decompress from the everyday stress of life and the stress of any issues in the relationship. Use this simple ritual to diffuse tension:

+ **Bring in light.** Begin by lighting a pink candle, symbolizing the light of love.

+ **Get in a loving mood.** As a gentle meditation and attunement, close your eyes and "remember" love. This is an easy way to connect, or reconnect, if you have been feeling separate or distanced from your beloved. Both of you can just picture a time, in your mind's eye, in which you were completely in love with each other. Doing this will help set the intention for the ritual as well as create a feeling of being openhearted.

+ **Reconnect.** Once you both feel centered, open your eyes and look deeply into the eyes of your beloved. Smile, giggle, feel whatever you feel yet keep your eyes connected. It is especially potent if you hold hands as you hold eye contact. This is an effective way to look right into the soul of the one you love and establish that soul connection.

+ **Talk to each other.** After a time of soulful connecting, open the floor to verbal communication. Each partner should have a designated period in which it is that partner's time to speak—especially if there is a crisis or challenge in the relationship. For that period of time (ten to thirty minutes each), there should be no interruptions or excuses from the other side—just listen to what your beloved has to say. After that, the partner listening should have a chance to share his or her view and experience on the topic (or whatever is on that partner's mind and heart).

+ **Communicate responsibly.** Take time to discuss needs, using *I* statements: "I really need this" or "It would support me if I could have that." Make a strong effort to never accuse or blame each other by using "*If only you would . . .*" or "*You never . . .*" statements. Each partner should take responsibility for expressing needs, without an expectation of them being fulfilled by the other person. This gives both the space to say what they really want, without putting pressure on the other partner. Sharing pent-up feelings will take the steam out of them. Being able to do that with your partner, without retribution or shame, creates great freedom and an opening for giving and supporting one another.

+ **Be present for each other.** This process helps couples reconnect to one another and the power of their relationship on an emotional, physical, intellectual and spiritual level. You can use it anytime. But when you really need time out with your partner, it's useful to just get a hotel room (or some other private, quiet place), hide away from all the distractions and just focus on being in the moment, together, for a day or two. It clears the mind, and the sinuses, as this ritual can lead to a wonderful "make up" intimacy.

It is helpful, after sharing individual needs, to reiterate your commitment to each other, as well as to ideas, projects and experiences you want to create and share. There are many ways to reaffirm love and express the joy you feel. You can also do this as a separate ritual.

2. Renew your vows or create a new intention for your relationship. If you are married, you might want to repeat your wedding vows to one another while maintaining direct eye contact and holding hands. If you are in an exclusive, committed relationship but not ready for legal marriage, consider sharing "commitment" vows. You can recommit to one another in the most casual way, just by speaking your heart and by allowing feelings for each other to be expressed by touch, movement and eye contact.

How to Keep Isis with You

Wear matching ankhs. The sign of the gods and goddesses of Egypt is the ankh, which means eternal life. Get matching ankh rings or pendants to symbolize the eternal life of your love for each other.

Always communicate to one another. While Isis scoured Egypt for her beloved, she continued to speak to him. Though separated, they weren't that far apart. People in love have the ability to communicate on many levels. Keep the channels open.

Send e-mail kisses during the day. The distance communication takes to travel between the two worlds is simple for a god and goddess. As modern day Isis and Osiris, you can send love messages, thoughts, concerns, things that are hard to say in person and many, many kisses and hugs via e-mail all day long! (Just watch out for bosses and nosey co-workers who might read your honey's e-mail kisses!)

ISIS AFFIRMATION:

"I am in you. You are in me."

Part Five

GODDESSES
OF FRIENDSHIP
AND
FAMILY LIFE

16

TRANSFORM YOUR RELATIONSHIP TO YOUR MOM WITH THE GREAT GODDESS

"What unites all people of all times is not that we are all mothers, but that we have all been born of a mother who was born of a mother who was born of a mother . . ."

—Donna Wilshire, *VirginMotherCrone*

We've all probably had our rocky roads with our mom. In fact, from the time we are teens to about our thirties (and beyond), it is tough to be in the same room with Mom and feel like a grown-up. Just the sound of her voice is a hypnotic cue that can cast us back into childhood and to that old sense of being little again. She can get on our nerves like no other, yet perhaps there is no one we'd rather run to when there is a problem or call when there's a success to be shared.

As we mature and go off to do our thing, we may find ourselves vacillating between desire to be closer to Mom and disappointment in who she is or how she is (can't wait to get home for the holidays . . . and can't wait to leave). Odd as it may seem, it's a completely natural phenomenon to long for our mothers and at the same time feel let down by them. One of the reasons is that we tend to place impossible, goddesslike expectations on our mothers, forgetting that they are only human.

The mother-daughter connection is a sacred bond like no other. Although the umbilical cord has long been cut, there's an invisible power line that will always pull us back home. Even if we have difficulties or a painful relationship with Mom, we are tethered for life to the one who brought us into the world. Although you may have spent years rejecting her worldview, when you begin to explore the path of the goddess, your yearning to be closer to your mother might intensify and you might just find yourself seeking a deeper connection to your female ancestry. Even for women who have rejected their mothers or who have been rejected by them, things can change greatly in the mother-daughter relationship, and with all other women, when you realize *we all* come from the goddess.

The Great Goddess is a girl's best friend when it comes to embracing your mother, as well as your longing for *the mother*. She shows you the power of the feminine that connects you to your mother, all ancestors and all women, and helps you accept your mother's love and devotion as it is offered, while accessing a higher love from your divine mother. She represents unconditional loving, nurturing and positive parenting.

Who Is the Great Goddess?

"In the beginning people prayed to the Creatress of Life, the Mistress of Heaven. At the very dawn of religion, God was a woman. Do you remember?"
—Merlin Stone, *When God Was a Woman*

The Great Goddess is the great mother of all things, the source of all that is. She has been worshipped from the beginning of time, and her worship continues today, by practitioners of goddess spirituality and priestesses of Wicca and other earth-based religions. She is the earth we stand on, the air we breathe,

the fire we cook with, the waters of life that sustain us and the spirit that lives inside us and all around us. She can be found in the history, mythology, sacred texts, spiritual practices and folklore of every culture. Stories are the same, yet she is known by many names. She was Mother Nature, the very energy of a planet filled with life, and she was life itself. She was fertility, death and regeneration, the cycles of life witnessed in the flowers and trees, the moon and the ocean, humans and nature. Experienced and known in so many diverse forms—fluid like the ocean, strong like the ground, light as air, angry as the hurricanes, gentle as the first sign of spring—she was capable of adopting any role. The earliest artifacts of goddess worship date back more than 30,000 years. Many believe that the first god worshipped was a woman. She is often depicted in ancient stone carvings and icons as a full-figured female with round, fecund belly, or as the earth herself.

How to Invite Her into Your Life

Like our own mothers, the Great Goddess has always been in our lives, but her presence is not always acknowledged or announced. Just as our moms are there for us, the Great Goddess has stuck around—through all our rejections, tantrums, fits and taking her for granted. Understanding her role in our lives connects us more deeply to our own mothers. You may have come to the conclusion that your mother comes from *another planet,* but in truth, she hails from the same source as you . . . and all women.

1. **Insights to help you with Mom:**
   + **Mothers are human.** One of the reasons we become disappointed by our own mothers or feel that they are not all we want them to be is because we have a hard time accepting that they are human and imperfect. As babies, we see Mom as all-powerful; as kids we tend to see Mom as godlike. She is the all-knowing, omniscient

mother goddess who knows all. She seemed to be a master of the mysteries of life and of healing. Yet being human, she perhaps could never give us the kind of all-embracing spiritual sustenance we seek, or maybe she just is not as hip or *with it* as we'd like. It is very humbling when we realize that Mom really cannot be all things to all people at all times or always offer all the comfort we need. She cannot be the absolute everything the divine mother is. You may even discover that while she is the personification of a mother goddess to you, she is not your "spiritual mother." And that's okay.

+ **Learn to parent ourselves.** Our mother used the resources she had to be the best mom she could be. But she cannot be expected to provide the magic and evolution that the Great Goddess instills in us when we look to her for empowerment; she is, after all, divine. Ultimately, the Great Goddess shows us *we can parent ourselves* the way we wish we were parented and rely on ourselves. She encourages us as we strive for independence, trusts us to find our own way in the world, helps us to see the world is abundant and full of resources and has faith that we can take care of our own needs. This leads us to a more authentic, relaxing and enjoyable relationship with our mother because she doesn't feel she has to take care of us all the time, and we don't feel compelled to ask her to help every time we get into a bind.

+ **Mother's mysteries.** Our mothers teach us about the first mysteries of life—menstruation, the birds and bees, simple things about how the world works. But the key to the "something bigger in life" goes beyond just our one mom. There are religions and spiritual practices that call out to the Great Goddess with the same reverence that other faiths call out to Christ, Allah or Buddha. There are many options to connect with her in ritual, in celebration and through nature. Just as you are connected to life, so is your mother.

2. Reunite with your mother. Many ancient religions focus on honoring the ancestors as a way of healing family relationships and rebirthing ourselves. You become closer to your mother when you honor the source of who she is and own it as the source of who you are. These exercises help you connect to your mother via family roots.

✦ **Honor your mother and female ancestors.** Ask your mom to help you in your special project to honor family roots by creating an "ancestor table." This will be a special altar table in part of your house or apartment with pictures of women in your family—your mom, grandmothers, sisters, aunts and relatives from Mom's side—and special heirlooms or reminders. Also include a childhood picture and a more recent shot of you and your mother. The purpose of this ancestor table is to give you a visual link to your past, get in touch with the humanity of your family and connect with the great power of the feminine that the ancients believed connected us to the Great Goddess, mother of us all.

✦ **Share some girl talk with your mother.** Get Mom talking about family history—the basic background, as well as scandals and wild tales, especially stories that highlight the special traits of your female relatives. Was there a warrior queen or a preacher in your background, a farmer or an exotic dancer? Go back as far into the family tree as possible. Especially try to find out if the women in the family had any particular strengths (physical strength, the bread winner, great cook, could drive a tractor, a healer, a loving person, took a leap of faith and left home and family to get married, etc.). Take notes. Look for what was special about your relatives. And use this topic to gather a little more insight about your mother. Listen especially to how she talks about her mom; therein lies the key to how she learned to be a mother to you.

+ **Go through family photos.** Get your mom to pull out the family photo albums and, as you look through them, get her talking more about the women. Pick at least one picture of each relative to place on the ancestor table. Assure her you'll have copies made if she doesn't want to give up the originals. Realize that as you gather the pictures you are embracing the special energy of the feminine that birthed your mother before you, her mother before her, and so on.

+ **Put the pictures in beautiful frames.** If the originals are tiny, blow them up through the magic of photo-quality copy machines. Have your mom come over (if possible) and help you arrange them.

+ **Add family heirlooms to the table.** If you have a piece of jewelry, a hankie or china from any of the relatives, include it on the table as well.

+ **Represent the goddess via the elements.** Add the energy of the Great Goddess to the table by placing items that represent the four elements: air (a feather), water (in a small cup or bowl), fire (a candle), earth (a pot or bowl of earth, preferably from your mother's backyard or neighborhood).

+ **Pick out the best family traits.** Go over your notes about the special strengths of the women in your family. Type them and print them on a beautiful piece of paper like a scroll and title the list "The Strengths of Our Womenfolk." Buy two identical frames. Send one framed copy of the strengths to your mom for her home, and place one on your ancestor table.

✦ **Visit with the womenfolk.** Sit with them every day for a while. Bring flowers, favorite candies or a special offering to the ancestors. (For example, if your grandmother grew corn, bring her a stalk; if great-grandmother raised cows, bring her a cup of milk.) When you're having rough times (with your mother, your path in life, your comprehension of the Great Goddess) or feeling confused, ask the womenfolk to help soothe and improve things. When you are feeling low, read the list of family strengths and know *they are in you* as well. If you connect to the source of who you are, your relationship with your mom will naturally begin to improve and transform. Pray for what you need in the presence of your ancestors and ask for their help: *Ancient mothers and ancestors, please guide me, for you see what I cannot yet know. Let me take on your strengths and your spirit as appropriate to help me in daily life. Let me find my way in the world and still stay close to my own mother. Ancient mother, ancient spirit, please guide and protect me.*

3. Heal misunderstandings with Mom. Give misunderstandings over to the Great Goddess for healing. If your relationship with your mom is strained or troubled, if you are having a hard time communicating with her or if she has passed on and you feel incomplete about your relationship, it is important to try to heal it spiritually. Write down everything that is upsetting you. Roll up the list like a scroll and leave it on the ancestor table with a prayer requesting the ancestors' help. Take another copy to a place where you can bury it in mother earth—a park or your backyard. With a little prayer of thanks to the Great Goddess, bury your list of concerns and pray that the Great Goddess will take them into herself and transform them, bringing your relationship with Mom a rebirth when the time is right. The Great Goddess takes things into her body—the earth—and returns them renewed. Ask her to bless both you and your mother with a happy resolve. Then do something nice for your mom anonymously. For example, have a tree planted in her name in her hometown to symbolize earth or make a donation to her favorite charity.

4. Connect to the Great Goddess in prayful chant. In the practice of ancient earth religions, the people of earth would gather to ceremonially honor the Great Goddess and affirm their connection to her. They acknowledged themselves as her children. Today, many practitioners of earth religions and goddess spirituality sing her praises in brief, repetitive chants, sung over and over. These simple statements, such as the traditional "We all come from the Goddess," connect us to the mother of all things: *We all come from the goddess, and to her we shall return. Like a drop of rain, flowing to the ocean.*

How to Keep the Great Goddess with You

Hug your mother whenever possible. Reach out. She is a living link to the Great Goddess. She is the *first* mother of all things, in your life!

Keep a portrait of the earth. A beautiful shot from space of the planet we call home can remind you how precious and beautiful our universal mother is.

Spend time in nature. A walk in the park, a talk on the patio, a hike up a mountain, a moment gazing at the full moon or a swim in the sea all bring you closer to her.

Praise her in song. A wonderful way to stay in touch with the many traditions of the Great Goddess and to honor the divine ancestry of your mother is with the CD *Ancient Mother,* by On Wings of Song with Robert Gass. It's an inspiring collection of goddess chants from many traditions, performed by traditional singers and priestesses. Also from On Wings of Song, *From the Goddess* is a weaving of three well-known goddess chants that plays like one long-running chant.

THE GREAT GODDESS AFFIRMATION:

"We all come from the Great Goddess."

CHANNEL YOUR ANGER AND HEAL HOSTILITY WITH PELE

"Holding on to anger is like grasping a hot coal with the intent of throwing it at someone else; you are the one that gets burned."

—*Buddha*

Nothing can stimulate our anger like a family function. Weddings, funerals and even baby blessings are notorious for stirring up the fires of family hostility and rage; a simple holiday gathering can do the same. Much as we love them, our families somehow knows how to push all our buttons. There are certain family members and even close friends who do it to us every time. The result is usually us getting angry—whether we direct that anger outward or, worse, inward.

Some of us are like volcanoes ready to pop—fiery, angry, permanently pissed off and not afraid to show it and shout it. Others need some inspiration to spew out some of the feelings stimulated by family members, as well as to learn how to protect ourselves from the wrath of others. Anger can be useful when acknowledged and utilized to propel self-development and change for the better in family life. But unchecked anger literally makes us sick. Excessive, unexpressed rage can raise stress levels so high that blood pressure can boil over. If we express rage excessively and live angry lives, we fare no better; studies show it wreaks havoc with the heart. There has to be a middle ground for acknowledging the pain that anger protects and healing the hostility that is sometimes generated by unresolved and unexpressed issues with family and close friends.

Pele is a girl's best friend when it comes to dealing with anger and hostility. She expresses her rage without holding back and yet she is a natural equalizer of anger. If you blow your top too easily, Pele can soften your temper; if you never quite express yourself, she helps you find your voice. She represents the power of fiery anger and hostility, passionate self-expression and responsibility over rage.

Who Is Pele?

"Pele is often thought of as a cruel goddess. This is untrue. Yes, she has a temper and possesses the power to vent her anger in a spectacular fashion, but her worshippers accept this as part of her nature."

—Scott Cunningham, *Hawaiian Religion and Magic*

Pele (*pay-le*) is the ancient Hawaiian goddess who lives on the Big Island of Hawaii, in the famous Kilauea Volcano, the world's most active volcano. She was a pivotal deity in the ancient Hawaiian religion that reined in Hawaii until Christian missionaries came and converted the native peoples in the 1800s. But her spirit lives on, and she is widely regarded. Her legend and stories abound, and the volcano is considered by many to be her permanent temple. There is a vast history of worship and sacrifice at her fiery altar. It is said that when she was a small child she did not like the water, as her sisters and brothers did; eventually, as she came into her power, she shaped and formed her abode into the Big Island of Hawaii, where her red-hot lava seeped down to the sea, creating lava rocks, jagged cliffs and black-sand beaches that still exist today. The story of Pele's rage reflects the love-hate relationship between sisters. It speaks of sibling rivalry and, ultimately, forgiveness. When she was young, Pele met the young chief of Kauai, Lohiau. They fell in love and promised themselves to one another. But Pele missed her fiery home and headed back to her volcano. She pined for Lohiau and realized she could not do without him and sent her trusted sister, Hi'iaka, on the perilous journey to the neighboring isle of Kauai to get him. As the two traveled back to Pele, her sister fell in love with the handsome prince. In anger, Pele killed him, *twice,* and Hi'iaka revived him. Pele spewed her angry lava to and fro and banned her sister from her island. Her sister stole her beloved, and she expressed her anger without apology. It took some time, but she eventually settled down and forgave Hi'iaka. Having a new lover, Kamapua'ua, whose temperament matched her own, helped quell Pele's jealous anger. Pele is pictured as mistress of the Kilauea volcano. It is considered her center, and the lava is often seen in art as her red, flowing hair.

How to Invite Her into Your Life

You can tell when Pele is pissed. Yet beneath the surface of her fiery eruptions is a great, bright light. Pele lives in the spirit of fire, a glorious element that brings warmth, excitement, healing and a sense of sacred. Fire also burns. It can ravage, destroy and ruin our lives if not handled responsibly; its fierceness must be respected and carefully monitored. Over the years, and as recently a major volcanic eruption in 1983, people have watched in awe at how the fiery temper of Pele can destroy all that is in her path. The same is true of our anger. When we direct anger at others, words can slice through them, and the feelings associated can have a painful impact. If we are the recipients of someone's anger, we, too, are wounded. Words of anger can destroy our relationships, friendships and opportunities. Yet anger and hostility that is not expressed, acknowledged and healed can burn away at our insides. The great sages have warned: Master anger, or it will master us. The ancients made offerings to Pele to appease and please her and settle her fury. It is important that we too offer up our anger to Pele so we can learn to utilize it, channel it appropriately and heal its consequences in our lives.

IDENTIFYING AND UNDERSTANDING ANGER:

1. **Know thyself—and who pushes your buttons.** If you get queasy, nervous, moody or jumpy right before a family function, or before a designated time to be spent with certain family members or friends, chances are that you are reacting to anticipatory stress based on memories of family gatherings, and traumas, of the past. You may know exactly who and what gets your goat when you are with your family, or it might just be a dull ache somewhere that gets activated when you are around certain people. It is essential to somehow demystify the things that you are angry about and investigate why you feel so angry. Look at each situation from all angles and pick it apart until it is no longer mysterious or frightening so it loses it charge.

+ **Clearly identify your hot spots.** Don't feel bad about admitting who makes you angry. List the family members you have issues with and how you feel around them. Does Dad drink too much? Is Mom overcritical? Do you have siblings who get on your nerves? Get in touch with what they do that triggers unsettling emotions in you.

+ **Get clear on your own reactions.** Do you overeat, drink or smoke like a chimney at these events? Do you fall asleep, withdraw, go unconscious and essentially avoid hot spots? Do you cry, whine, get cranky and explode with anger like a child having a tantrum? Do you desperately want to flee but feel sentenced to family hell, and go home feeling unhappy, drained or depressed?

+ **Pretend you are a reporter taking notes for a documentary on dysfunctional family gatherings.** Pull back for a moment and become an observer in your own mind and memory. See if you can make the connection, for example: *When Dad drinks and gets nasty, I feel like I want to leave, but because I can't, I eat too much food and fall asleep* or *Whem my brother tries to hit me up for money, again, I bite his head off, he insults me and we fight all afternoon.* If you map out some of the *cause and effect* of behaviors that trigger anger and hostility in your family, you may be shocked to find that there are some very specific behavior dynamics and that by identifying them you can gain more control over the situation and begin to heal it.

2. Leave a peace offering and memorize a prayer. The ancients would make the ultimate offering to Pele, giving to her the remains of their loved ones and utilizing her fire as the funeral pyre. They also gave her pigs and other offerings to quell her anger and keep her peaceful. If you feel her volcanic action may rage in you or family members, try to quell it in advance with this simple ritual:

+ Before heading to a family event, leave a flower on your alter, or near a picture of yourself, to energetically cast a peaceful vibe and as a gift for the goddess.

+ Make an offering to her in prayer: *Pele, Goddess of the fiery volcano, lady of the light, I give to you my anger at (name). I give to you my fear of (name) anger. I give to you that which keeps me angry/keeps me from expressing how I feel.* Tell her "Mahalo" (Hawaiian for "thank you").

+ Memorize a short peace affirmation and speak it to yourself, or in your head, over and over on your way to family events. It can be as simple as this: "*Pele, queen of molton lava, this is too hot to handle. I give it over to you.*"

3. Manage emotions: Historically, Pele has poured down upon her people in the form of uncontrollable volcanic eruptions. Some of us have personalities like that, or relatives like that, with rage problems. There is such a thing as a "rageaholic." You can't change another's behavior; but if it is you who rages uncontrollably, you've got to get a grip. If you are about to fly into a rage or if someone is raging at you, do a reality check: Is someone in your family being a complete and offensive idiot? Or are you feeling out of control because something has been said or done that has triggered vulnerability in you? Sometimes we attempt to defend our raw spots with anger and a warring spirit in order to hide truer feelings. Sometimes we go on automatic pilot and, quite predictably, get reactivated by someone's hostility.

+ **Assess before you react.** Learn the difference between a true fear of being in harm's way that presses you to act aggressively and having "your buttons pushed." Even if you have spent your entire life in battle with certain relatives, break the habit of angry or defensive reactions. Here's a three-step breathing exercise to help you hang in there:

a) Take a moment to breathe, deeply, before you say a word or react in any way. Just stop everything and breathe. On that first exhale, choose to let go of confusion and illusion, so you can see the problem rationally and clearly. Think: *What is* really *going on here?*

b) Breathe in again, deeply and fully. Don't be afraid to take the time to breathe, even if all hell is breaking loose. And when you exhale, hold the intention that you are breathing through your desire to react instead of getting reactivated—which is what perpetuates the problems. Just breathe.

c) Breathe the third breath and imagine there is a switch within you that can turn on your internal cooling system, an air conditioner for the soul. Feel the cool air come on, fresh, delightful, cool enough to make the heat die down. Relax. Stand firm in your sense of calm.

Repeat these steps as needed and learn to use your breath to center yourself. There is no harm in breathing, and you can breathe through the urge to react. If you find that breathing and staying put does not quell the heat of the moment, take time out. Take a walk, go to the store, leave the premises—and detach temporarily from what is going on.

4. **Release yourself from pent-up anger.** Some of us store anger in our bodies and turn it into illness and self-hatred. Things can simmer and boil for years and eventually erupt, either inside us or onto others.

✦ In general, whenever possible, take your issues right to the source. If you conquer anger at its source, it will not conquer you. Tell the truth using "I" statements rather than blaming or accusing. Then, let the chips fall where they may. The person will either "get it," or not. For example, if Dad turns into an obnoxious drunk who berates or teases you when he's had a few too many, it may be time to tell him, when he is sober, before the next function, "*I will not visit again when you are drinking. You have six other days of the week to drink. If you want to see me, don't drink during our time together.*" He may not respond the way you want him to and he may be in complete denial, but just by bringing it up, you take the charge off the situation; the anger will no longer be sitting in your gut, because you have made his drinking problem *his* responsibility to deal with. Maybe just finding the courage to *say it* will help avert undue stress. There is no need to step in Pele's path of molten lava if you can draw a line in the sacred black sand and stay away from trouble spots. Sharing honestly, when possible, is a way to release pent-up anger so it does not come out in inappropriate ways.

+ **Let the steam out of hostility and anger.** Not everyone can go to the source and tell them how angry they make us. But we can all take the edge off anger in some way other than through self-destructive behavior and wild bursts of anger. To chill out after a family gathering, engage in physical activity:

  a) Run, go the gym, swim, play volleyball or go for a walk.

  b) Go home and hit pillows.

  c) For heavy-duty release of pent-up anger, try kickboxing or learn to (safely) punch a punching bag.

  d) Dance to your favorite music.

5. **Share the story of your anger and hostility in a safe space.** Pele has always made her wrath a public spectacle; at the very least, she communicates her feelings. It helps

to share and allow others to bear witness to your pain (the pain that stimulates feelings of anger and hostility) in real life. Group therapy or a professionally supervised spiritual group is a good start; twelve-step programs are always an option as well. Always make sure you share in a group that will treat it as sacred and honor you in whatever place you are at in your healing process.

6. **Sing and chant out your shame and give it over to Pele.** Musical prayers and songs take the shame out of us and into the hands of the divine and uplift us so we can be healed. Hawaiian music that evokes the spirit of Pele can be very soothing, even though you may not know the words or understand them. The people of Hawaii still "melo o Pele" (sing and chant for Pele) and Kilauea. Try this simple ancient chant:

> *"E ola mau, e Pele e! 'Eli'eli kau mai!"* Ee-o-la-mao e Pay-lay ee! E-lee-e-lee ka my, *which means "Long life to you, Pele."*

You might also want to chant anything that comes to mind or talk to yourself in jibberish. It brings intense, pent-up, hostile energy out of you and disperses negative feelings that might arise when you inventory your pain and hostility.

How to Keep Pele with You

Meet her in her homeland. Pele's home, the Big Island of Hawaii, is one of the most breathtaking of the Hawaiian Islands. You can visit the island as a tourist and get ever so close to her, standing in the volcano crater itself and watching aspects of her fiery, smokey nature. If you can't make it there, catch her on video. *The Wrath of Pele, Fire Goddess of Hawaii,* is a wonderful Reader's Digest/A&E video narrated by Leonard Nimoy that takes you right to her world.

Gather her special tools. It's said that Pele had a magic "Pa'oa" stick to help her find fire at her new home. Her mother gave Pele a magic egg. Try to get a piece of driftwood and an egg-shaped rock from one of her beaches on the Big Island and keep them near.

Name a star after the ones who've passed on. If you are holding anger in your heart for someone who is deceased, heal hostility from high above by joining with loved ones in an eternal cosmic dance where the soul knows no anger. It is said that Pele followed the northern star and found Hawaii. Perhaps you can follow a star and find greater healing. The International Star Registry can name stars and give you the paperwork to prove you have devoted a part of the heavens to someone you cared about. Maybe from that perspective you can imagine they are watching over you and know they will never hurt you or make you angry again.

PELE AFFIRMATION:

"My fiery spirit is a healing force."

18

BRING LIGHT TO YOUR FAMILY WITH ST. LUCY/ LUCINA

"She would rather light a candle than curse the darkness."

—Dag Hammarskjold, about Eleanor Roosevelt

Perhaps you love and adore your family, but you realize they need a little . . . work. No family is perfect and not every family is as conscious as you'd like them to be, but there is hope. You can be the bringer of light in your house, the one who shines a light and tries to bring healing to the tribe. Oftentimes, in family situations, we harbor ancient hurts and injuries and use the pain of the past to build a wall between us. It just takes one person, willing to boldly go where no family member has gone before, to try to heal family rifts and establish a little more "awareness" within the fold.

First, we have to open our own eyes and see our family in a different light. Rather than accusing them of this and that and holding history against them, perhaps we can see them as who they are in the world. This is not foolproof at all times and with all people. Sometimes our greatest awareness about certain family members and situations is that we can do nothing to heal them, that we must move on, let go and focus that light on healing ourselves. An organic benefit of self-healing is that it's sometimes catching, and as we allow our light to shine, it touches others and inspires them to let a new light shine through them.

St. Lucy/Lucina is a girl's best friend when it comes to opening our eyes and shedding new light on old situations. She has the ability to see with spiritual eyes, and she teaches us to do the same. She represents bringing the light and seeing things as they are . . . and as they can be.

Who is St. Lucy/Lucina?

Santa Lucia, thy light is glowing
Through darkest winter night, comfort bestowing.
Dreams float on dreams tonight,
Comes then the morning light,
Santa Lucia, Santa Lucia."
—Italian devotional song

St. Lucy is the popular medieval martyr who fought religious oppression and insisted on a life of light-bringing and devotion to Christianity and humanity. Reputed for her resistance to marrying and reportedly tortured in hideous ways for her belief in Christ, she is the heroine of the famed devotional song Santa Lucia (Saint Lucy). One of the losses she suffered—if only temporarily—was her eyes, or her sight. Many believe the genesis of Saint Lucy can be found in the mythology of the Roman goddess Lucina, a birth and light goddess who later merged with mother goddess Juno. Juno Lucina combined the feminine power of Roman mother goddess Juno with the sweet energy of the goddess of first light, Lucina. Juno protected the people of Rome and was a special patron to women in matters of marriage, fertility and all aspects of pregnancy and childbirth. Lucia was the deity of birth and light; she brought good things to light—like babies—and a baby's first sight. When merged over time with Juno, she became a more full-bodied divine female, responsible for opening every new baby's eyes to see the world for the very first time. Juno Lucia, also known as the mother of lights, was celebrated in a festival of torchlights and bonfires in early December. St. Lucy's feast day is December 13 and early celebrations included "the fires of St. Lucia." Because number thirteen is affiliated with the feminine, many practitioners of women's spirituality have adopted her as a patron of women. The tradition of honoring St. Lucy seeped into the Scandinavian culture a thousand years ago, and to this day, celebrations include pageants of women dressed like the saint; activities begin December 13 and last for one month. In prayer cards, St. Lucy is often pictured with her eyes sprouting like flowers, sometimes on a plate. On ancient coins, Juno Lucina was pictured with a child in her arms and two babies at her feet.

How to Invite Her into Your Life

There are many legends about Juno Lucina's successor St. Lucy, and in all she stands as a symbol of light and hope. Her coming on December 13 marks a time of feasting, merriment, singing and the spirit of friendliness and goodwill that lasts all through the holidays. Whether it is holiday time or not, it's a good time to practice being nice to your relatives. Even if you think they are lame, rather than insisting on always being right, consider seeing them in a new light. Having lost her physical sight, St. Lucy's strong suit is her ability to see through spiritual eyes. Although her mythology suggests that her eyes and eyesight were magically restored, this is symbolic of receiving a new set of eyes and a new way of seeing things, which can lead to a new way of being. By the same token, in opening a baby's eyes for the first time, Juno Lucina had the power to give a new soul a fresh start, innocent and

"Christ Sophia"

@ 1989 Robert Lentz

Kuan Yin

courtesy of Kuan Yin Unlimited

Green Tara from a silk embroidered Tibetan "Thangka"

"Oshun"

©2002 by Joanna Powell Colbert

Mary Magdalene
photogravure

from a painting by
W.A. Bouguereau

Isis

courtesy of The Egypt Store

"Artemis"

Lakshmi modern lithograph

Durga vintage print from British India period

St. Térèse of Lisieux

©1998 Janet McKenzie

Bast

courtesy of The Egypt Store

wide-eyed. These are qualities we all need to bring home to our families.

1. **Shine a light of love.** The flashlight is a powerful metaphor for bringing something to light. Your eyes will often adapt to darkness and will become comfortable being in the dark. Suddenly, there's a glimmer of illumination that's especially powerful for seeing the things right under your nose! This is a perfect tool for being able to see family, or just particular members, in a new light. Just your *willingness to try* will make a difference in your relationship with your family or particular members you're focused on. As we heal, they can heal, too. Do the flashlight exercise on your own, but shine a light on those you love and those with whom you have a love-hate relationship. Meditate or ruminate on the following:

+ **Try to see at least three of their redeeming qualities.** Think of it this way: If you were to write a eulogy for this loved one, which of his or her positive qualities would you acknowledge and highlight?

+ **Think of what you need to tell them.** If this person were gone from you tomorrow, what would you wish you had said, done or completed with them? Shine a light on old grudges, missed communications and miscommunications. For your own edification, create an awareness of what you would like to say "if you had the nerve or opportunity."

+ **What is one risk you'd be willing to take?** Not every family member is receptive to healing old hurts, but what if they are and you just don't know it? What action or communication would you risk to find out? If you reached out and they reached back, how would you feel? Let St. Lucy/Lucina give you second sight to see where your efforts to patch things up will be greeted warmly.

+ **Look at the mirror they hold up to you.** Oftentimes we are aggravated by our closest family members because they remind us of parts of ourselves, our history or our lives that we would rather not look at. Be willing to see where you, too, could use a little work and improvement. Fair is fair.

2. **Family-friendly offerings.** There are many ways to evoke a sense of warmth, joy and light. Try some of these simple, generous gestures to bring you closer to the people you care about:

+ **Say grace.** Whenever possible while gathered, hold hands and say a prayer of thanks over the meal, something that acknowledges the value of family ties:

> *Divine spirit of all there is, we thank you for this opportunity to gather together.*
> *Please grant us the opportunity to continue to be there for each other*
> *In good times as well as not-so-great times.*
> *Give us strength and fortitude to ride the tides of change,*
> *And empower us always to be nurturing and loving with one another.*
> *We thank the divine for this delicious dinner, prepared with love.*
> *May all consumed here tonight fill us with health and well-being. Amen. Dig in!*

+ **Help out.** Do things that assist with the ease of a gathering: Come early, leave late, set the table, clean up, do the dishes or take the trash out. Or extend yourself in other ways: Pick someone up from the station or help your mom shop and cook.

✦ **Contribute something sweet.** Bake a cake or a special dessert with your own hands and fill it with love and the secret prayer that everyone who tastes it will have sweetness and joy in their lives. If you can't bake it, buy it, and say a prayer over it before serving.

✦ **Contribute to good feelings.** Buy or locate a piece of music that is part of the family history and lore, something that has many good memories associated with it—Dad's big-band music, Mom's Sinatra tunes, etc. Play if after dinner as a special surprise. Music stirs the soul and conjures good feelings that can bring everyone closer together as they remember good times. Even if there is no talking, the music will elevate the energy in the room.

✦ **Hug a loved one and tell them something you admire about them.** Showing physical affection and expressing appreciation in the form of authentic and loving compliments is a powerful way to bring light, love and smiles to loved ones. For example, just hug your sister and say, *"I really love the way you cook,"* or *"I am so touched by the patience you have with Granny . . . you're so good with her!"*

3. **Random acts of kindness.** If family lives far away or if you don't have much time to socialize with them, stay in touch with simple gestures to let them know you are thinking of them:

✦ Call Dad, Grandma, Sister or anyone in your family just to let them know you love them or to share some good news that will bring a smile to their faces.

+ Send a card that expresses your feelings.

+ Write a letter that acknowledges something you are touched by or appreciate in them.

+ Send an e-mail with a goofy smiley face or picture.

+ Send a book you know will be helpful.

+ Mail a special present, for no particular reason.

+ Always remember to say "I love you."

+ Say a prayer for those you love whenever they are in need and even when they are not, just so you can send good energy their way.

How to Keep St. Lucy/Lucina with You

Wear a St. Lucy medal to family functions. Icons and sacred jewelry abound in church stores and Catholic boutiques. Get a medal on a chain and wear it as a sacred amulet.

Celebrate St. Lucy's feast day. Sweden and all Scandinavian countries especially celebrate Lucia Day on December 13. Usually the eldest daughter in the house dons a white gown with a red sash and a crown of candles. Saffron buns and gingerbread cookies are served. There are gatherings at school and workplaces; there are pageants and parties. The lights go dim and the Lucia maids sing the old song "Santa Lucia." Just light a candle and remember her!

See with new eyes. Practice seeing your family with new eyes and with spiritual eyes at every opportunity.

ST. LUCY/LUCINA AFFIRMATION:

"I see all with my spiritual eyes."

19

CELEBRATE FRIENDS
WITH THE MUSES

*"The real life Muses that show up in our lives are usually found
in our relationships . . ."*

—Angeles Arrien, from *The Nine Muses*

Our best friends and our sisters can be our most intimate, important and closest companions. They've been there for us through thick and thin, trying to figure out boys, parents, school and life. Female friendships and "girl talk" were even more important than those magical moments we spent in the presence of that special male person. Over the years we've seen, time and again, that while men and jobs come and go, our girlfriends are always there for us.

Our friends have been our solace and strength; they are an informal board of directors to help solve the common problems of being women, and there's nothing like being surrounded by a group of women who truly care about your life. It is with our girlfriends and sisters that we can get down and dirty and tell the truth of what is in our hearts, minds and souls. We can be ourselves and become more of ourselves.

Women need each other. We need to honor our sisters

and "soul sisters" and make sure those relationships are nurtured and cared for as we get older and farther away from those days of being an essential part of a "gaggle of girls." As we get older, busier, more successful and more involved in the world of whatever business or career we are in, life in the real world gets more complex, yet the bonds of female friendship remain simple. What's usually hardest is finding the time, which is why it is so important to find the time! A special gathering with our female cohorts can be powerful and meaningful for all!

The muses are a girl's best friend when it comes to gathering in small groups of women. Because there are nine, the muses represent so many aspects of creative female power and possibility. They guide our gatherings with joy, merriment, mirth and the bliss of being together. They represent joyful self-expression, sacred sisterhood and the bonds that link women everywhere.

Who Are the Muses?

"I believe that the moment I open to the gifts of the Muse,
I open myself to the Creation. And become one with the
Mother of Life Itself."
—Jan Phillips, from *Marry Your Muse*

The Muses, Greek deities who presided over the arts, are among the most familiar mythical women and goddesses. Although the numbers varied from region to region, the classical period in Greece established them as nine, including their mother, Mnemosyne, a Titan who was said to have spent nine nights with the top-gun god, Zeus, producing nine daughters, all beauties with long tresses. The Greek poet, Hesiod, suggested that the muses were the ultimate party girls of Greece, "their hearts set upon song and their spirit is free from care."

Taking great pleasure in merriment, good food and celebration, they helped mortals lighten up and allow their creativity to flow. They were closely associated with the Three Graces, but each had their own distinct area of expertise: Calliope was muse of epic poetry; Clio, history; Erato, the lyre; Euterpe, the flute; Polyhymnia, hymns and mime; Terspsichore, dance; Thalia, comedy; Urania, astronomy; and their mother, Mnemosyne, tragedy and memory.

How to Invite Them into Your Life

The muses met at Helicon, a mountain near the Gulf of Corinth in Greece. It was sacred to the muses and to their special cohort, the god Apollo. They found this place more pleasant than the hustle-bustle of Mt. Olympus, and it was also a temple of sorts, because this is where they keep replica statues of themselves. They would often gather there with poets, orators, artists and theater folk and enfold them in their joyous revelry, freeing their creative spirits to soar. Like a meeting of the muses, invite your favorite females for a spiritual sleepover and creative ritual where you will all get a chance to feel like goddesses and make choices for the futures you want to create.

A*muse* them with a pajama party. Make of a list of your best friends and favorite female relatives, and invite them for a pajama party with a twist. The theme is "come as your favorite muse." Send an invitation that includes a description of the muses' special qualities—from sexy Erato, to funny Thalia, to brainy Urania. Encourage your girlfriends to dress up like goddesses—and you do it, too!

1. **Have fun, food and music.** Treat it like a party for girls, with yummy snacks and great music. But tell the gang that there will be a special "sacred circle" where you will all gather like the muses on Mt. Helicon and focus on joy and creativity.

2. Create a sacred circle. Ask everyone to gather for the formal part of the evening and give everyone a chance to participate. The ancients knew how to call to the muses and cultivate ongoing relationships. In ancient societies, it was customary to first invoke the inspiration and protection of the muses for all creative pursuits. You can call the energy of the muses to your gatherings with friends and sisters.

3. Start with a prayer/invocation:

God, Goddess, all there is . . .
Let us feel your presence here with us.
Reconnect us to our highest selves, our personal muses.
Let us all be empowered as a family of soul sisters
And take the journey together toward prosperity, success
and creative self-expression.

4. Bring light to the gathering with this candle-lighting ritual. Light one eight-inch taper candle, and place it on the center of the coffee table or table closest to where you are gathered. Speak the following:

Let us light a candle to shine light on this gathering of
goddesses

To inspire the light of the muse that lives within each of us.

To fill our hearts and souls with brightness and glory.

To heal the hurts of the past and to embrace forgiveness.

To forgive ourselves for hurting other women in the past.

To declare we are ready to allow the power of gathering
to be part of our lives.

To declare we are ready for satisfaction and balance in
all areas of our lives.

*To agree that we support one another in being successful,
happy and fulfilled.*

*To acknowledge we are ready to help one another
achieve our mightiest goals.*

*To our fears, for making life an adventure, and to a new,
improved, productive relationship to fear.*

*To all the muses within us and to allowing them to assist
on our journeys.*

*To everyone's personal truth and authentic self-expres-
sion in the world.*

*To request special guidance for any of us in the room,
and in the world, who want spiritual assistance and still
are not sure how to choose it, ask for it and receive it.*

*Let us light a candle to thank the goddess of all that is
and the muses for bringing us together, guiding us out in
the world, protecting us, teaching us, moving us through
our next steps and helping us claim our birthright as
daughters of the divine.*

5. Spend some time with the muses. Let everyone talk about their outfit and why they picked their particular muse. Explore the mythology of the dancing sisters and how important they were to every creative endeavor executed by the ancients. Explore ways they can help modern women improve their lives. If your friends did not wear muse costumes, talk about which muse she *would have chosen*, if she had the nerve!

6. Evoke the muses. Call them into the circle with you to bless your goals, dreams and desires.

We call to the muses ...

Mnemosyne, muse of tragedy and memory
Please deliver us from sorrows and grief
And help us remember all that is good about ourselves
And our world.

Calliope, muse of epic poetry
Please inspire us with your fine, strong voice.
And create a sacred space in which we can share our stories.

Clio, muse of history and the written word
Please help us honor our history together
And let us write a new chapter in our lives,
Beginning tonight.

Euterpe, muse of the flute
Make our lives like beautiful music,
Full, rich and sweet with wonder and grace.

Terspsichore, muse of dance and song
Bring your joyous expressions to this circle
And let us dance and sing and enjoy one another,
And the new lives we will be creating.

Erato, muse of the lyre and love poetry
Bring your sexy stirrings and wild imaginings
To our hearts and loins and let us
Look forward to your presence in our lives.

Polyhymnia, muse of hymns and mime
Bring us prayers and soulful messages
And help us live more sacred lives.

Urania, muse of astronomy
Show us all your stars and

Let us dance in the heavens
And know the sky is not the limit!

Thalia, muse of comedy
Let us hear your jokes and wild ideas
And bring us to the point of sidesplitting laughter and joy
That we may smile and fully enjoy your presence.

Amen. And so it is.

7. **Give everyone a chance to make a wish.** Pass out tea-light candles that can be lit from the taper that's already lit. Have a large, sturdy plate to rest the lit tea-lights on. Let everyone take a candle, light it and then declare a special goal or desire. Have them think of something they will initiate and would like to have happen in their creative lives (or work, love or home lives) in the very near future. For example, "*I will start on that book I've been wanting to write,*" or "*I will open my own business.*" Encourage them to go for big goals, because this will set forth the possibility for a new reality. While each woman declares her goals, the rest of the group should just bear witness and listen.

8. **Thank the muses.** When everyone has spoken, thank the muses, God, goddess, all there is, and your friends. Suggest they work with the muse they came as (or who is their favorite) in partnership for thirty days to begin to move their goals forward.

9. **Ask the group to support one another.** Now that you have all heard one another's goals, see if there is willingness to support one another in attaining those goals. Be each other's muses! Suggest phone and e-mail contact to help each other along.

After your sacred circle and ritual, eat, drink and be merry! A new wheel has been put into motion.

How to Keep the Muses with You

Stay in touch with your muse. Once you've identified your muse, evoke her for every creative and business endeavor. Ask for her help. Keep her emblems around you—tools of the creative trade, such as pens or instruments, anything that represents her.

Be in touch with your human muses. Look for ways you can help one another in the world.

Gather again. Keep the energy going with additional gatherings and candle-lighting ceremonies.

MUSE AFFIRMATION:

*"My life is filled with muses who
inspire me in all ways."*

20

SURVIVE THE LOSS OF A LOVED ONE WITH MARY MAGDALENE

"We are healed of suffering only by experiencing it to the full."

—Marcel Proust

Losing a loved one is one of life's most difficult and devastating transitions. It is never easy to say good-bye. Death, or any kind of separation from someone we love, is an experience that can rattle us to the very core, shake up our entire lives and uproot us from the life we know. The pain of loss is oftentimes too unbearable for words; it leaves us dazed, dumbfounded and shocked. However, there will come a day when we wake up, see the sunshine and say, "Hey, there is a light at the other side of the tunnel." It just takes time.

Loss is part of life we must all face during our time on earth. We will lose people we love and adore, those that we are close to and those who we have come to know in the public eye. We will lose people we didn't even think we cared for anymore and be shocked at how much impact their death has on our lives. We will grieve with our nation and the world for tragedies and loss that reach universal proportions and affect all people. We will mourn ended relationships and significant personal losses that herald the end of an era. While each and every one of us will face grief in our own personal way and in our own time, there is a universal principle: There is no way over grief, only through it.

We must cry and feel the pain, as searing as it is, and get to the end of it, to the place we can surrender and let go. Mourning and grieving is a project unto itself. Grieving takes us through a time in life where emotions are unpredictable, erratic and odd. One moment you are wracked with inconsolable sorrow, the next you laugh hysterically at a joke, the next you're feeling reflective and filled with loving memories of the person who has gone on. It is a complex process, a healing journey. Psychiatrist Elisabeth Kubler-Ross described the classic pattern of coping strategies of terminally ill patients as a five-stage process. These five stages are widely viewed as stages we all go through when faced with loss: denial and isolation, sometimes experienced as shock; anger or resentment; bargaining; depression; and, finally, acceptance.

Death and loss are one of life's most profound and challenging "classrooms." Somehow, in the loss, we ultimately can find a gain in the form of lessons, self-awareness, completion, healing and a new life. When someone or something dies, a part of us does as well, and this ending births a new beginning.

Mary Magdalene is a girl's best friend when coming to terms with loss. When your heart is aching, breaking and hurting so bad you can't imagine anything worse, no one will understand better than Mary Magdalene. She shows us the power of a woman's love, the challenge of the healing heart and the willingness to go on in the face of deep loss. She represents the right to grieve and the ability to survive and grow beyond any loss.

Who Is Mary Magdalene?

"There were three who always walked with the Lord:
Mary, his mother, her sister,
and Magdalene, the one who was called his companion."
—Gospel of Philip, Gnostic Gospels

Mary Magdalene, also called "the Magdalen," was the first disciple of Jesus Christ. She was the disciple he was closest to and, as many believe, the one he loved most. In the Gnostic Gospels, Mary Magdalene appears as a disciple, singled out by Jesus for special teachings. Although most of us were raised to believe she was a whore saved by Jesus, some modern feminist theologians believe she was his wife—rabbis of the day had to be married, Jesus' closest consort. "When she cried," it was said, "so did he." At the very least, she was his spiritual wife and soul mate. It was Mary Magdalene who many believe anointed Jesus with the spikenard from the famous alabaster jar, in what Jesus said was preparation for his death; this was a duty that fell to the womenfolk in one's family. Mary Magdalene has been called a whore, a hedonist and a sinner and has the rep of being a femme fatale. Although it is said Jesus cast seven demons from her, there is nothing that confirms her "sins" were sexual in nature, and there is no place in the Bible that actually identifies her as a prostitute. Although we all know about the twelve apostles, we hear little about the posse of women who also traveled with Jesus, who funded his ministry, who ministered to him, who were with him at death. Mary was chief among them and obviously had the family financial status to travel with him. She is credited with helping keep the Christ crusade alive after his death. She is often depicted in robes with her head covered with the desert attire of the time; some portraits show her as sexy and seductive.

How to Invite Her into Your Life

If Mary Magdalene could somehow get through the unbelievable gut-wrenching pain of her loss and go on to keep the work and spirit of Christ alive, she can help you get over your pain, too. Sometimes death comes after a long, arduous battle, and we are, in some ways, relieved our loved one is free of the physical body. Other times, people we love are taken from us suddenly, with no warning. Mary Magdalene could do nothing more than watch helplessly as her beloved Jesus died on the cross. A loss so devastating leaves us in fragments; confused, stumbling about wondering "why" as we try to also figure out how we can go on. Healing from this is a process that takes time. The following exercises can help you through the death of a loved one, and are also for those who are going through a breakup or divorce:

1. **Honor your feelings.** Denial, yearning, disbelief, anger, confusion, humiliation, shock, despair, sadness and guilt are all typical feelings associated with loss. The tricky part is that they can hit you when you least suspect it and impact your life in all ways as you go through the process of grieving. It takes time to fully absorb and heal from the impact of a major loss. You may never stop missing— or loving—a lost loved one or friend. However, time does heal. The pain will ease, and you will go on with your life. But you must give yourself time. As much as you might want to believe that loss of love is fate tossing you a curve ball, remember that love shared is love that exists in your heart forever. The love you once shared is as real in death as in life.

2. **Carry on.** Serious loss heralds a time of great transformation, sometimes as dramatic as the proverbial phoenix rising from the ashes. It gives us a chance to reevaluate our own lives. It makes us think: *If it were my last year on earth, where would I want to be? How would I spend*

my precious time? What would I want to say to the people I love? You might ask yourself those questions and answer them introspectively (just mulling them over) or proactively (taking action or communicating about your thoughts).

3. Soothe yourself with water. Take a dip in salt water whenever you feel sad, overwhelmed or depressed. The ocean or a salty body of water is a great natural healer. You can use your own tub by filling it with sea salt. Take many, many warm baths and include bubbles and uplifting scents. They will soothe your soul and have a healing, calming effect. The shower can be like a temple for your tears—you can have a good cry, and it's refreshing, cleansing and revitalizing. In addition to all else, make sure you drink lots of water; it will keep you hydrated as it cleanses from within.

4. Be part of a support community. After Jesus died, Mary was with the other women. They shared a common bond of loss that held them together as they plunged into the depths of despair. Gather in informal groups or join an existing grief support group. There are lots of Internet sites that help people get through loss, including www.iVillage.com, which has many message boards.

5. Build an altar to the one you love. Create a memory table. Fill it with pictures of your beloved. Include objects that honor and recall his or her life. You can also create an altar for a deceased pet or adapt this for a relationship that has ended.

+ Light a candle. Get a special beautiful candle or a plain white one.

+ Resolve issues. If you have an unresolved regret or issue, write a letter and leave it under the picture of your beloved.

+ Sit and talk with your beloved as you did in life. This may sound crazy, but just imagine that the one you lost is not far away, just a shout off in the distance.

+ Work toward closure and forgiveness. Embrace them wherever they are. Share any concerns. Tell stories about your life.

+ Feel the safety and sacredness of the moment. If you can bring yourself to go through this process, you will find it will take less and less time to heal. This processes grief and offers a healthy approach to closure.

+ Don't hold on forever. Let go when the time comes. Pack up the pictures and the mementos, and put grief away. A new day will dawn. There are many schools of thought that say excessive grieving of a loved one or grieving to the detriment of your well-being holds the soul of the departed to us and prevents that soul from going to the light. Allow yourself to come to trust that your loved one is safe and where he or she is meant to be.

6. Honor the gifts of loved ones. Many people come to know that they have received a great gift from a beloved who has departed. There are many who believe that the beloved soul of those we lose continues to watch over us. How warming that thought is! Ponder this: What is the gift that your loved one has given you. Thank her or him for the lesson and the opportunity.

7. Taking over the mantle of a loved one. It has been said that when a loved one passes on, we can take over his or her mantle. One of the ways we do this is to look deeply at how this person has contributed to us, and the world, and see the part of them that we are best meant to carry on. In life, Mary shared the ministry of Christ and helped develop it. After Jesus' death, she helped keep his mission alive and, it is believed, went on to play a huge role in the development of early Christianity.

How to Keep Mary Magdalene with You

Embrace your pain. Whenever you feel the pain of loss or a broken heart searing through you, remember that the only way to heal the pain is through it. It may seem like a tunnel of torture to travel through the depths of how you feel inside, but remember, "This, too, will pass."

Keep her symbol near you. To represent the masculine and the feminine, keep a beautiful picture of Christ's sacred heart and an alabaster jar near you.

Anoint your heart with spikenard. A special Mary Magdalene nard and a Christ nard are available from World Light Fellowship. This is a replica of the healing unguent that Mary anointed Jesus with.

MARY MAGDALENE AFFIRMATION:

"I will survive."

CREATE A COZY HOME WITH VESTA

". . . A woman needs money and a room of her own."

—Virginia Woolfe, *A Room of One's Own*

We all need a place to call home. Whether we live with roommates or live alone, whether it's our first apartment or one of many, home is a place that offers security and rest, alone time and separation from the world. Whether home is a cottage or a castle, a studio or a duplex, it matters not. As long as you have a room to call your own that is comfortable, you have a sense of stability and place in the world.

Celebrities build huge mansion fortresses because they have so little privacy. Their homes are a complete shelter, a place to throw a curtain up to the world. Nuns and monks live cloistered so they can focus on prayer and sacred living, untouched by the stirrings of the outside world. Some people use their homes to entertain and gather with others. Some people love having guests, animals and kids clamoring through all day; others revel in quiet splendor of a moment alone. It's important to assess the kind of place that is home to you. Then set about finding it, building it, living in it and making the rest of your life's dreams come true.

Vesta is a girl's best friend when it comes to creating a home that is a personal haven and sanctuary. It is Vesta who made Mom's house into home, and she will bring her spirit to your dwelling place, too. She brings warmth and *that personal touch* to the place you call home. She can help you find an apartment as well as pick the right furniture, art and all the little touches. She represents sanctuary and feeling nurtured and empowered in the place that is home.

Who Is Vesta?

"[Vestal Virgins] had the sacred duty of tending the sacred hearth of the state in the Temple of Vesta in Rome. On March 1, the fire was rekindled ritually by rubbing two sticks together; if the fire went out, it had to be lit the same way."
—Lesley Adkins and Roy A. Adkins, *Dictionary of Roman Religion*

Vesta (*vest·a*) is the Roman goddess of the hearth. Although she started out as a spirit of the home who tended the hearth, she went on to gain importance in the Roman pantheon as the goddess to whom prayers for a safe and happy home and home life were addressed. Although she was personified as a female, she was represented only by flame. In homes, it was the fireplace or hearth flames that called forth her warmth and protection. The Temple of Vesta was fashioned in the round, like a home, similar to the earlier thatched huts of Rome. Six vestal virgins kept constant vigil over the flame of the goddess. No men were permitted to enter the temple, and, as sacred flame keepers, the vestal virgins had a strict code of conduct to follow. Roman families would gather together once a day to honor Vesta and perform sacrifices in her name.

She is represented in hearth fires. Although the ancients never portrayed her in statues, relief or arts, modern renditions of Vesta show her as an older, gray-haired woman, usually with a kind face.

How to Invite Her into Your Life

To the ancients, Vesta's hearth magic transformed a hut into a sanctuary. The first thing you have to do to whip your home into shape is "clean house."

1. **Organize your home.** Before you can rebuild or re-create, you have to let go of anything that stands in the way. If your life is too cluttered or filled up with "stuff," if your house is messy or disorganized, it's very hard to feel connected to Vesta's warmth.

+ **Toss.** As a symbolic step, make a sacrifice to Vesta in the form of one messy desk or bureau drawer. Clean it out, toss old stuff and reorganize it. The energy of release will move you toward the next drawer, closet, file and cleanup task.

+ **Clean.** Once you've de-cluttered, scrub and wash with love. Treat this as a sacred act, not just a grungy chore; make it an offering to the goddess of the hearth.

2. **Create magical surroundings.**

+ **Buy candles.** Get candles that will burn safely and responsibly to light in Vesta's honor. Or make it even more special by making your own candles!

+ **Fill your home with the sacred.** To you it may be holy icons and arts or pictures of movie stars. Surround yourself with things that feel special and spiritual.

+ **Document the great times.** Surround yourself with positive memories, such as photos and momentos of good times. Trash any reminders of ex-boyfriends, broken hearts, failed jobs or bad experiences.

+ **Build into the future.** Create a home that reflects who you are and also where you intend to go in life. Don't get pulled into the past with old furniture or family relics—unless you are in love with them. Choose household items and furniture that advance your life, not keep you stuck in history or negative consciousness.

+ **Have fun stuff.** Include things that bring you joy and that are a pleasure for visitors, such as a pool table, a basketball hoop, a chess set or a large-screen TV. Home entertainment and enjoyment is just as important to Vesta as fire. It brings pleasure and joy into the abode.

3. To find a new home:

Let Vesta help. If you are looking for a first apartment or a new place to live, petition her to help you get there.

+ **Clarify.** Make a list of all you seek in a home. Include number of rooms, whether you want to rent or own, location and cost.

+ **Visualize.** Cut out pictures or renderings of your perfect home and paste a photo of yourself inside the new abode.

+ **Focus.** Create an altar to Vesta, along with a special candle that acts as the flame of the goddess. For thirty days, go to the altar with an offering of bread or baked goods, light the flame, read your list, look at the rendering and pray to Vesta to please bring it closer to you while bringing you closer to it. Snuff out the candle when you are done. Offer the bread or baked goods to birds when you replace it with fresher food; this way mother birds can bring the food to their homes too!

+ **Believe.** Set a goal for yourself and trust it will come true. For example, buy a six-bar package of soap and affirm, before the flame of the goddess, "Before this six-pack is done, *I wish to have my new home lined up . . . or the lease signed.*"

+ **Trust even more.** If the goal is not fulfilled exactly on time, that's okay. Start again, with another six-pack of soap. Honor the notion that as Vesta seeks the perfect digs, there may be some delay.

+ **Celebrate.** When the goal is fulfilled, thank her, and make sure you continue to honor her in your new home.

4. Honor Vesta at meal time:

+ **Cook and eat dinners at home.** When you turn on a pilot light or light a barbeque, know you evoke her nurturing energies in the fire. Let her cook a good meal with you. Mix affirmations about your future into dinner. If you cook, do so with intention, placing prayers into every step of the preparation. If you don't, take on simple food-preparation tasks, such as crafting a beautiful salad or cutting up a delicious fruit salad with all your favorite fruits. Pour prayers for your "hearth's" desire in as you mix. Talk to the food as if you are talking to the goddess, petitioning her for all your needs. *I want to eat good food . . . have enough space and rooms in my home . . . enjoy giving parties and soirees,* etc.

+ **Put prayers into all your food.** If dining with others, begin with a dinner prayer whenever possible. Or quietly place the palms of your hands just above your plate and zap the food with good energy while saying a prayer of thanks to Vesta. If you take the time to radiate healing light and bless your food, you will always slow down and eat in a healthy manner.

+ **Eat happy thoughts.** Never talk about anything nasty, negative or depressing while eating. When you discuss these things during a meal, you literally eat them and take them inside you.

How to Keep Vesta with You

Clean up your room. Vesta comes to cleanliness, neatness and order. She seeks the open space and sanctified environment as a temple for her warmth.

Celebrate her on her sacred day. Vestalia, the Festival of Vesta, was essentially a holiday for bakers and millers. They honored Vesta with bread and other baked goods on June 9. You can, too, by baking a loaf of bread in her honor and breaking bread with female friends that night.

VESTA AFFIRMATION:

"I feel safe and happy in my home sweet home."

Part Six

GODDESSES
OF WORK
AND
FINANCE

PURSUE YOUR CAREER GOALS WITH ARTEMIS

"My aim is true."

—Elvis Costello

Launching a new career, pursuing advancement or taking on a new opportunity that will lead to professional evolution is a wonderful, juicy time. It is often a time when we exert our independence and capabilities and when our energies need to be channeled into the attainment of an important goal or opportunity. It's a time of laserlike focus, creativity and almost lustful desire to make something happen, to make it come to life.

Taking a proactive approach to career building is a way to take charge of your professional destiny. It may be a little daunting to put yourself out in the world and try things you have not yet experienced in life, but it is the act of giving it your best shot, with all your heart and soul, that makes an experience so gratifying. Like taking a ski lift to the top of a mountain and stepping off the slope to ski for the first time, it's exhilarating, risky and occasionally terrifying. You might or might not have all the training needed for the task. But the trick is to approach it *as if* you can, and will, pull it off.

The pursuit of big projects and career goals requires much love, nurturing and attention, and there's often a period when the dedicated, busy careerwoman will want to ditch the rest of the world and focus only on her work. It can be an isolating and single-minded pursuit. It may leave little time for family, and less time for love affairs; friends at work, people who we can learn from and who can help our careers along, will be of utmost importance. There will be plenty of challenges to test your mettle, such as procrastination, inability to focus, fear of failure or success, lack of self-esteem and the inevitable failures and mistakes. Embrace the things that don't work out well; they teach lessons that bring strength. If you are willing to take risks, you can rise above any roadblocks to success. The key is to aim high—and be true to yourself!

Artemis is a girl's best friend when it comes to setting sights on bigger targets and passionately hunting career opportunities and advancement. She helps you go after your mark with passion and focus and is a free spirit who empowers independence as she shows you how to make no apologies for going after what you want. She's no man magnet, by choice, so she is especially helpful in those times when you don't want to dilute your career focus with romance. She represents independence, self-reliance, and the ability to aim high and hit the mark.

Who Is Artemis?

"I sing of Artemis, whose shafts are of gold,
who cheers on the hounds,
the pure maiden, shooter of stags,
who delights in archery . . .

*Over the shadowy hills and windy peaks she draws her
golden bow,
rejoicing in the chase, and sends out grievous shafts."*
—"Homeric Hymn XXVII," from *The Homeric Hymns*

Artemis (*ar-te-miss*), Greek goddess of the hunt, was one of the first feminists of the Mt. Olympus set. A huntswoman by skill and divine profession, she was chief hunter of the gods, known as "Lady of Wild Things." A virgin goddess who is fiercely independent and would let no man have her, she knew her territory well and had many friends to help her along the way. She spent her days in the forest with her posse of animal guides and virginal wood nymph companions. She was famous for *always* reaching her target with her golden arrows, which "moaned" as they sped toward her prey. She understood the ways of the wild, and the nature of beast and bird and could gently speak the language of the wild, yet she was fierce and a force to be reckoned with. She was not afraid to make the kill. With her nymphs and hounds, she hunted in the deepest wilderness, slaughtering stags and lions. For recreation, she would gather with her brother, Apollo, and their favorite friends, the nine muses, to sing and dance. She is often pictured as a young woman in a short toga with bow, arrow and animal friends in tow.

How to Invite Her into Your Life

Artemis wanted nothing to do with men (except her brother, Apollo, perhaps), and the penalty for getting a peek of the virgin goddess could be instant death. A Centaur hunter once stumbled upon—or deliberately sought out—the goddess while she was bathing naked in a stream, and with a single word and gesture, the outraged Artemis turned him into a stag and watched him turn into dinner for his hounds. She could be nasty with the very animals she protected, and at the same time, she was extremely protective and would take out anything or anyone who sought to injure her posse of forest friends. She had her own agenda! Artemis is an excellent source of inspiration when you want to put men and most other things in life on hold and channel all your energy into getting your career off the ground or going after *the big job* or project. Swiftly did her arrows fly. Yours can, too.

Artemis had the focus and attunement of the senses as laser-sharp as piercing arrow; her arrows were associated with light. Arrows also represent the piercing, masculine principle; they are virility and power. Although Artemis is a divine female, she largely called upon her male energy to accomplish her work in the world. You, too, may find that there are times when you operate more on "yang" than "yin" energy in order to accomplish a goal. Although Artemis was an expert archer who packed a weapon, your greatest weapon is your mind. Your thoughts and your intellect are as potent as golden arrows when you give them power, language and life and focus them in the right direction. Consider this: Everything human-made that exists in the world began as a thought in someone's mind. You can call Artemis to you by adopting her skills as a mighty archer and independent woman and go after what you want in life!

1. **Create a career treasure map.** Visualizing the results you want to create in your life is a powerful way to get there! As they say, "If you can dream it, you can create it!" A career treasure map is like a road map to your future.

+ **Clarify your goals.** Just as Artemis must have known her target before she let her arrow take flight, you must know your outcome before you take aim, otherwise you can end up exerting a lot of energy in the wrong direction and missing opportunities. Be as specific as possible about what you want your career and work life to look like.

+ **Make a collage of your desired career.** Get these materials: a big piece of oak tag or poster board, stick glue, scissors and magazines that you can cut pictures from. Use magazines you have around the house or buy new ones that have many images related to your goals. Include any aspects of particular projects or advancements you are after. Cut, paste and create your career treasure map with your own hands, heart and spirit. Go through the magazines and clip out enough pictures and images to fill the whole board; just flipping through the pages and selecting images will heighten your visualization skills. Images can be pasted on in any way you like, including overlapping each other and at angles. Have fun and be creative! Include anything that relates to your goals: images of success, fun at work, financial security and prosperity and professionalism or images that reflect the way you want to look, feel, be, behave, travel and live. Include headlines, quotes and neat sayings that give language to your thoughts. For example, if appealing, you might pick a photo of a businesswoman relaxed and flying first class and a headline that says: *"First class, all the way."* Or find your motivation in the famous Nike ad that heralded female power and said, *"Just do it!"* You might also find articles and pictures of people in the public eye who represent the kind of success you would like in your life. It's fine to utilize their images as symbols of the success you desire.

+ **Display it proudly.** Your treasure map is a very personal and sacred blueprint for your career and business goals. Place the map somewhere you can see it daily, even if in passing. The career treasure map supports your internal visualization by placing images that represent goals, dreams and hopes right in front of your face. It stimulates conscious awareness and conscious creation of goals, and it acts as a visual messageboard for the brain. In a gentle and quiet way, it feeds images of the success you choose to your subconscious mind in a way that draws you closer to your dreams and draws those dreams closer to you. (If you are an extremely private person and have a roommate, this can be done in a low-key way and kept in a closet, or it can be done on a smaller scale, in a notebook.)

2. Treat your efforts as a sacred act. Devote yourself to following your treasure map and making it come to life. When you devote yourself so fully to the creation of something meaningful, and do it as it is as if you are building something sacred, it's an offering to the goddess. What you put in will come back, plus some. Ask Artemis for her blessing: *That I may be as skilled and devoted to your targets as you!*

3. Sharpen your focus. Keep your eye on the goal—don't let it out of your sight—as you clarify all the appropriate actions you need to take. If you focus on the end result you are working toward, all the steps to achieving it will seem more natural, allowing you to more easily accomplish the practical aspects as well as the more daring.

4. Dedicate yourself to your most important goal or goals. While you wouldn't want to turn into a work-addict who has nothing else in life, at the crucial stages of development, any project of importance will require *all of you*. When Artemis would disappear into the forest to do her work, the rest of the world faded away. Be a workaholic for the time it takes to make a dream come true; pour all your energies into your special goal. Live, breathe and sleep it until you nail it down. Like everything in life, there is a time and a season for this kind of focused devotion.

How to Keep Her with You

Carefully craft your language. Your words are like golden arrows that can create "thought forms" and can be targeted to help you "sell" your ideas to the right people—bosses, supervisors, clients and people you want to be working with. Communicate in a positive, forward-moving manner when talking about important projects. Avoid complaining and groaning about how tired or stressed you are; focus instead on the benefits and importance of what is being created.

Keep an arrow on your desk. Be reminded of reaching goals by keeping an arrow, an archer or even a statue or picture of Artemis in view.

Enjoy the hunt. The greatest way to evoke the presence of the goddess of the hunt is to pursue it with passion, as she did, and enjoy every nuance of the experience.

ARTEMIS AFFIRMATION:

"I take responsibility for reaching my goals."

FIND YOUR INSPIRATION
WITH BRIGID

"Imagination is evidence of the divine."

—William Blake

ometimes good ideas elude us, or we feel our minds are clogged up somewhere between "concept" and reality. It's too hard to "get into the mood" to be creative, or there's not enough motivation or support to get a project cooking and completed. Good intentions are sometimes thwarted by anxiety about starting—and finishing—a project. You might be used to accomplishment via deadline-induced inspiration, fueled by adrenaline and panic. Maybe you just don't know how to open up to divine inspiration.

Many of us romanticize creativity as something that we evoke only when the spirit moves us, but the real world dictates that things get done on deadlines and according to contracts. While it is always nice to wait for divine inspiration to strike, we also have to learn to evoke inspiration and draw it to us—and to catch it and utilize it when it comes. The amazing thing about the creative process is that one moment we may be completely stumped, and then suddenly, as if a switch has been flipped, the lightbulb in our brain turns on. The heart opens the mind, and anything seems possible. And so it is.

Every project, in every profession, has a creative element. It begins with a flutter of inspiration, and it becomes bigger, greater and more fully formed in our minds. But a woman cannot live on ideas alone! Once the flame of creativity is alight, an idea can easily grow wings and take flight and manifest as reality. We have to honor the process of creation, yet continue to consciously fan its flame.

Brigid is a girl's best friend when it comes to creativity, self-expression and bringing new ideas into the world and giving them life. When at a loss for stimulation and motivation and tearing your hair out with anxiety, she lights the fire in your creative soul with her creative magic. She will freshen your ideas and bring her fiery spirit to your life. She represents the passionate flame of creativity and inspiration.

Who Is Brigid?

"Brigit, excellent woman; flame golden, sparkling.
May she bear us to the eternal kingdom; she the sun,
fiery, radiant."
—Seventh Century Hymn of St. Brigid

Brigid (*bridge·jeed*) is the Celtic triple goddess known as keeper of the sacred fire. Her name means "exalted one," and she is sometimes referred to as a "bride." Goddess of poets, blacksmiths, brides and childbirth, she watched over the hearth, fire, fertility, creativity and healing. As a triple goddess, she represents the three aspects of the divine feminine and three stages of a woman's life —maiden, mother and wise woman—all in one. When Christianity took hold, she survived the fall of the "old religion" and was adapted as a Catholic saint and got a slightly different spelling of her name. She was, and continues to be, the much-loved St. Brigit of Kildare, said to be founder of the first female Christian community and abbess of a large double monastery in Kildare in the Middle Ages. She is touted as midwife to the virgin Mary and has long been invoked by women in labor and viewed a great supporter of birthing new ideas as well. As a goddess, Brigid is always represented as youthful and beautiful, all three aspects of her the same age; she's pictured with flaming red hair, often holding a flame as her symbol. In her incarnation as a saint, she is seen with cattle and is affiliated with dairy and milk especially. It is said her cows were milked three times a day and could fill a lake with their milk. She is also affiliated with water and wells. There are still many wells in Ireland devoted to her as sacred shrines.

How to Invite Her into Your Life

Brigid is the symbol of eternal light. In the days when Celtic paganism was the main religion of Ireland, nineteen priestesses tended the flame of the Goddess Brigid. They rotated, one each day, and it is said that on the twentieth day, the goddess herself tended the flame. This evolved into an early Christian tradition whereby nuns in the abbey she founded were considered guardians of the "Fire of St. Brigid." After her death, it's said the fire burned continuously and took a great deal of wood, but the ashes did not increase—until the church outlawed the practice. The Sisters of St. Brigid order continue to tend "the eternal spiritual fire of St. Brigit," and members of a worldwide organization called Ord Brighideach continue to maintain the twenty-day rotation schedule, keeping "Brighid's Flame" alive. You can, too.

FOR LONG-TERM PROJECTS:
Light her fire. Just by lighting a candle, you can evoke her energy and kick-start an endless flow of ideas, solutions and creativity. If you commit yourself to a twenty-day program of lighting a flame in honor of the goddess, you ensure twenty

days of focusing on creating something important and you'll have the chance to "work" with Brigid every day.

You can go back to the very ancient roots of the tradition in everyday life in a number of ways. If you happen to have a fireplace or an outdoor fire pit, you can light any of these daily for twenty days in honor of the goddess. Candles are fine, too. You can use one large pillar candle that you light daily for an hour and then snuff out until the next day or twenty small candles. Votives will burn for about ten hours; tea-lights for about two. The color orange is particularly powerful, because orange is the color of Brigid's flaming hair and also represents the color of the energy center in the body affiliated with creativity and birth (known as second chakra or the sexual chakra). Needless to say, any way you choose to honor her, you must absolutely do it safely and carefully.

+ Pick an appointed time *every day* for twenty days to light the fire in honor of Brigid, and try to keep the sacred schedule. If your timing is off, light the flame when you can, but do it daily. As you do, visualize the project you want her inspired blessings for and say it out loud if you can, as you ask for her help.

+ You can ask in your own personal way for what you need, or use this prayer: *Brigid of the golden flame and fiery inspiration, I welcome you. Please bring me the inspiration and motivation I need to (fill in your need). On this day I pray that this sacred flame lead me to your light. Amen.*

After your prayer ritual, snuff out the candle with a candle snuffer, rather than blowing it out (spiritually, blowing could mean blowing away the intention of it). Thank the goddess for being with you on that day and always.

Over the course of a few days, you will feel the energy of inspiration begin to sizzle within. Seize it, ride its wave and get your work done! Brigid's gifts will come, naturally, in the course of your days. By the time you reach the twentieth day, you may find yourself in especially good spirits, as you have had almost a month of intimate communion with the goddess of inspiration. On the day Brigid is believed to tend the flame herself, approach the lighting of the fire with great reverence, and thank her for every small gift she has given you in these twenty days. Recount every idea, inspired moment, creative experience and finished project that has come about in twenty days, and thank her for her part in it. When you acknowledge divine co-creation, you build a bridge of gratitude that can lead to greater confidence in the creative process and continued inspiration.

FOR SHORT-TERM INSPIRATION:

+ **Let her waters inspire you.** Because of her affiliation with sacred waters, you can also call Brigid to you with the help of water. Anytime you can get out and sit by a lake or the ocean, your mind will clear and ideas will flow. If you can't spend time around a body of water, try a home water fountain, sometimes called tabletop fountains or feng shui fountains, they can be purchased in drugstores these days. Set it up in a part of your home or office that is not in your direct working area. When you need a little inspiration, you usually need a little relaxation. Turn on the fountain and sit and gaze at the running water; it is hypnotic. Let the sound take you on a relaxing journey, and as it does, imagine the goddess Brigid washing over you with her sacred, cleansing, healing waters. Ask her to help you with whatever it is you're working on. When you feel refreshed, turn off the fountain and go back to work.

+ **Ask her to bless your handkerchief.** It is an old custom to leave a white cloth out on the table for the goddess to bless (at her holiday, Imbolc). To this day, people continue the tradition of honoring her with pieces of cloth that hang near her shrines and springs, such as the Well of St. Brigit in Fouchart, Ireland. Keep an "inspiration hankie" handy. When you need a little help with a project, leave the white hankie on your table at night and, with a little prayer of thanks, ask the goddess to help with your need. Be specific. Then take the hankie to work with you the next day. Take it with you into any meetings, or keep it by you at your desk. Anytime you feel the need, hold it in your hands and visualize that whatever you are trying to create or work through is done, completed.

How to Keep Her with You

Keep the flame of Brigid's inspiration flowing. Light candles when you want to get in touch with Brigid. This invites her to not just visit, but to stay with you.

Get the Cross of Brigid for your home or office. Often made with straw and uniquely shaped, it is widely available and affordable and can be purchased at most Irish-American gift shops. The cross can also be constructed at home.

Listen to Celtic music. Tunes from the homeland of Brigid's birth will evoke her energy in your soul. New Age tunes and anything from Enya can call forth her warm and inspiring spirit.

Partake in her annual celebration. Brigid is honored on the eve of February 1, known as Candalmas, and the day of February 2, Imbolc, with fire and prayer. It's a time to acknowledge her light, the increasing power of the light of day and the first seedlings of spring. As she blesses nature in bloom, we ask her to bless our creative ideas and ventures. This holiday of Brigid was precursor to Groundhog Day, the predictor, and also conscious awareness of coming spring.

BRIGID AFFIRMATION:

*"Inspiration fills me. My creativity
flows easily."*

INCREASE YOUR INCOME WITH LAKSHMI

"A girl needs cash."

—Joan Perry, financial advisor

Many of us dream of making a lot of money. Some of us are quite talented and savvy about finances; at an early stage of our careers we figure that success involves striving toward financial security that includes sound investments, savings and the wise use of resources. But most of us grapple with money issues of one sort or another: we don't make enough or we spend too much; we crave financial power yet fear taking responsibility; we get overwhelmed or sloppy with bills or are basically clueless about finances; we're just starting out so we don't really know our worth or perhaps still think a man or Dad will show up to save us financially. Maybe we just don't believe we can make it on our own because we simply were never brought up that way.

Whatever the issue, when we're younger, our financial priorities tend to be based on short-term goals, such as making it to the next payday or saving for a vacation. We don't always think in terms of building long-term wealth, developing our credit ratings or securing enough money to buy a house or start a business of our own or even having money so we can contribute to good causes. We may not pay bills on time because our records are sloppy or there never seems to be enough money, and you can bet the credit cards get used more than we'd like. Some of us just haven't developed the foresight to see into our financial future and plan for it. Many of us also suffer from a self-worth issue that makes it impossible to see ourselves as women who can earn, save and invest money so it grows.

One of the most important skills we will have to develop in order to succeed is to learn how to create our own prosperity. This means we have to rise above feelings of unworthiness, fear of finances and the fantasy that it will "all be taken care of" in order to see that responsibly managing, making and investing money are an act of self-love. And we have to get into a mind-set of planning for the future in addition to living for today.

It may seem that one of our biggest problems with money is that there is never enough. And so it is, if we tend to keep our focus on "lack" and "not having" enough, rather than working on our "issues" and developing the grace, wisdom and sense of personal responsibility needed to build a sound financial future. Building a career that brings a great income can take time. Learning to save, invest and spend wisely is also a process. One of the first steps to success is to expand our sense of having the ability to build prosperity and begin to build it, one small step at a time, until we embrace it and come to see that there is plenty of abundance to go around.

Lakshmi is a girl's best friend when it comes to money. We need all the help we can get in surrendering poverty consciousness, increasing income and investing for the future. But before you ask for that raise, try to elevate your position at work or even think about underselling your services just to make money, ask for Lakshmi's help. She grants and delivers good fortune in material and spiritual realms. She represents abundance, plenty, good fortune and beauty.

Who Is Lakshmi?

"I invoke Sri, the blissful goddess, who is sweet-smiling, who lives in a hall of gold, who is full of compassion and drenched with it from the heart, who is resplendent at the seat of the lotus, is lotus-hued, and who bestows all pleasures to her devotees."

—Sri Sukta, from the *Rg Veda*, a Hindu holy text

Lakshmi (*lock-schmee*) is the Hindu goddess of good fortune and beauty. She is actively worshiped around the globe by millions of Hindus and interfaith practitioners of goddess spirituality and is considered the personification of abundance, prosperity and wealth. It is said that three millennia ago, Lakshmi was born, fully grown, on a pink lotus that rose from the milky sea. She was immediately bedecked, bejeweled and worshipped by the gods and sages. They prayed that she would come to their abodes and to their worlds, because they believed that where Lakshmi is you will find riches and fulfillment. "Believers" of all faiths trust that praying to the goddess of fortune brings all things good to life. Her eternal consort is Lord Vishnu, "the preserver," and her cohort is Ganesh, the elephant-headed Lord of Obstacles. Lakshmi, like many Hindu deities, is often pictured as a beautiful Indian woman with big, dark eyes and four arms. Most Hindu shopkeepers and businesspeople keep her image in their place of business because they believe she brings them luck. Clad in a sari, with a form that is very feminine and full, she sits or stands on her lotus throne. She usually has two lotuses, in both of her back hands. Her front arms offer blessings and what are known as "boons," or favors from the gods. Her ability to enhance good fortune is symbolized by the gold coins pouring from her hands back into the ocean of life.

How to Invite Her into Your Life

Lakshmi will work with you to increase your income—when she feels welcomed. But first, she asks you to do your part to make your life and your financial situation a welcoming environment for her magical touch.

1. **Clean up and organize your room.** The first step to inviting Lakshmi is to clean up your home environment and remove excess clutter. Lakshmi is attracted to cleanliness. At Diwali, the Hindu festival of lights, which falls in October or November, women clean their houses the night before the new moon to help attract Lakshmi. On Diwali, they light oil lamps to invite her, because it's believed that she is drawn to the sparkling cleanliness and the sparkling lights. It's easier for her to bring good things to life when our lives are organized and when we're making an attempt to be more organized. Organize your files and desk and put financial records in order. Even if you can't pay all your bills, *know what you owe* and put a system in place for being financially accountable.

2. **Praise her and pray to her.** Before Hindu people ask for Lakshmi's assistance, they evoke Ganesh (Gah-nesh), Lord of Obstacles, and ask for his help in removing barriers to the success Lakshmi can bring. You can do this by saying Om Ganesh, Om Ganesh, Om Ganesh. Then praise Lakshmi's powers and attributes and petition her for help:

Dearest Maha Lakshmi (Mother Lakshmi),

who resides in the pink lotus, who wears a red sari and who is gifted with great beauty, please come into my life. Brilliant Lakshmi, who is loved by Vishnu, the gods and the sages, please bring your light into my life. Generous Lakshmi, who has four arms, who carries two lotuses,

*who wards off evil and who pours forth the abundance of
the universe, please bless me with your bounty and help
me increase my finances, now. Shanti. Shanti. Shanti.*

3. Build a Lakshmi bank. Lakshmi is attracted to her own
image, and she is honored when you place her picture or
icon in your home. Get a small statue or postcard of Lakshmi in a local Hindu store, temple or on the Internet,
and build a small "bank" in honor of the goddess of fortune. It should be positioned somewhere you can see it
every day—next to your computer, your dresser or in a
closet if you need to stash it out of sight.

+ Get a clear glass bowl, vase or cup. This will be your
  Lakshmi bank, and as you fill it with coins, you will see
  your prosperity grow.

+ Place Lakshmi's picture or icon alongside your bank. If
  you are not able to or don't feel comfortable or ready
  to use her picture, try to just view the bank as a vital
  essence of Lakshmi's prosperous energy and dedicate it
  to her.

+ Start your bank with four shiny new quarters, to represent her four arms. Symbolically, the new coins will
  initiate financial flow. Taking the time to quiet yourself
  and feel relaxed, offer the coins to the goddess as if you
  are giving a divine gift. As you place them in the clear
  bowl, thank her for all the good fortune that she will
  now bring and for all areas of your financial life that
  she will empower and help you develop.

+ Put at least one coin of any amount of money into the
  bank every day, whatever you can manage and whatever feels right. Just make sure you share your good
  fortune with the goddess daily. Spend a moment of
  sacred silence every time you drop a coin in and ac-

knowledge the increasing finances. The sight of your money growing and the sense that *you are growing it with your own hand* and with the help of the goddess will instill you with greater confidence and inspiration.

+ Carry out all your financial tasks in front of the bank shrine. As you add money to it, it is adding power to your financial life, so it becomes a sacred space in which to take care of all your money-related tasks. Write your checks, pay your bills and go over your credit card bills in front of Lakshmi. If you don't yet have a checking account, fill out the forms for a new checking account in front of the bank shrine. When you are feeling brave, balance your checkbook. Get in the habit of evoking Lakshmi in all things financial.

+ When the bank fills up, take the money out and count it. First, following the spiritual law of tithing, and put 10 percent aside for a worthy cause that you would like to support. Put the rest in a savings account and dedicate it as an offering to the goddess Lakshmi.

How to Keep Lakshmi with You

Keep things clean. Lakshmi revels in cleanliness and order—and you will, too! You may start out keeping your home, your head and your finances free of clutter to attract her support and energy, but in the long run, your financial life will be so much healthier!

Wear gold or silver and precious jewelry. Lakshmi loves things that sparkle and shine. Beautiful jewelry will draw her to your being—and make you feel like a goddess!

Eat healthful foods that are symbolic of Lakshmi. If you like yogurt, honey and milk, eat, drink and be merry in the name of Lakshmi, because these are the offerings made to her as part of worship. Every time you ingest one of these foods, imagine she is nurturing your very being with foods that sustain life and that you are taking in the empowering energies of beauty and good fortune.

Experience a Lakshmi puja. Hindu people honor Lakshmi with a worship service known as a "puja." People of any faith can attend whether it's at a Hindu Temple or in a private home with a Hindu priest. Prayers are uttered repeatedly, and devotional songs are sung. Celebrate her during the special holidays, Navarathri (October) and Diwali (November New Moon).

LAKSHMI AFFIRMATION:

"My life is rich in so many ways."

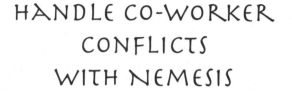

HANDLE CO-WORKER CONFLICTS WITH NEMESIS

"No one can make you feel inferior without your consent."

—Eleanor Roosevelt

M any of us have a "nemesis" at work. Perhaps it's a co-worker who makes our blood boil, an incompetent colleague who charms her way into the good graces of the powers that be and edges in on our territory or a boss who takes our ideas and presents them as her own. If you haven't come across this person yet, you likely will some day, because friction in the workplace was invented long before the workplace itself, and even the nicest of us will, at some point, work with someone we don't like and someone who does not particularly care for us, either!

How many lunches with friends, phone calls with loved ones or drinks with office pals have you spent trashing the person you consider the bane of your professional existence? How much have you complained and, yes, whined, about the one person who is always impinging on your territory, treating you like crap, pulling power plays, sabotaging you behind your back, making you do more than your fair share of work, stealing your ideas or making your life at the office hell?

One of the most difficult steps in healing from the offenses and attacks of people we work with is to recognize how they are holding up a mirror to us about something we need to look at in life. Usually this has to do with the way we sabotage ourselves and sometimes self-destruct our own good work, good fortune and opportunities. It's a hard mirror to gaze into. It spotlights self hatred and a wound you may not even know is there. It is human nature to see the problem as a defect in the other person, but because you may be stuck with your office nemesis for some time, it is important that you work on yourself. Your archrival may be reflecting your own worst behavior or your own worse attacks on yourself, pushing you to evoke your power in a way you never have before.

It's tempting to fantasize of retaliation for any perceived or actual wrongs. But if you are dealing with an individual who is angry, arrogant, competitive, resentful, manipulative, nasty, sneaky, deceitful, paranoid or slightly insane, you must assess if there is anything in that person that is also in you. Experiences with difficult people often show us a side of ourselves that is buried in the unconscious and bring up old wounded parts of us that need healing. In many cases, this person represents a classic case of "your problem is your best friend."

Nemesis is a girl's best friend when it comes to dealing with confrontations and conflicts with work associates. She helps us recognize when someone in front of us is reflecting something within us and helps us heal self-sabotage. She represents the internal mechanisms of judgment, retribution and revenge and how they can backfire on us if we do not have a clear concept of so within, without.

Who Is Nemesis?

"Goddess of Righteous Anger (Justice, Unhappiness). She is a primordial deity who emerged from Chaos. She's an avenger because she takes away happiness if she thinks her sister Tyche has been given too much."

—Martha Ann and Dorothy Myers Imel,
Goddesses in World Mythology

Nemesis (*nem-e-sis*) is the Greek goddess of retribution, revenge and moral indignation for evil deeds and undeserved fortune. She was in charge of putting "evildoers" in their place and kicking butt when it came to untamed, arrogant and unscrupulous behavior. She also was not at all big on allowing people to have what *she* viewed as excessive wealth, happiness or even self-confidence. Her name means "one who distributes or deals out retributive justice," and that's what she did for the ancients—anyone who tried to get one over on her was eventually under her thumb. She was somewhat of an "instant karma initiator"—you stole, you hurt another, you committed a crime or you ended up with something you did not deserve and she was on you. She was the daughter of Erebus and the night goddess Nyks. She is said to have had a rip-roaring affair with the king of all gods, Zeus, which produced the beautiful Helen of Troy; but some stories say she only laid an egg containing her daughter and refused to nurture it, leaving the hatching to someone else. Nemesis was represented, often in tragic art, as a serious and thoughtful young woman, sometimes seen with wings of a griffon and sometimes with a sword and whip.

How to Invite Her into Your Life

The *American Heritage Dictionary* points out that Nemesis is not only the goddess of retribution in Greek mythology, but her name has come to symbolize "a source of harm or ruin . . . an opponent that cannot be beaten or overcome . . . and one that inflicts retribution or vengeance." But the goddess Nemesis is not the one who is out to get you; she's there to guide you. She views your enemy at work as someone who can teach you more about your *inner nemesis,* the one who criticizes and negating everything you do, making you vulnerable around office bullies. Nemesis holds a mirror to us so we can uncover our own dark side and heal ourselves. We can't change the people around us—and it's not up to us to do so—but we can expand our understanding of frustrating situations, and we can change our own reactions and behaviors.

1. Create a Nemesis awareness chart. Start with a plain piece of paper. Make three columns. Write down the name of your work nemesis in the first column, your name in the middle column and "Family" in the third column.

+ **Let it all out.** Proceed to write down all your issues with this person in the first column. For example: *She or he is nasty, arrogant, a liar, manipulative, backstabbing, etc.* Complain and let loose. Just the act of discharging some of your pent-up feelings on paper will be helpful.

+ **Is this me?** Next, ask yourself honestly if you can relate to any of those qualities. Do you see them in yourself? If the person you take issue with is overly competitive, envious or intentionally covert, could it be that you have any of those traits, too? If so, write them down in your column, beginning with, "*I am . . .*" and own up to the quality.

+ **Check the family tree.** Then, under the heading of Family, see if there is anyone in your family who exhibits the kinds of behaviors you find so problematic with your work nemesis. Maybe you had a parent who was very critical and judgmental, or a sibling with whom you experienced great rivalry or who was always vying for attention and taking it away from you.

+ **Review your lists.** Take a deep breath and ask Nemesis to guide you as you go over the completed three-column list to seek clarity and illumination. See if you can identify all the specific ways you feel attacked and aggravated by your work nemesis; also look to see if there is a corresponding behavior in you or someone in your family.

+ **Don't be shocked!** Most everyone will find a little bit of their work nemesis in themselves and their families; some will find more similarities than others. This list helps you see that your situation at work may be just the icing on the cake, that it is triggering painful or disturbing behaviors you developed or were exposed to in childhood. Healing these things is a process. The first step is to illumine them and begin to notice what sets off the difficulties at work. For example, perhaps you felt out of control at home as a child, and now you have a boss who is very dysfunctional. Every interaction with the boss would include not just the current drama they are creating, but it would restimulate the old dramas and traumas you grew up with. In many ways, these difficult work situations cause us to revert to childhood and feel like children again—it's very hard to put in a decent days' work when you feel three feet tall!

2. **Keep doing a self-sabotage reality check.** Use the list as a launchpad to get to know yourself, your patterns and your emotional, psychological and spiritual makeup a little better and explore family history that may affect you at work. Perhaps you come from a family that encouraged you to feel more comfortable with confrontation

and hardship; you might be repeating that pattern at work. Or you might have a family that did not empower feelings of worthiness and, thus, Nemesis may show up like a bully in the workplace who challenges you to own your power. Be gentle with yourself as you muster the courage to sort all these issues out.

3. Identify where you are your own worst enemy. The most difficult and dark side of Nemesis is that she also represents the part of us that is lacking in self-esteem, self-appreciation and self-love. Nemesis is sometimes pictured with a sword and whip to emphasize her power to punish those who misbehave. How often do you use that sword and whip, metaphorically and emotionally, to punish yourself? How often do you retreat into a critical self-image when someone at work gives you a hard time? How often do you judge yourself and take the blame when it is not yours to take? How many times have you compulsively tried to "fix things" and "make things better" at work with people who mistreat you? And how often do you berate yourself for how *you* respond to difficult people or for any ill feelings you may have toward them for being mean to you? Ask yourself: *If someone were physically beating me up, the way I beat myself up, wouldn't I fight back?* If so, it may be time to take on the challenge of Nemesis and begin to free yourself from her grip. She only wants you to stop being cruel to yourself!

4. Purge some of the negativity. Cleanse other peoples' negative energies and your own every day after work. Take a warm mega-saltwater bath in kosher salt or sea salt and a cup of Epson salt; it will help relieve stress, aches and pains and restore electrolytes when you are stressed. Dunk your entire body—hair, too—as many times as you feel you need to. With each dip in the water, feel negativity washing away. Make an offering to the goddess at every bathtime; surrender to her one negative quality you have discovered within yourself that you would like to heal. Feel free to have a good cry and allow your salty tears to go into the water, which represents the salty, healing water of the sea. Release, release, release into the water. Say a prayer: *Nemesis, I surrender (name of quality) to you. Please help me learn the lessons of this situation and move on. Please help me find balance at work and peace in my heart. Please bring the right remedy to me now. Please heal this situation, me and all involved for the highest good. Amen.*

How to Keep Nemesis with You

Limit self-judgment. As critical as you are with yourself is how critical you are with others. Oftentimes people act out when they feel they have been put on the defensive. If you are less defensive, people around you are less likely to reflect that to you.

Give up the ghosts of betrayal of the past. If you have been fired, pushed out of a job, hurt by an alleged friend, skipped over for a promotion or given a smaller bonus than a co-worker, you have felt the sting of Nemesis trying to get your attention. Focusing on offending parties and making the experience about them is not useful. Try to use disappointing experiences to grow and learn how you can improve yourself.

Seek professional support when needed. Counselors and therapists can help you through the rough spots; it's always good to get an emotional tune-up when you're in the throes of a situation that's depleting your energy. Twelve-step programs, such as Co-Dependents Anonymous (or others related to specific family issues), are a way to safely process a magnitude of Nemesis-type issues and feelings.

Enlighten yourself. Debbie Ford's books on understanding our shadows are excellent for anyone who wants to explore this further. Check out *The Dark Side of the Light Chasers: Reclaiming Your Power, Creativity, Brilliance and Dreams* and *The Secret of the Shadows: The Power of Owning Your Own Story.*

NEMESIS AFFIRMATION:

*"I can choose my actions and
reactions to all things."*

DRAW YOUR BOUNDARIES WITH DURGA

"Be your own palace, or the world's your jail."

—Anonymous

Drama, dysfunction, assorted crises and just plain "bad energy" generated by difficult people can drive a sane woman straight to the bar after work if she doesn't stay balanced and grounded. Some businesses just seem to thrive on a constant state of chaos and emergency. Perhaps you work with a perfectly nice but slightly "emotional" or "creative" crew of people who are big on drama. Maybe you are just having one of those days where you are barraged by a series of activities that, in the course of a day, begin to wear you down: The boss is in a bad mood and barking at you; co-workers are having personal problems they've brought along to work; people keep coming into your office to ask annoying questions; the phone is ringing off the hook; or employees need more hand-holding than you can handle.

When people are getting in your face and into your space it's tough to draw the line and limit their access to you. You have to have a strategy for staying focused and strong, a way to avoid getting dragged into other people's drama and any other shenanigans that are a drain on your energy and disruptive to your productivity. Office politics, imbalances or chaos can turn an eight-hour workday into a prison shift—unless you know how to draw your boundaries and keep a healthy distance from the craziness.

Durga is a girl's best friend for those days—weeks, extended time periods—when people are getting on your nerves, intruding on your space, draining your battery and giving you a hard time at work. Durga helps you define and create boundaries—physical, psychological and spiritual. She shows you how to psychically protect yourself from intruders and ward off anyone who does not wish you well. She represents valor, the warrior spirit and the ability to be mistress of your environment.

Who Is Durga?

"The demon threatens even the might of the gods, who call upon Durga to save them from the chaos it represents. By slaying the demon, Durga restores order to the cosmos."
—from the *Anthology of Sacred Texts by and About Women*

Durga (*dur-gah*) is the great mother and warrior goddess of the Hindu tradition who symbolizes strength, valor and protection. Worshipped by millions over the world, she is a particular patron to women, who regularly direct their morning worship and daily prayers to her attention. She was the first personification of the divine female in the Hindu pantheon, having emerged from the cumulative powers of all the gods, who called her forth—and conjured her, some say, by breathing fire—when they could no longer fight *Mahisasura*, the buffalo demon who threatened the world. Brandishing the weapons given to her by the gods and representing their fiercest forces of good, she set off on her lion to find and destroy him. Durga, in Sanskrit, means "a fort" or a place that is protected and difficult to reach. With her eight arms and numerous weapons, ornaments and apparels, she was the only one who could reach the nasty demon and stop him. In addition to being an evil-slayer, she is the great mother, a nurturer, comforter and loving protectress. Durga is typically seen as a beautiful Indian woman with eight arms, sometimes ten, dressed in a sari; she rides a lion and sometimes a tiger, each hand holding a weapon or poised in a sacred stance.

How to Invite Her into Your Life

Durga embodies the very powerful warrior aspect of the divine mother, yet she is also the all-powerful, very nurturing mother who wants to safeguard her children from harm and look after their well-being. She unifies the male and female principles because she represents the ultimate divine power of the feminine, called *shakti,* and also embodies all the energies of the divine male. She protects the universe and is protected by the universe; therefore, when you come under her auspicious shield, she's got you covered! She has the very special power of being "unreachable" because the boundaries she sets are impenetrable. With her help, you can keep negative people, vibes and happenings out of your personal space or at least deal with them in a way that allows you to feel more in charge. Bring Durga to work and let her be the fort:

1. **Call her to you with a special mantra.** For thousands of years, this mantra has been used to evoke the help and protective power of the goddess and can be your secret weapon at work: *Om Dum Durgayei Namaha* (pronounced *om dumb dur gay nam-a-ha*). Memorize it, chant it out loud when possible, keep it in your head or write it on yellow stick-ems and put them on your computer, your phone or your desk. Anytime you feel your

boundaries being impinged upon, start chanting it over and over in your mind. Repeating this mantra will strengthen your personal power and help you endure difficult situations. It will call her energy to any situation. It means, essentially, *"Om and Salutations to that feminine energy who protects from all manner of negative influences, and for which Dum is the seed."*

2. Pray to her. The Hindu tradition is rich with prayers, odes and devotional songs to the goddess. These hail her powers, exploits and traits. You can recite this ancient ode to *Durga Mata* to offer praise and ask for her attention to your needs. You might also copy it and tape it to the backside of an image of her, or rest it under the frame, beneath her feet, which is where people typically leave offerings to the goddess in temples:

Oh mistress of the universe, whose nature is the world,
filled with all powers.
Save us from dangers.
O goddess Durga, praise be to you.

3. Keep Durga's image on your desk. It is typical in Hindu culture to use an icon or image to bring in the energy of the goddess. The image of Durga with eight arms, packing all those weapons—yet with such a sweet and beautiful face, and with a lotus in one hand—is a wonderful visual reminder of warring power, woman-style. Although she is generally pictured on a tiger or lion and often portrayed stomping on the buffalo demon, she is so peaceful. It is believed that having her image handy helps you focus on her powers and enlist her in your aid. If you cannot keep her picture on your desk, keep one in your wallet and keep a miniature toy tiger on your desk to represent her.

It is helpful to understanding the spiritual significance of her weapons. She has an awesome arsenal. She lovingly holds out one hand, decorated palm facing outward, to ward off negative vibes. The rest of her accouterments are sacred objects that represent powerful aspects of the protective qualities of the divine. Her bow and arrow represent the male and the female; her sword is a symbol of wisdom and the battle against ignorance; her three-pronged trident, an attribute of the god Shiva, symbolizes the three aspects of the divine as creator, protector and destroyer; her snake is a symbol of the eternal cycle of time and immortality; her conch shell, an attribute of the god Vishnu, is a musical instrument that is sounded to ward off demons, and the spiraling of the shell represents infinite space; the wheel she spins on one finger is a symbol of life and death; the lotus is a powerful symbol of beauty, fertility, happiness and eternal renewal and is the throne of all the gods and goddesses. It is important to note that she packs a lot of good in those weapons, so her assistance serves everybody for the highest good! Tune into her true energy, and you can tell she seeks not to harm but to heal by casting away demons and blocking negative influences.

4. Imagine her as your force field. Durga's weapons physically put space between her and opponents, and they can *spiritually* put space between you and yours. Having a rough day and want some time and space to get work done? Put the "spiritual seal of Durga" on your door and around you. Call in her divine protection by visualizing yourself surrounded in pure white light; then use your imagination to visualize her powers creating a wall of protection between yourself and others. Try it someday: Imagine she is stationed at your office or cubicle door, weapons poised sitting on her tiger. She will not let anyone too near you because you have work to get done or because your bad-mood boss is bumming you out too much. Imagine she makes sure that any bad moods or vibes bounce off you. The slang equivalent is "Talk to the hand."

5. Keep a bell on your desk. In Hindu temples, priests ring bells during worship to eliminate distracting sounds and help the mind concentrate and to acknowledge worship of a deity. Bells are also used to "clear energy," because a bell can change the focus. When things are tense in your office, or if people are stuck in a fruitless debate or a creative struggle, why not ring the bell? You can even become the person in your office known for ringing the bell to cut the tension. If your office is too stuffy or corporate for that, ring the bell in your mind. Hear it ring and ring. Secretly, you will be calling Durga to the rescue.

How to Keep Durga with You

Burn sandalwood incense at home. In the evening, unwind with a scent that is used in temples and conjures the energy of Durga, as well as spiritually cleans you from a challenging day.

Get a Durga Yantra. This is the magic triangle of the goddess, a diagram that is often seen on postcards and posters, often beneath the foot of the animal she rides. You can get one from an image of the goddess and also purchase the Yantra in shiny brass or as an amulet. It is used for protection, as if the goddess has her eye on you.

Visit her in a temple. Most will have an icon of Durga or one of her sister goddesses you can visit during normal temple hours.

Experience a Durga puja. Durga is celebrated during the Hindu holiday of Navarathri, which honors the divine mother. For nine days, usually in October, people honor the goddess with puja and washing of her icon. In India, huge icons are taken to a body of water and immersed, given back to the source, in honor of Durga. You can experience it online at the website for New York's Shiv Shakti Peeth temple, at www.shivshaktipeeth.com/jai_mata/durga_pooja.wma.

Be a warrior princess. Durga has eight arms (sometimes ten), and they are symbolic of her ability to defend herself and all people in all ways and bring enlightenment and transformation at the same time. Imagine that she is your backup and your partner in business battles.

Get a "What Would Durga Do?" shirt. It's a cool T-shirt or tank top from Snake and Snake Productions you can wear like Superman's "S" on your chest. Or write yourself a note, tack it to your computer and anytime a boundary challenge arises, ask yourself: What *would* Durga do?

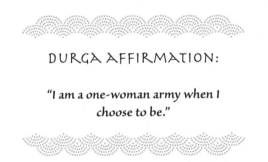

DURGA AFFIRMATION:

"I am a one-woman army when I choose to be."

27

GET THE JOB DONE
WITH ST. TÉRÈSE

"Live every moment as if you are building a temple."

—Sri Ram

We all have our grueling days at work, those times when we must complete a project, honor a responsibility or follow a directive that makes us want to run screaming from the office. You know the kind . . . it feels *so* difficult and *so* unpleasant that just the thought of it makes your skin crawl. Sometimes we simply cannot conjure up the energy and enthusiasm needed to complete a task, or we get annoyed at having to do menial labor that seems to have nothing to do with the career path we are pursuing— like fetching something for a boss or spending all day making copies or tracking down information for a super dull report.

If you are a procrastinator by nature, especially when confronted by an unpleasant task, you enlarge it into epic proportions, make it bigger and more overwhelming than it really is and create a lot of drama. Then, you do your darndest to avoid it, dance around it, make excuses for not having it done and suffer the consequences for delays. Unfortunately, not every step on the career path is lined with a bed of roses, yet you can learn to smell the flowers anyway! Wouldn't it be nice to have the inspiration to approach even the mega-mundane and annoying tasks as if they are an act of love for the divine?

St. Térèse is a girl's best friend when it comes to completing even the most boring tasks in a simple manner without a lot of conversation about whether we like it or not. She was known for her knack of approaching everything she did in life as offering to God. She represents the power to do many small tasks with lots of love and giving up complaining as a temporary sacrifice to the divine.

Who Is St. Térèse?

"Instead of becoming discouraged, I said to myself: God cannot inspire unrealized desires. I can, then, in spite of my littleness, aspire to holiness . . . I want to seek out a means of going to heaven by a little way, a way that is very straight, very short, and totally new."
—Saint Térèse of Lisieux, The Story of a Soul

One of the most beloved of Catholic saints, St. Térèse of Lisieux, a.k.a. "the Little Flower," is a very cool spiritual heroine for women of all faiths. She is not a goddess, but in the Catholic faith, she is widely prayed to and revered. She advocated that all of life was best conducted as a simple devotion to God. Born to parents who yearned for religious life but instead had a brood of children, St. Térèse had the fervor in her blood from an early age and had many spiritual ambitions. In childhood, she had a vision of the Blessed Virgin that was said to heal her; as a girl she wasn't wild about domestic tasks, but would spend hours kneeling in contemplative prayer.

After an emotionally vulnerable childhood, she prayed to be stoic and insisted on becoming a nun; she was finally accepted into the Carmelite order. She learned to flow with the rigors of convent life and give herself over to quiet obedience and devotion. In her eloquent biography, *The Story of a Soul,* she stressed the pleasures of performing small tasks; as opposed to striving for major feats or thinking that greatness lies only in big accomplishments. She reveled in God's small graces. She died at age twenty-four yet saw her pending death as yet another blessing in the wheel of life. She is most often pictured in her nun's habit and yellow cloak, clutching a bouquet of roses and a crucifix; born in 1873, there are also photos available of her.

How to Invite Her into Your Life

Térèse's popularity transcends religion. Although she spent her young life in mystical communion with Christ and addressed her prayers to the Virgin Mother, you do not have to devote yourself in the same exact way—or become a nun, for that matter—to benefit from her approach. She didn't label one task more important than another; all were equal in importance. Life becomes a living grace when you allow each action to bring you closer to the divine. Evoke St. Térèse for especially tedious projects that you have trouble dealing with. Life will be lived with far more ease when lived in a state of gratitude. Your energy level will change dramatically if you say thanks to the divine throughout your day, for every task you accomplish—from your morning shower to going to bed at night.

1. Evoke her with scent:
Legend tells us that if she agrees to help, St. Térèse will send you a rose. Many have claimed to smell the fragrant flower after praying for her intercession. So why not in-

vite her with a rose? When faced with ~~a nasty task~~, see if you can take a moment to ~~go to a shop~~ and buy a single red rose as an ~~offering to Térèse~~. For those times when you can't get ~~out, keep~~ a small bottle of rose water or essential ~~rose oil~~ around. Dab some on your wrists to symbolize that you are reaching out to the Little Flower for her help. You can tune into her energy from anywhere and let her guide you. Once you get past your self-imposed limitation, she is like "cosmic coffee," urging you to get things done . . . and with a big smile on your face.

2. Literally, take three steps forward. Imagine you are moving from your complaints to a state of grace. Take three steps accompanied by a declaration to St. Térèse, and this will create a shift in energy:

St. Térèse, I take this step into the day that has been given to me and ask you to give me the ability to see all tasks as equally important.

St. Térèse, I take this step into the day that has been given to me and ask you to empower me to do my best.

St. Térèse, I take this step into the day that has been given me and ask you to step forward with me.

3. Say a little prayer:
Count your blessings. When faced with a nasty task or a dull duty, saying a little prayer of thanks can never hurt. In addition, if you make a point to start blessing everything you do, you might find, buried in the most hideous tasks, the divine inspiration to do a good job and move on. While completing a task, bless each aspect and express gratitude (i.e., *thank you for this functioning copy*

machine . . . thanks for the nice weather so I don't get rained on while out on this errand).

4. Keep it simple, Sweetie. Simplicity was St. Térèse's approach to life, and K.I.S.S. is the motto of most twelve-step programs, where people with addictions learn, among other things, how much they complicate their lives by dramatizing and blowing things out of proportion. Dissect any task into its simplest components and identify the beginning and the end. Approach it systematically and with the intention to just get it done.

5. Complete everything. For inspiration, post this inspirational "Thought for Today" from the Brama Kumaris next to your desk: "A task left undone remains undone in two places—at the actual location of the task, and inside your head. Incomplete tasks in your head consume the energy of your attention as they gnaw at your conscience. They siphon off a little more of your personal power every time you delay. No need to be a perfectionist—that's debilitating in an imperfect world, but it's good to be a 'completionist.' If you start it, finish it . . . or forget it."

How to Keep St. Térèse with You

Always keep a rose on your desk. One lone flower will call to mind the Little Flower and make you feel better every time you catch the scent of or look at it.

Celebrate her traditions. Her feast day is on October 1. There is a nine-day St. Térèse Novena that you can get online or in most Catholic churches, that tells you how to commune with her and request her help according to her tradition.

Get closer to her. Around the country, you will find shrines to the much-loved saint and, because she was a living heroine, you can also view her relics. You can purchase a St. Térèse medal in any Catholic gift store.

Light a St. Térèse candle. If you want to light a candle of remembrance, yellow is her color. For a super-charged spiritual candle, try the St. Térèse blend from World Light Fellowship, an interfaith ministry that markets high vibrational candle oils said to evoke the energies of the masters of light.

ST. TÉRÈSE AFFIRMATION:

"I approach each task, big or small, with grace, gratitude and love."

Part Seven

GODDESSES OF PLAY AND LIGHTHEARTEDNESS

BE PLAYFUL AS A PUSSYCAT WITH BAST

"You have to sniff out joy, keep your nose to the joy trail."

—Buffy Saint-Marie

Some of us know how to party and how to enjoy life; we're good at making plans to party, setting up play dates with friends and making sure our calendars are filled with fun things and fun people. Then there are those of us who are so locked into an "all work and no play" ethic that we bore ourselves or find we are becoming increasingly grumpy and stressed. Many of us are just professional women who are so anxious to "make it in life" that we forget it is supposed to be fun along the way.

While you may crave responsibility and may be tempted to jump on every opportunity presented in life, you can't spend all your time being so serious and so adult that you forget how to take pleasure in life. If you work too many hours, worry about too many things, spend most nonoffice hours at work-related functions, work on weekends and barely have any personal time, you may find yourself straddling the thin line between devotion to career and being a workaholic. Time to lighten up and learn how to play!

Bast is a girl's best friend when you are ready to come out and play. A goddess who is revered by having fun, she brings out the pussycat in you. Felines represent the feminine, and they are sacred to Bast. She represents surrendering to pleasure, fun and seizing all of life's opportunities to meow.

Who Is Bast?

"Bast became an important national deity about 950 B.C., and her festival was among the most popular in Egypt. Vast numbers of men and women were in attendance . . . There was singing and dancing people clapped their hands or played castanets."
    —Anthony S. Mercatante, *Who's Who in Egyptian Mythology*

Bast (usually pronounced *bost*) is the Egyptian goddess of play, pleasure, frolic, fun, music, dancing and partying. She's also known, more formally, as Bastet. She was the ruler of the holy city of Bubastis, which was a city in lower Egypt devoted to all of those playful qualities—and cats. Almost everyone in Bubastis had a cat, and they all knew how to party! Bast was so cherished by her people that cats were considered sacred creatures, bejeweled in life by their owners and mummified like humans in their death. In addition, many of the Bubastic temples bred sacred cats that lived like pharaohs inside the temple, worshiped as the personification of Bast on earth. Her feast day was celebrated with unbridled enthusiasm each October 31, as thousands of Egyptians came from near and far on barges to pour into her city to party, drink wine until they dropped, sing and often dance lewdly. It was a religious festival with Mardi Gras–like energy—lots of letting down of hair and letting loose. Partying and gaiety were rampant. In addition to fun and felines, Bast was a noted patron and protectress of pregnant women, female fertility and cats. She originated as the lion-head goddess Sekhmet, who represents the raw power of the sun and presided over healing. Sekhmet, a powerful deity in her own right, is now considered the firier, fiercer aspect of Bast. Bast is often pictured with a trim female body and a cat's head, often holding a sistrum, a famous musical instrument of ancient Egypt that was said to drive away evil sprits. She is also quite often pictured as a cat, black or gold, with beautiful collar and jewels.

How to Invite Her into Your Life

The cat goddess of Egypt is a kitten to be reckoned with when it comes to playfulness. She began as a lion goddess whose image grew tamer over time—as will you, when you connect with her wonderful energy. Bast is famous for encouraging her celebrants to be light, happy and self-expressive. Where there is a party or celebration there is Bast. You can evoke her just by singing in the shower or dancing to a snappy beat, by getting a kitten . . . or just acting like one. Bast was revered in the act of having fun and enjoying life's pleasures, and she is present in all forms of good, old-fashioned enjoyment!

1. **Be a kid again:** If you are rusty at having fun, observing and partaking in some of life's simplest pleasures will remind you how to have fun again.

+ **Watch children play.** One of the best ways to remember how to play is to watch kids play. They *just do it*—no agenda, no schedule and nothing to do *but* play. Kids never want to leave the park or stop the game, even though many games have no goal other than just the act of playing itself. They explore, trip, fall, get up, throw a ball, chase a butterfly, make mud pies in the sand—and love every moment of it! If we can connect to playing through the eyes of a child, we will have a new sense of the purpose of playfulness. Just as kids need to play—to blow off steam and be entertained—we need to play and honor the part of us that wants to be part of a fun game or a goofy moment in time! If you can't get to a park, watch a cat play. The playful nature of a kitten is a sight to behold!

2. **Be nice to cats:**

+ **Honor your cat.** Bast comes to life in all felines, so if you already live with a cat, the cat goddess is close by. If not, perhaps a friend has a kitty you can spend time with. Cats were sacred to the goddess; they were highly revered and treasured and treated like royalty by the Egyptians. They were among the first domesticated animals, kept as pets and beloved family members, and also the official family destroyer of pesky snakes, mice and rats. In ancient Egypt, snakes especially were a threat in the home, so the family cat was a lifesaver. At the very least, the cat was considered the household guardian. Cats were also considered demi-gods because they protected the royal food supply from vermin. So find a cat and play with it or offer to take care of a friend's.

+ **Adopt a cat.** If you do not have a pet and are ready to care for one, getting your cat from an animal shelter or rescuing it from an environment where it is not cared for will bring even more brownie points from Bast. Good homes for all cats are a priority for her; she weeps over the fact that there are more cats than good cat homes to go around.

+ **Fill your home with cat knickknacks.** The Egyptians were big on cat tzkchies. You can see in any museum with an Egyptian collection many cat-shaped amulets, ornaments and many cat statues in honor of Bast. Cat mummies were big as well. The cat things you can buy in the general marketplace can accessorize your home and body. Wear cat earrings, necklaces and pins or enjoy cat statues, art and fancy feeding bowls.

3. Fill your life with joy. Look at your schedule to see how many fun things you have planned and how many play-dates you have scheduled. If your schedule is a balance of work, play, romance and family life, congratulate yourself for being so balanced! If it's filled with meetings and work appointments, begin to pencil in play. If there is nothing much happening, decree that you are ready to play and find the things that fill you with joy.

4. Expand your play options. If you had no limitations of time, money or energy, what would you do? Just to get your imagination going, list your ideas of fun and adventure: *Travel afar, take singing lessons, try ballet, get a summer beach house . . .* whatever your dreams, put all your secret fantasies on the list. It is for your eyes only.

5. Find good playmates. One of the first ways to invite playful Bast into your life is to begin to liberate yourself from people who bring you down. While it is difficult to ditch old friends and family members, you can opt to spend less time around them and more time with people who empower the joyous spirit in you. Make it a point to develop friendships, alliances and social contacts with people who are positive and joyous and who have similar interests.

6. Enjoy good old-fashioned fun. With less interest in noisy clubs and more interest in fun you can have at home, arrange play nights for groups of friends, to partake in classic games. The big hits are board games such as Trivial Pursuit, activity games like Twister and the mime and draw game Charades. Serve some snacks and have fun.

7. Play outdoor games. If you are one of those people who like to strategize on everything, it may not be that easy to just *play*. It is often easier to play with other people, so look for courses that offer structured play, such as Outward Bound, which has a super-fun outdoor rope course, or army skirmish games where you shoot each other with paint! Or just plan on going to a ballgame or a sporting event.

8. Fill the air with the sound of music. The sound of joyous music echoing through your home is reverence to Bast. Stock up on favorite CDs and let them play every moment you spend in your abode. If you are not feeling playful, music can take you on a journey through pain and lift you high above it. Be sure to play some music that makes you want to cha-cha or belly dance or move your body in some way.

9. Have a good laugh. Rent hilarious and fun movies, see a hysterical play or comedian or just be a comedy couch potato and watch your favorite TV sitcoms and shows. Seek entertainment that lifts your spirits and makes you laugh. Studies have shown that laughter is good for the soul. Besides, those who laugh spread good cheer. When we allow ourselves to feel good and filled with joy, we radiate it. A good mood can go a long way; just the act of smiling can adjust your whole attitude.

How to Keep Bast with You

Honor a cat. If you like cats, daily care of and playing with a cat will keep Bast present in your life.

Wear cat jewelry. There is perhaps no animal more revered in modern jewelry than the cat. Get a cat broach, ring or necklace to keep her with you; you can even get ancient Egyptian replicas of the cat goddess herself.

Sing in the shower—and beyond. Song is a tribute to the cat goddess. Just the expression of joy that comes through singing, and the physical release of tension that accompanies it, show reverence to Bast.

Get a cat suit. Not only will it give you that one-piece sleek cat look, it will make you feel playful and free, ready for fun!

BAST AFFIRMATION:

"I love to play, and I am having a lot of fun."

ADD COLOR TO YOUR LIFE WITH IRIS

"And then, in the blowing clouds,
she saw a band of faint iridescence . . .
She looked for the hovering colour and saw a rainbow forming
itself."

—D. H. Lawrence, from *The Rainbow*

We all get the yuckies, those times in life when things feel dark, drab and dreary. They hit us when we go through life's rough spots—a loss, a challenge, a sad mood—and they can be exacerbated by nasty weather, spending too much time cooped up at home, not having enough positive contact with other people or even just being under fluorescent lights at work day in and day out. Sometimes we just get so blah that the color seems to drain out of life.

Environmental factors can impact moods and sense of harmony, especially if you're spending too much time indoors, out of touch with nature or if home is not colorful or light-filled. Sometimes, just a little splash of light and color will bring on the cheer and help you refocus your vision on a brighter view of life. For example, yellow is a color that is known to be uplifting and sunny, and green brings about feelings of abundance, rebirth and growth. Also, letting the natural light shine in, or spending time sitting by a window, can help lift your spirits. There is a time and a season in everyone's life for exploring and embracing the blahs . . . and then there are those times when we need to construct a more colorful, uplifting and eye-opening approach to life.

Iris is a girl's best friend when it comes to chasing away the blahs and bringing color into your life. She brings her light touch to dark days and raises your vision over the rainbow as she carries your hopes and dreams to the heavens. She represents hope, vitality and the power of colorful communication with the divine.

Who Is Iris?

"Homer calls her 'fleet Iris of the Whirlwind Feet' and she travels so fast that all we usually see is the trail of her multicoloured passage across the sky."
—from *She: The Book of the Goddess*

Iris (*eye-ris*) is the Greek goddess of the rainbow and divine messenger of the gods and goddesses of Olympus. Considered a handmaiden to Hera and a close aide to Zeus, it was her job to run messages to and from the "eye of heaven." A female counterpart to Hermes (Mercury), she, too, is winged (symbolizing swiftness) and carries a caduceus (symbol of healing and divine communication). Her name means "rainbow" or "an appearance resembling a rainbow," and the Greeks believed each rainbow heralded her arrival. She was known to travel over its arc, without a chariot, in a robe of many colors; she bolted so quickly that all you could see were the colors of her robe rushing through the sky, hence, the rainbow. She was daughter of Titans, Thaumas and Electra, and by most accounts she is considered the bright-eyed sister of the Harpies, who were notoriously dark and gloomy. Though she was sometimes called upon to deliver difficult news, she was known as a sweet-tempered goddess, with no enemies. This gave her an all-access pass to the universe and made her welcome in all corners of the earth and beyond. Iris' duties included the sacred responsibility of leading the souls of dead women to the Elysian Fields. To honor her in this role, the Greeks planted her purple iris flowers on the graves of the deceased. She is usually pictured as a golden-winged maiden in a long, flowing garment that is colored like the rainbow, or as a rainbow itself.

How to Invite Her into Your Life

The rainbow is viewed in many cultures as a symbol of hope and vitality. As the embodiment of the rainbow, Iris helps bring color and cheer to our lives. On golden wings, she takes our heartfelt desires to the divine and brings glad tidings that help us pep up, lighten up and feel peaceful. She also symbolizes the idea that a colorful existence is part of our divine nature and birthright, and that color brings a bit of heaven to earth.

1. **Catch her in rainbows.** A rainbow is one of nature's most glorious sights. The Greeks deified them because they believed they signaled Iris streaking the sky. Rainbow sightings may seem to require a bit of serendipity, but there are just three simple ingredients needed: showers, sunshine and sight. Technically speaking, a rainbow occurs when light is refracted (or bent, so to speak) through millions of raindrops. The drops act like prisms, catching the sun and reflecting it back in vivid colors. The bigger the drops of rain, the more vivid the rainbow, but you can find the rainbow goddess and her hues in even the tiniest drop of water. A willingness to seek her out will expand your ability to see the colors of life and view life through new eyes!

2. Place a rainbow crystal on your window. Buy a multi-faceted Austrian crystal and let the sun shine through, filling your home with a dancing spectacular of all the colors of the rainbow goddess. The principle behind rainbows also applies to an Austrian crystal with many facets. The sun refracts through it and casts an array of rainbow-tinted light and spots around your home.

3. Bring more color into your home. If your abode is drab, dark and needs a splash of color, try some of these ideas.

+ **Pick the colors to suit the mood you want to create.** Studies show that certain colors have specific effects on mood and attitude, and interior designers regularly take this into consideration when designing home and office environments. In addition, color therapy is accepted as a modern mood enhancer, and spiritual design practices, such as Feng Shui, take into consideration that colors have a very specific impact on your life goals, happiness, love life and prosperity. The basic idea is to use the colors that bring the "right energy" to each room in your home (and office) so your environment supports you in all you do and want to achieve. Here are some colors and their effects in a room:

A) **Purple** creates mystery in a room and can help you feel closer to the divine.
B) **Blue** helps you relax, feel peaceful and makes a room seem cool.
C) **Green** brings on the feeling of being in nature and also is healing.
D) **Yellow** cheerfully energizes and expands the size of a room.
E) **Orange** also a cheery color, but it may make you hungry, so use only in the kitchen.
F) **Red** is the color of courage, daring, aliveness and sexuality.

G) **Pink** promotes affection and makes you think of love. It's soothing.

+ **Paint your way to happiness and wholeness.** A fresh paint job can change your outlook on life! The six colors of the rainbow are purple (which is the highest arch) blue, green, yellow, orange and red (the bottom arch). But use whatever colors empower you and make you feel good. Paint one room, or paint them all. Not up for a paint job? Then paint one small item, a symbolic gesture of colorful change.

+ **Choose colorful household items.** Curtains, shades, pillows, throw rugs and even towels can do wonders to cheer up a drab house or apartment. Colorful plants and flowers can also bring a burst of color. Even candles of different colors can help provide an attitude adjustment. Start in a small way, and before you know it, your home will become more colorful—and so will your life.

4. **Wear colorful clothing.** Color therapy gains deeper meaning from the world's religions and traditions. For example, the Eastern traditions believe that the human body has energy centers known as chakras, and that each of the seven chakras is represented by a very specific color that has a specific meaning and healing ability:

+ Red is the first chakra. Located at the base of the spine, it represents life force and vitality. Red also means daring. For courage and vitality, wear a red skirt or pants.

+ Orange is the second chakra. Loacted at the groin, it symbolizes sexuality and creative energy. It's a color that warms and energizes. To inspire creativity, wear orange underwear.

✦ Yellow is the third chakra. Located at the solar plexus, it is a color that can elevate mood and reduce exhaustion. For a pick-me-up, try a yellow T-shirt.

✦ Green is the fourth chakra, also known as the heart chakra—for healing, harmony and love. To connect to your own heart, wear a jade pendant.

✦ Blue is associated with the fifth chakra, also called the communications chakra. To inspire your true voice and clear speaking, wear a blue scarf.

✦ Indigo is the sixth chakra, also known as the third eye. To open intuition, wear glasses with an indigo frame or a scarf of that color on your head.

✦ Violet is the seventh chakra, which is the energy center closest to the divine. It is higher understanding and a sense of calm. To connect to your divine self, wear a violet cap or hair ornament.

USE COLOR IN A PLAYFUL AND FUN WAY:

5. Create a message board to the goddess. Create a colorful communications center for uplifting messages and ideas. Buy a rainbow poster, place it at the bottom of the bulletin board and leave room on the top, somewhere over the rainbow, for messages you'd like Iris to take to the "eye of heaven." On multicolored notepaper or index cards, write brief prayers, goals and hopeful thoughts such as "Today I move forward" and "I will have a divine time today" and tack them on the board. You can also pin up pictures and art—smiling people, women who look happy and colorful or art that represents the cheerier life you choose to experience. Consider them cosmic memos to the goddess. Gaze at it for a few moments every day.

6. Counteract darkness with crayons and doodles: Anytime you are feeling low, out of sorts or sad, you're more vulnerable to the Harpies, but you can balance it out by drawing and doodling your way to a more colorful moment.

+ Keep a set of rainbow-colored Magic Markers or crayons around along with some white paper. Draw anything! Let the colors swirl and twirl and fill the page. Write things you just feel like saying: *I am happy, I am beautiful, today will be so much fun, sunshine fills me, happy days are here again* . . . If you don't feel those things inside, keep at it anyway, because you can write and draw yourself out of a funk.

How to Keep Iris with You

Let her bloom in your life. The iris flower was dedicated to the goddess because it blooms in all the shades of the rainbow. It has a long history of special significance. Irises look and smell beautiful and come in many uplifting colors and styles.

Buy a new lipstick. Nothing cheers us like a fabulous new color— or two. Studies show that when women want to make a change, they often start with a new lipstick.

Quit complaining. Just for one day, do not moan, groan or complain about anything at all. See how you like it. If you do, try it again . . . and again . . . and again. You might find you've developed a new habit that helps keep the Harpies away!

IRIS AFFIRMATION:

"I can always see the rainbow past
the storm."

TRANSFORM YOURSELF
WITH
BUTTERFLY MAIDEN

"There came a time when the risk to remain tight in a bud was more painful than the risk it took to blossom."

—Anaïs Nin

There will be many times in life that we will find our-selves in a "waiting period" or "holding pattern" meant to be a time of transition that prepares us for the next stage. Sometimes it is as if we are incubated; just like the infant in the womb, being readied for life. Although still attached to the umbilical cord that sustains us, birth is immi-nent. It happens early in life, when we crawl from the com-forting cocoon of family life and suddenly have the desire and ability to spread our wings. It can happen when we find our-selves in those in-between times. During a time of incubation, we may feel separated from the world and as if nothing is happening; in truth, a new possibility is being developed and nurtured as an old stage is being outgrown. For everything there is a time and a season.

Problems come when we find ourselves squished into a situation that we have definitely, without a doubt outgrown, yet we can't seem to leave behind. It's become so familiar that it's comfortable and we don't want to budge. Some people call that the "fly in the garbage pail syndrome"—a fly has the great big world to traverse yet she swirls around the same garbage pail over and over. She may swoop down on your neck and circle your apartment, but when you open the window, she will not leave. She's stuck. In order to grow, we are continually called to surrender a part of the lives we have known and shed the old skin to be born anew. We have to stretch beyond the place we were before. It is as if a part of us must die to allow something new and vibrant to be born. Sometimes we struggle through it, the way a baby chick breaks out of a shell or a butterfly emerges from its cocoon; this is a natural process of growth. When the time comes to let go and fly free, it is a glorious moment of rebirth.

Butterfly Maiden is a girl's best friend when it comes to emerging into your fuller state of being. She teaches you to gain strength from your struggles toward transformation and how to surrender to nature's will when it's time to become the beautiful butterfly you're meant to be. She represents transformation, emergence and taking flight in life.

Who Is Butterfly Maiden?

"Butterfly Maiden is the Hopi Kachina who governs Spring. A Kachina is a Nature Spirit. They are sacred spirits living in the plants, animals, and female ancestors who link the human with the divine."

—Nancy Blair, *Goddesses for Every Season*

The Butterfly Maiden is a Native American fertility goddess who brings her pollen from one place to another, bringing about transformation, new beginnings and fresh starts. Like a fresh breath of spring, she is witnessed on the wings and in the soul of a butterfly, the beautiful creature that can transform herself from caterpillar to flying work of art by following nature's simple calling to create a cocoon and then emerge from it when the time comes. She is the spirit that moves the butterfly to produce the tiny eggs that will become little larvae and that allows the caterpillar to know when to fashion its cocoon and when its transformation is complete. The Hopis believed she pollinated the world of nighttime dreams, carrying the life force from dreamtime to reality, in essence, making dreams come true. She is a creative force, a symbol of rebirth and regeneration, and the one who heralds new beginnings. Hopi legend says that the butterfly is the best messenger for making wishes come true and that they are taken to heaven on the wings of the butterfly, hence, Butterfly Maiden. She is pictured in modern art as a young Native American woman, dressed in or surrounded by butterflies.

How to Invite Her into Your Life

In the Native American culture Butterfly Maiden hails from, it is believed each animal, plant and insect has an energy and spirit; the healing qualities in each are referred to as *medicine*. "Butterfly medicine" is about transformation and our personal power and responsibility to transform ourselves. It requires us to become skillful at understanding and honoring our own nature and rhythms, to know when to build a cocoon and when it's time to fly! When we follow the ways of butterfly medicine, we know that while growth is sometimes painful, lack of development makes us feel worse!

LEARN FROM NATURE:

1. **Understand the natural transformation of butterflies:** Some of us might think that caterpillars are ugly, but they are obviously a required aspect of transformation. You might also be surprised to know that the yuckiest-looking caterpillars are usually the ones that become the most beautiful butterflies. There is no fuller beauty, no flutter-

ing wings, no soaring flight without it first being a cater-pillar. They begin as tiny eggs left on a leaf by a mature butterfly. The eggs hatch into tiny larvae (caterpillars). These minute slinky things begin to chow down on na-ture's bounty and quickly grow into full-size caterpillars. The adult caterpillars then eat until their skin is fully stretched. It is then that they build their little shell-like homes—cocoons—also called the chrysalis. For ten days, the mystery of transformation quietly takes place, then slowly, almost magically, the butterfly appears. Butterflies are a miracle of nature. We, too, must allow ourselves the space to endure the less-colorful caterpillar stage of life in order to grow more fully, toward our own miracles.

2. Witness butterflies in flight. It is considered auspicious when you see a butterfly. They stir the soul and inspire us to recognize that we, too, can aspire to move freely from one place to another and that we can follow our highest aspirations. Because many species are endangered due to loss of natural habitats, butterfly conservatories are pop-ping up around the country (The American Museum of Natural History in New York City, Kansas State Butter-fly Conservatory, Butterfly Kingdom in South Carolina, to name a few). They have hundreds of varieties and of-fer an environmentally protected way to observe butter-flies in action, see cocoons and learn more about them.

3. Create a sacred ceremony to inspire transformation and change. If you find yourself in a holding pattern that has you a little stuck and you don't mind a little self-imposed darkness and restrictive clothing, you can symbolically move yourself forward by emulating the emergence of a butterfly from its cocoon:

+ **Gather uncomfortable clothing.** Find items of clothing in your closet that are way too tight and uncomfortable—jeans that are too small, a bra or bustier that squishes you or even a confining panty girdle or skirt.

+ **Prepare to spend some time in the smallest, darkest space in your home.** Somewhere you can be alone for at least a half hour, undisturbed, where you will wear some of those items for a short time to see what it feels like to be squished, uncomfortable and ready to emerge out of a small, dark space.

+ **Play music you love.** Set up a boom box and play soothing, beautiful music that makes you feel comfortable, safe and loved. This will help establish the dichotomy of being in a place you have outgrown but feel too comfortable to leave.

+ **Offer an opening prayer or invocation to Butterfly Maiden.**

I come in the name of new possibilities.
Butterfly Maiden, please join me, protect me and
fill my heart with the power and inspiration of butterfly
medicine.
Let me move forward from my cocoon and answer
spirit's call to fly.
May I trust my heart.
May I grow lighter, wiser and more skillful as I learn to
fly higher.
I thank you. So be it.

+ **Step into your cocoon and spend some quiet time.** Turn out the light, draw the shades or cover the window with a sheet, play your special music, begin to relax, and become soothed.

+ **Bring on the discomfort.** Once you are relaxed and feel good, begin to slowly add the tight items of clothing. In the darkness, put them on over whatever you are wearing—a tight bra over the bra already on your body, tight pants over whatever pants you are wearing. Feel the snugness and just sit in the dark with the feeling and let it get a little uncomfortable. In the silence, try to commune with the Butterfly Maiden, harbinger of transformation, as you prepare to take the first step toward a major change.

+ **Notice where your mind goes.** You will likely feel the clothing get tighter as the darkness of the room gets more annoying or restrictive. Feelings of "wanting to get the heck out of there" will not be long behind. When you get the point, turn on the light. Take off the extra clothing. Open the doors and the windows. Notice the difference between feeling stuck and being free.

+ **Declare your freedom.** Make a choice to get yourself unstuck from whatever situation has a hold on you. It is time for transformation. Think of one major goal that can truly change your life. Aspire to it. Hold it in your heart and mind. Let it take on life and promise.

+ **Close with this benediction:**

*I choose to believe in myself as the Butterfly Maiden
believes in her own nature.
I choose to trust my own heart, for it is a good and
pure heart.
I choose to trust I can find my own path and walk
it wisely.
I choose to believe in my dreams and follow them.
I choose to believe they are just waiting to be brought
to life.
I choose to believe in my strength and power to make it
on my own.
I choose to believe I am the keeper of my own destiny.
I choose to believe that I can fly!
Thank you Butterfly Maiden for guiding this ceremony.*

4. **Go fly a kite.** Native American legend tells us that butterflies can carry our wishes up to the heavens on the flutter of their wings. To enact an ancient custom, buy and fly a butterfly kite; there are many spectacular and reasonably priced versions on the Internet. The physical activity of putting the kite together is a metaphor for a butterfly leaving the cocoon; it comes rolled up, and you must put it together carefully in its fuller form. Then take some friends and go out and find a fabulous place to fly a kite—get it airborne and then run with the wind to keep it aloft. As you are running, think of that one special goal that will change, improve and transform your life, and send it soaring to the heavens on the wings of your butterfly kite. Imagine that the butterfly wing kite is the Butterfly Maiden, paving the way for the changes to come in your life.

How to Keep Butterfly Maiden with You

Grow a butterfly-friendly garden. You can keep her spirit close to home if you have a sunny spot in your garden and a green thumb. Find out what kinds of nectar plants attract butterflies and how to grow your garden through the American Museum of Natural History website, www.amnh.org/exhibitions/butterflies/.

Wear her on your heart. Her spirit lives in the wings of butterfly and S. Bosco Designs creates sacred jewelry utilizing the gorgeous wings of many species of butterflies that have expired naturally.

Get a dream catcher. This Native American sacred object is a branch fashioned into a circle, made with netting and feathers, in many sizes. It's believed that if you place one by your bed, the great spirit will catch all your good dreams and filter out nightmares and bad dreams. It will help you hold on to dreams of positive transformation.

Create a butterfly doll. The Hopi children were taught the spirit of the Butterfly Maiden lives in the Kachina doll. They are often made of ceramics or straw, but you can fashion one with clay and place a drawing or image of a butterfly on it.

BUTTERFLY MAIDEN AFFIRMATION:

"My time has come. I have arrived."

A GATHERING OF GODDESSES

*"A circle of healing. A circle of friends.
Someplace where we can be free."*

—Starhawk, *Dreaming the Dark*

There are a number of chapters in this book that offer unique, fun and productive ways to gather with small circles of women friends. I believe it's important for women to gather together, in a spiritual context and for a spiritual cause, and empower one another toward a deeper experience of their own divine nature. Like the muses on Mount Helicon . . . like the sisters in the Native American circle . . . like the women who have gathered together to honor the goddess for millennia, coming together with like-minded females for a goddess night is a great gift. Just as in the heyday of the women's revolution, more women seek the company of other women to raise consciousness and support one another in achieving greater spiritual wisdom and success. It is so important that we celebrate the goddess within, together.

I've had the good fortune to witness the power of women supporting one another on their spiritual paths in my personal life and my ministry. In the nineties, when I was the editor-in-chief of a national magazine, I invited a group of media friends together for a night of spirituality and girl talk. Each and every one of them was a very cool woman with a high-powered career and spirit. I called it a "Gathering of Goddesses." Everyone loved the idea that we were goddesses—beautiful, smart, powerful and able to affect change in our worlds. They were journalists, radio personalities, publicists, actresses, performers, TV spokespeople and authors. I called them Media Goddesses. We so enjoyed each other's companionship and support that first night, we decided to turn it into a monthly event. We affectionately called our gatherings "Goddess Nights."

In the course of facilitating these sacred gatherings for two years, my great reward was finding my calling as a minister and a facilitator of women's spiritual evolution. Each of the goddesses evolved in significant ways, too. Many of us wrote new books and took on significant media projects; some of us met our soul mates, made major moves or got fabulous new homes. We grew, and we empowered each other to grow more. Most important, we shared an extraordinary and lasting bond and friendship.

From the beginning of time, women have gathered to do things in small, supportive groups—from cooking and cleaning out the caves, to celebrating with clan members, to helping each other birth babies, to plotting revolutionary responses to oppression. When women gather with the intention to grow and heal and evolve—on a personal, professional and planetary level—everyone benefits including the women present, their families and the world. The ripple effect can really help, in some small way, to transform our world as it transforms our lives.

Life will change in leaps and bounds from the first day you call a bunch of friends together for a "Gathering of Goddesses." Your goddess group can be a light that shines and can always lead you back to yourself. You light the way for one another's journeys; you bolster one another's courage and confidence. You help each other to affirm, *"Yes, I can do this!"* I believe that when women gather together, it is easier for us to see ourselves as living links to the divine. Our first experience of bringing the goddess down to earth may be seeing her in the eyes of a goddess friend we admire, trust and respect.

There is great magic in having a spiritual family of women to share the experience of healing, growing and evolving together.

As the traditional goddess chant goes:

> *May the circle be open, but unbroken*
> *May the peace of the goddess be ever in your heart.*
> *Merry meet, merry part . . . and merry meet again!*

Bright blessings,
Rev. Laurie Sue

BIBLIOGRAPHY

ARTEMIS

Hamilton, Edith. *Mythology: Timeless Tales of Gods and Heroes,* New American Library.

Hesiod, Evelyn-White, H.G. (Translator). *The Homeric Hymns and Homerica/Loeb,* Harvard University Press, 1936. "I sing of Artemis," quoted from Homeric Hymn XXVII.

Weave, Robin M. *The Dark Goddess,* www.LiberalMafia.org.

BAST

Marashninsky, Amy Sophia, and Janto, Hrana (artist). *The Goddess Oracle: A Way To Wholeness Through the Goddess and Ritual,* Element Books, 1997.

Mercatante, Anthony S. *Who's Who in Egyptian Mythology,* Barnes & Noble Books, 1995.

Veggi, Anthony and Davidson, Alison. *The Book of Doors Divination Deck: An Alchemical Oracle from Ancient Egypt,* Destiny Books, Rochester, Vermont, 1995.

BRIGID

Green, Miranda J. *Dictionary of Celtic Myth and Legend,* Thames and Hudson Ltd London, 1992.

Jordon, Michale. *Encyclopedia of Gods: Over 2500 Deities of the World,* Facts On File, Inc, 1993.

BUTTERFLY MAIDEN

Blair, Nancy. *Goddesses For Every Season,* Element Books, 1995.

Estes, Ph.D., Clarissa Pinkola, *Women Who Run With The Wolves: Myths and Stories About The Wild Woman Archetype,* Ballentine Books, New York, NY, 1992.

Sams, Jamie and Carson, David. *Medicine Cards,* Bear & Company, Sante Fe, New Mexico, 1988.

The American Museum of Natural History, www.amnh.org/exhibitions/butterflies/. *The Butterfly Conservatory* section highlights butterfly facts, history and gardening.

DURGA

Jansen, Eva Rudy. *The Book of Hindu Imagery: The Gods and Their Symbols,* Binkey Kok Publications, Diever, Holland, 1993.

Kishore, Dr. B.R. *Durga Mata,* Diamond Pocket Books, New Delhi, published in the USA by Nataraj Books, P.O. Box 5076, Springfield, VA 22150.

Seth, Kailas Nath and Chaturvedi, B.K. *Gods and Goddesses of India,* Diamond Pocket Books, New Delhi, India. Available in the USA by Nataraj Books, P.O. Box 5076, Springfield, VA 22150.

Young, Serinity, editor. *Anthology of Sacred Texts By and About Women,* The Crossroad Publishing Company, New York. Durga quote.

EVE

Ball, M.A., Carolyn M. *Claiming Your Self-Esteem: A Guide Out of Codependency, Addiction and Other Useless Habits,* Celestial Arts, 1995.

Cooper, Rabbi David A. *God Is A Verb: Kabbalah and the Practice of Mystical Judaism,* Riverhead Books, 1997.

Gelberman, Rabbi Joseph H. *Kabbalah As I See It,* (self published).

Raver, Miki. *Listen To Her Voice: Women of the Hebrew Bible,* Chronical Books, San Francisco, 1998.

Rosenblatt, Naomi H. and Horowitz, Joshua. *Wrestling with An-*

gels: What Genesis Teaches Us About Our Spiritual Identity, Sexuality, and Personal Relationships, Delta, 1995.

Todeschi, Kevin J. *Edgar Cayce on Soul Mates: Unlocking The Dynamics of Soul Attraction,* A.R.E. Press, Virginia Beach, Virginia, 1999.

Weyrick, Rev. Jeannie. *World Light Fellowship, The Order of Melchizedek: Handbook and Study Guide for Ordination and Initiation,* published by World Light Fellowship, 36 South Avenue, Wappingers Falls, NY 12590. (Apple juice ritual is adapted from "The Liturgy.")

FREYA

Blum, Ralph. *The Book of Runes,* St. Martin's Press, New York, NY, 1993.

Bowes, Susan. *Life Magic,* Simon & Schuster, New York, NY, 1999.

Monaghan, Patricia. *The New Book of Goddesses and Heroines,* Llewelyn Publications, St. Paul, Minnesota, 1997.

Dictionary Mythica. www.geocities.com/Heartland/Ridge/1983/freya.html.

Freya, Goddess of Love and Beauty. www.moggies.co.uk/html/freya.html.

What Life Was Like When The Longships Sailed: Vikings, AD 800–1100. Time-Life Books, 1998.

GAURI

Kingma, Daphne Rose. *Weddings From The Heart: Contemporary and Traditional Ceremonies for an Unforgettable Wedding,* Conari Press, 1991. Seven Steps reading excerpt.

Pandya, Meenal Atul. *Vivah: Design For A Perfect Hindu Wedding,* MeeRa Publications, Wellseley, MA, 2000.

Schuler, Stephen. *Meeting God: Elements of Hindu Devotion,* Yale University Press, March 2002.

Hindu Prayer To Mother Gauri. The Hindu Universe. www.hindunet.org/god/Goddessesses/gauri/index.htm.

GREAT GODDESS

Mutén, Burleigh, editor. *Return of The Great Goddess,* 1999 Engagement Calendar, Stuart, Tabori & Chang, New York, 1999.

Quote on mothers from Wilshire, Donna from *VirginMother-Crone.*

Redmond, Layne. *When All the Women Were Drummers,* Three Rivers Press, New York, 1997.

Starhawk. *The Spiral Dance: A Birth of the Ancient Religion of the Great Goddess,* 10th Anniversary Edition, HarperCollins, 1979, 1989. "The Charge of The Goddess," pp. 90–91.

Stone, Merlin. *When God Was A Woman,* Harcourt-Brace, 1976.

HATHOR

Ellis, Normandi. *Feasts of Light: Celebrations for The Seasons of Life,* based on the Egyptian Goddess Mysteries, Quest Books, Wheaton, Illinois, 1999.

Roberts, Alison. *Hathor Rising: The Power of the Goddess In Ancient Egypt,* Inner Traditions International, Rochester, Vermont, 1997.

What Life Was Like On The Banks of the Nile: Egypt 3050–30 BC, Editors, Time-Life Books, Alexandria, Virginia, 1999.

IRIS

Garland, Linda and Roger (illustrations) and Suckling, Nigel (text). *She: The Book of The Goddess,* Lakeside Gallery, Cornwall, UK, 1998.

Repro-Tech Printing and Digital Media Services: Online Printing Services For The World. www.webprintcolor.com/colour-moodtest.htm. *"Colors by Mood: Is There A Connection Between Color and Your Mood?"*

Rose, Patricia. "Chakra Colors," article, *Woman Spirit Rising,* www.womanspiritrising.nu/Resources/chakra.htm.

"Finding Rainbows" article. http://www.angelfire.com/tx/CZAngelsSpace/Rainbows.html.

ISIS

Houston, Jean. *The Passion of Isis and Osiris: A Gateway To Transcendent Love,* Ballentine/Wellspring, New York, 1995.

Mercatante, Anthony S. *Who's Who in Egyptian Mythology,* Barnes & Noble Books, 1995.

Veggi, Anthony and Davidson, Alison. *The Book of Doors Divination Deck: An Alchemical Oracle from Ancient Egypt,* Destiny Books, Rochester, Vermont, 1995.

Wolkstein, Diane. *The First Love Stories: From Isis and Osiris to Tristan and Iseult,* from "Isis and Osiris, The Sunboat of a Million Years," page 10, HarperPerennial, 1992.

"Relationship Rescue" communication exercise adapted with permission from a ritual co-created with Richard Cohn, Ph.D.

KUAN YIN

Boucher, Sandy. *Discovering Kwan Yin, Buddhist Goddess of Compassion,* Beacon Press, Boston, MA 1999.

Research and wisdom on Kuan Yin contributed to this chapter by Rev. Vic Fuhman, M.S.C., R.M. www.energvision.org.

LAKSHMI

Debroy, D. *Laksmi Puja,* Hindi Pocket Books, Delhi, India, 1996.

Dhal, Dr. Upendra Nath. *Goddess Lakşmi: Origin and Development,* Eastern Book Linkers, Delhi India, 1995.

LILITH

Bronznick, Tr. Norman (with Stern, David & Mirsky, Mark Jay). *The Story of Lilith: The Alphabet of Ben Sira,* http://ccat.sas.upenn.edu/~humm/Topics/Lility/alphabet.html.

Garland, Linda and Roger (illustrations) and Suckling, Nigel (text). *She: The Book of The Goddess,* Lakeside Gallery, Cornwall, UK, 1998.

The Lilith Shrine. www.lilitu.com/lilith/.

MARY

Harvey, Andrew and Baring, Anne. *The Divine Feminine: Exploring The Feminine Face of God Around The World,* Conari Press, 1996. "Ancient Prayer of Protection," translated by Andrew Harvey, p. 113.

Lovasik, S.V.D, Rev. Lawrence G. *Our Lady of Lourdes,* Catholic Book Publishing Co, New York, New York, 1985.

Novena To Our Lady of Lourdes, from The Lourdes Center, Marist Fathers, Kenmore Box 575, 698 Beacon Street, Boston, MA 02215.

MARY MAGDALENE

Ford-Grabowsky, Mary, editor. *Sacred Voices: Essential Women's Wisdom Throughout The Ages,* HarperCollins, 2002.

Haskins, Susan. *Mary Magdalene: Myth and Metaphor,* Riverhead Books, NY, 1993.

Ricci, Carla. *Mary Magdalene and Many Others: Women Who Followed Jesus,* Fortress Press, Minneapolis, MN 1994.

Robinson, James M., editor and MacRae, George W., translation from the ancient text. *The Nag Hammadi Library,* revised edition, HarperCollins, San Francisco, 1990. *The Gnostic Gospels,* selection from "The Gospel of Philip."

Mary Magdalene, An Intimate Portrait, V.I.E.W. Video, New York, shown on Lifetime Television for Women.

Wisdom and insights on Mary Magdalene contributed to this chapter by Rev. Jeannie Weyrick, founder, World Light Fellowship, www.worldlightfellowship.org.

MUSES

Arrien, Angeles. *The Nine Muses: A Mythological Path to Creativity,* Tarcher/Putnam, 2000.

Hamilton, Edith. *Mythology: Timeless Tales of Gods and Heroes,* New American Library.

Hathoway, Nancy. *The Friendly Guide To Mythology: A Mortal's Companion to the Fantastical Realm of Gods, Goddesses, Monsters and Heroes,* Viking, 2001.

NEMESIS

Apostolos-Cappadona, Diane. *Dictionary of Women in Religious Art,* Oxford University Press, New York, 1998.

Imel, Martha Ann and Imel, Dorothy Myers, *Goddesses In World Mythology: A Biographical Dictionary,* Oxford University Press, 1993.

The American Heritage Dictionary of the English Language: Fourth Edition. 2000.

NIKE

Apostolos-Cappadona, Diane. *Dictionary of Women in Religious Art,* Oxford University Press, New York, 1998.

Greek Mythology. Historical writings on Nike from "Nike." http://www.theoi.com/Ouranos/Nikc.html.

"Nike and Her Impact on Greek Art and Culture," article, art and commentary at http://apk.net/nike.html.

OSHUN

Badejo, Diedre. *Òsun Sèègèsí: The Elegant Deity of Weath, Power and Femininity,* Africa World Press Inc., 1996.

Brockway, Laurie Sue. *How To Seduce A Man and Keep Him Seduced,* Citadel Press/Kensington, New York, NY, 1997.

Omifunke. *"Keys To Feminine Empowerment: From The Yoruba West African Tradition,"* article at www.voiceofwomen.com/omi. html.

Ossiac, Rodica. *"Orisha Oshun,"* article from www.themestream. com, February 28, 2001.

OYA

Gleason, Judith. Quoted in "The Awakened Woman" e-magazine, from her book, Oya, *In Praise of The Goddess,* 1997.

Marashninsky, Amy Sophia, and Janto, Hrana. *The Goddess Oracle: A Way To Wholeness Through The Goddess and Ritual,* Element Books, 1997.

Omifunke. *"Keys To Feminine Empowerment: From The Yoruba West African Tradition,"* article at www.voiceofwomen.com/ omi.html.

Insights on an organized approach to change adapted with permission from the planning technologies of change consultant, Theodore A. Hagg, Ableman Management, New York City and Wurtsboro, New York.

PELE

Cunningham, Scott. *Hawaiian Religion & Magic,* Llewelyn Publications, St. Paul Minnesota, 1995.

The Wrath of Pele: Fire Goddess of Hawaii, Ancient Mysteries, New Investigations of the Unsolved, video Narrated by Leonard Nimoy, Produced by Filmroos for A&E Network.

Thought for the Day, on managing emotions, from www.relax7. com, used with permission from the Braham Kumaris.

Hawaiian Volcano Observatory website, USGS: Science for a changing world, http://hvo.wr.usgs/kilauea/summary/.

Kilauea Volcano, information sheet from Hawaii's Big Island tourism website, http://www.gohawaii.com/VacationPlanning-hawaii/Destination/General/Volcano.

PERSEPHONE

Reukauf, Diane. "Seeds of Change," *Skirt Magazine,* 2000. www.skirtmag.com/0100/feature2.asp.

Schaeffer, Brenda. *Signs of Healthy Love,* Hazelton Educational Materials, Center City, MN, 1986.

J&T's Pomegranate Jelly. "The Edible Ornament," www.pomegranatejelly.com. Insights into the pomegranate.

SOPHIA

Powell, Robert A. *The Most Holy Trinosophia and the New Revelations of the Divine Feminine,* Anthroposophic Press, Great Barrington, MA, 2000.

Robinson, James M., editor and MacRae, George W., translation from the ancient text. *The Nag Hammadi Library,* revised edition, HarperCollins, San Francisco, 1990. *The Gnostic Gospels,* selection from "The Thunder, Perfect Mind."

Russell, Letty M. and Clarkson, J. Shannon, Eds. *Dictionary of Feminist Theologies,* Westminster Press, 1996. From "Sophia/Wisdom."

Schayp, Suzanne. *Sophia: Aspects of the Divine Feminine, Past & Present.* Nicolas-Hayes, Inc, York Beach, ME, 1997.

The Wisdom of Solomon, King James Bible, 6:12.

The Old Testament, Book Of Proverbs, 28:27 to 30, one of the first references to Sophia as a feminine entity unto herself.

Research and wisdom on Sophia contributed to this chapter by Rev. Vic Furhman, M.S.C., R.M. www.enervision.org.

ST. TÉRÈSE

Beevers, John, translator. *St. Thérèse of Liseiux: The Story of a Soul,* Doubleday, New York, NY. 1957.

Bramhas Kumaris. "Thought for Today," from Sunday, November 25, 2001, http://www.brahmakumaris.org.uk/thoughts/ and attributed to www.relax7.com.

Flinders, Carol Lee. *Enduring Grace: Living Portraits of Seven Women's Mysteries,* HarperCollins, 1993.

La Plante, Alice and La Plante, Claire. *Heaven Help Us: The Worriers Guide To Patron Saints,* Dell, New York, NY, 1999.

ST. LUCY/LUCINA

Adkins, Lesley and Adkins, Roy A. *Dictionary of Roman Religion,* Facts On File, Inc., New York, NY, 1996.

Bernstein, Ph.D, Frances. *Classical Living: Reconnecting With The Rituals of Ancient Rome.* HarperCollins, New York, NY 2000.

Colbert, Joanne Powell. School of Seasons, Waverly Fitzgerald, "December 13 St. Lucy's Day." http://www.nas.com/jpcolbert-art/seasons/lucy/html.

Catholic Encyclopedia. http://www.newadvent.org/cathen/0941a.htm.

"Santa Lucia Day," http://www.unkc.edu/imc/stlucia.htm.

TARA

Beyer, Stephen. *The Cult of Tara: Magic and Ritual In Tibet,* University of California Press, 1978.

Research, wisdom and Tara Meditations contributed to this chapter by Rev. Vic Fuhrman, M.S.C., R.M. www.enervision.org.

VENUS

Adkins, Lesley and Adkins, Roy A. *Dictionary of Roman Religion,* Facts On File, Inc., New York, NY, 1996.

Bernstein, Frances. *Classical Living: Reconnecting With The Rituals of Ancient Rome.,* Ph.D., HarperCollins, New York, NY, 2000.

Hamilton, Edith. *Mythology: Timeless Tales of Gods and Heroes,* A Mentor Book, Little, Brown and Company, 1940, 1942.

VESTA

Adkins, Lesley and Adkins, Roy A. *Dictionary of Roman Religion,* Facts On File, Inc., New York, NY, 1996.

WHITE BUFFALO CALF WOMAN

Cathbadh, Morgan. "White Buffalo Calf Woman—Prayers for Peace are Being Answered," reprinted from *Main Well Being,* October 1998, at http://wwwmindspring.com/~what/whitebuff.html.

Looking Horse, Arvol. "The Story of White Buffalo Calf Woman," excerpt from a Speech to the Unrepresented Nations and People's Organization, January 1995, The Netherlands. www.thefoundation.com/redroad/keeperof.htm.

The Foundation. www.thefoundation.com/redroad/PeacePipe.htm and www.thefoundation.com/redroad/ceremony.htm. A wealth of information on traditional Native American ceremonies, and the peace pipe.

Wisdom and insight on White Buffalo Calf Woman and Native America tradition contributed to this chapter by Don Evans, www.thefoundation/com/redroad.

A GATHERING OF GODDESSES

Starhawk, *Dreaming the Dark,* Beacon Press, Boston, MA, 1982.

Christina Baldwin, *Calling The Circle: The First And Future Culture,* Bantam Books, New York, NY, 1998.

GODDESS RESOURCE GUIDE

Specific Resources Mentioned in the Chapters:

Comprehensive listing of resources related to items and ideas in these specific chapters

BUTTERFLY MAIDEN:
For information on how to buy adult butterflies for a butterfly release.
International Butterfly Breeders Association, Inc. (IBBA)
P.O. Box 14012
Columbus, OH 43214
(614) 288-5677
http://www.butterflybreeders.com/

Butterfly jewelry made with real butterfly wings.
B. Bosco Designs
21475 Boston Crosscut Road
Hancock, MI 49930
TEL/FAX: (906) 482-6888

TOLL FREE: (800) 936-6110
http://www.bboscodesigns.com/

DURGA:

What Would Durga Do? T-shirt.
From Snake and Snake Productions
307 Dixon Road
Durham, NC 27707
(919) 401-9591
Fax: (919) 493-7210
http://www.localweb.com/snakeandsnake/order.htm

Desktop Toy Tiger
Safari Ltd.
P.O. Box 630565
Miami, FL 33163-0565
www.safariltd.com

Tiger watch. Image of tiger with tiger-striped band, from Zoobee.
(800) 815-1306
www.zoobee.com

FREYA:

Athena Pheremone 10:13
The Athena Institute
1211 Braefiled Road
Chester Springs, PA 19425
(610) 827-2200
www.athenainstitute.com

THE GREAT GODDESS:

"Ancient Mother," by On Wings of Song with Robert Gass, 1993, available on CD Spring Hill Music, (P.0. Box 800, Boulder, Colorado 80306).
Chants from many traditions that include the feminine divine, with traditional women singers and priestesses. "From The Goddess," by On Wings of Song, three traditional chants woven together.

GREEN TARA:

"Green Tara Mantra" by His Holiness the Dali Lama
Prayer: A Multicultural Journey of Spirit

From Sounding of the Planet
P.O. Box 4472
Bellingham, WA 98227
(800) 93-PEACE
www.PeaceThroughMusic.com

Brass Tibetan Tingsha, from The Manda Collection: Tools For Soulful Living
www.themandalacollection.com/tools_toys.com

Green Tara Incense, available on www.ebay.com or in any Tibetan store

HATHOR:
Feet First by Laura Norman teaches the art of reflexology. Considered the country's premier foot reflexology, Norman offers "Be Treated Like A Goddess" reflexology and facial sessions, and she also has a reflexology training program and a shoe line.
(212) 532-4404

LAKSHMI:
Lakshmi lotus wands. These can be specially made by Pamela Richardson of PAMELA.
150 West 28th Street, Room 1004
New York, NY 10001
(212) 255-8233

LILITH:
"Bitch Goddess" T-shirt.
Feline's Out There Wear
www.fetishtees.com/tspages/516.html

MARY:
Lourdes Water, bottles of water from the Shrine at Lourdes, $1.50 per bottle donation.
Available from Lourdes Center, Marist Fathers
Kenmore Station, Box 575
698 Beacon Street
Boston, MA 02215-2594

Goddess Sites: Europe, by Anneli S. Rufus and Kristan Lawson, HarperSanFrancisco, 1991

MARY MAGDALENE
Mary Magdalene Spikenard from World Light Fellowship
Biblical healing balm for the heart, soul and body.
P.O. Box 425,
Wappingers Falls, NY 12590
(845) 297-2867
www.worldlightfellowship.org

OYA:
Cowrie shells available from Shell World.
(888) 9-SHELLS
www.seashellworld.com

PELE:
International Star Registry
The Original Star Naming Service
www.starregistry.com/

Tourism and Vacation Planning Hawaii:

Hawaii's Big Island Official Vacation Planner
(800) 648-2441 from the United States or Canada.

Hawaii Volcanoes National Park Headquarters and Eruption Update info:
(808) 985-6000
www.nps.gov/havo

Kalapana Safe Viewing Program, to view Kilauea lava flow
www.hawaii-country.com/information/lava_news.html

PERSEPHONE:
Seeds of Desire, serigraph on canvas, from the artist Yuroz.
Stygian Publishing
1250 Long Beach Avenue #326
Los Angeles, CA 90021

(800) 423-1631
(213) 622-6416
Fax: (213) 622-8030
www.yurozart.com/hp/home.htm

ST. TERÉSÈ:
High Vibrational Candle Oil from World Light Fellowship
P.O. Box 425
Wappingers Falls, NY 12590
(845) 297-2867
www.worldlightfellowship.org

VENUS:
Venus from Gillette for Women
http://www.gillettevenus.com

Where to find illustrations featured in the book:

CHRIST SOPHIA
Christ Sophia © 1989 Robert Lenz, courtesy of Robert Lenz.
Image available at www.BridgeBuilding.com

KUAN YIN
The Water and The Moon KuanYin Bodhisattva.
Nelson-Adkins Museum of Art, Kansas City, Missouri, courtesy of
Kuan Yin Unlimited
Image available at www.Kuanyinlimited.net

GREEN TARA
Image from a traditional, silk embroidered Tibetan *"Thangkas"*
Similar images available at www.dharmaware.com

OSHUN
Oshun © 2002, by Joanna Powell Colbert, courtesy of Joanna Powell Colbert.
Image available at www.jpc-artworks.com

ISIS
Winged Isis reproduction of an ancient statue.
Image courtesy of The Egypt Store
Statue available at www.theegyptstore.com

ARTEMIS
Artemis © 2002, by Joanna Powell Colbert, courtesy of Joanna Powell Colbert.
Image available at www.jpc-artworks.com

ST. TÉRESÈ
St. Téresè of Lisieux © 1999 Janet McKenzie, courtesy Janet McKenzie.
Image available at www.BridgeBuilding.com

BAST
Bast reproduction of an ancient statue.
Image courtesy of The Egypt Store
Statue available at www.theegyptstore.com

General Resources for Goddess Art, Icons, Images, Supplies:

LAKSHMI INTERNATIONAL
Beautiful Hindu art of all Hindu Goddesses and online temple.
www.motherKali.com

EXOTIC INDIA ART
Icons, brass statues, batiks and art of Asian deities
www.exoticindia.com

JPC ARTWORKS
Goddess and mythological art by Joanna Powell Colbert www.jpc-artworks.com

GODDESS ICON SERIES
by Hrana Janto
www.hranajanto.com

SACRED SOURCE
The best one-stop shopping, online source for multicultural goddess statues and deity images, sacred CDs and jewelry.
P.O. Box 163WW
Crozet, VA 22932-0163
(800) 290-6203
(434) 823-1515
Fax: (434) 823-7665
email: spirit@sacredsource.com
www.sacredsource.com/

THE EGYPT STORE
Fabulous authentic merchandise direct from Egypt, including ancient Egyptian reproductions, statues, papyrus, and ceremonial objects, all specially blessed.
213 S. Illinois St. #4
Anaheim, CA 92805
(714) 817-9053
(800) 616-7206
Fax (714) 817-9054
Lauren@TheEgyptStore.com timetravel@thegrid.net
www.theegyptstore.com/

THE ASIA SOCIETY AND MUSEUM
A leading institution devoted to fostering understanding of Asia and communication between Americans and people of Asia and The Pacific. Special events, exhibitions, gift shop.
725 Park Avenue
New York, NY 10021-5088
(212) 327-9211

FEMAIL CREATIONS
Fabulous and specially designed goddess jewelry, trinkets, art, spirituality enhancing "stuff" and unique gifts to celebrate women—and the goddess and queen within. These are items you won't find anywhere else!
(800) 996-9223
www.femailcreations.com

OM GIRL SHIRT FROM BAREFOOT YOGA CO.
Beautiful, hip, spiritual shirts with lotus, namaste, om and other rhinestone-studded spiritual symbols mentioned in the book.
3785 Balboa Street
San Francisco, CA 94121
(877) barefoot (227-3366)
www.barefootyoga.com

WORLD LIGHT FELLOWSHIP
High Vibrational Oils and Candle Oils that carry the divine essence of many gods and goddesses, including Isis, Lakshmi, Kali, Mary, Mary Magdalene, St. Brigid, St. Theresa, and White Buffalo Calf Woman. Recommended for healing, meditation and ceremonies.
P.O. Box 425
Wappingers Falls, NY 12590
(845) 297-2867
www.worldlightfellowship.org

eBAY
Online source for sacred objects, art, books and stuff from all traditions.
www.ebay.com

Sources for More Information On Goddesses:

Return of the Great Goddess, edited by Burleigh Muten (Stewart, Tabori & Chang, 1997).
  Art and inspiration/poems/ponderings about the feminine divine.

When the Drummers Were Women, by Layne Redmond (Three Rivers Press, 1998).
  Terrific history of Goddess worship via tracing ritual, drumming and gathering in community.

The Alphabet vs. the Goddess: The Conflict Between Word and Image, by Leonard Shlain, M.D. (Viking, 1998).
  Fascinating assertion and history of how the goddess was lost to left brain thinking.

When God Was a Woman by Merlin Stone (Harcourt-Brace, 1976).
  Classic ancient history text.

Men and the Goddesses: Feminine Archetypes in Western Literature, by Tom Absher (Park Street Press, 1990).
Interesting look at how Westerners view the sacred feminine.

The Myth of the Goddess, Evolution of an Image, by Anne Baring and Jules Cashford (Viking, 1991).
Compendium of goddess history that is delightfully comprehensive.

The Goddesses in Art, by Lanier Graham (Artebras, 1997).
A beautiful collection of Goddesses in art.

The New Book of Goddesses and Heroines, by Patricia Monaghan (Llewellyn Publications, 1997.)
Who's who in the world of the sacred feminine.

The Goddess: From Natura to Divine Sophia, by Rudolph Steiner (Rudolph Steiner Press, reissued April 2002).

Introducing A Practical Feminist Theology for Worship, by Janet Wootton (Pilgrim Press, 2000).

Encyclopedia of GODS—Over 2,500 Deities of the World, by Michael Jordon (Facts on File, 1993).
Who's who in all pantheons—half of the gods are goddesses!

Interfaith Roundup of the Divine Feminine:

An Anthology of Sacred Texts by and About Women, edited by Serenity Young (Crossroads Press, 1993).
Amazing collection of journalings, musing, sacred writings, speeches, reports.

Listen To Her: Women of the Hebrew Bible, by Miki Raver (Chronicle Books, 1998).
Brings the Goddess alive through the stories of the first females.

She Who Dwells Within: A Feminist Revision of Renewed Judaism, by Lynn Gottlieb (HarperCollins, 1995).
Shekinah and the sacred feminine in the Hebrew tradition.

The Devi Gita: The Song of the Goddess, Translation, annotation, commentary by C. Mackenzie Brown (SUNY Press, 1998).
Original sacred text of Hindu workshop of the great mother.

Devi: Goddesses of India by John Stratton Hawley and Donna
  Marie Wolf (University of California Press, 1996).
  In-depth study of Hindu goddesses.

The Goddesses' Mirror: Visions of the Divine from East and West,
  by David Kinsley (State University of New York Press, 1989).
  Excellent roundup of goddesses of many traditions.

*The Living Goddess: Reclaiming the Tradition of the Mother of the
  Universe,* by Linda Johnsen (Yes International Publishers, 1999).
  *The daily worship of the mother comes to life here in a way that
  Westerners can understand.*

Specific Goddesses and Discovering the Goddess Within:

The Book of Goddesses, by Chris Waldherr (Beyond Words Publishing, 1995).
  Beautiful picture book with brief bios on twenty-six goddesses.

*365 Goddesses: A Daily Guide to the Magic and Inspiration of the
  Goddess,* by Patricia Telesco (HarperSanFrancisco, 1998).
  *A goddess, her history/mythology and a ritual for each day of the
  year.*

The Mysteries of Isis: Her Worship and Magick, by Traci de Regula
  (Llewellyn Publications, 1995).
  The ultimate book about one of the most famous Goddesses.

Isis and Osiris: Exploring The Goddess Myth, by Jonathan Cott
  (Doubleday Books, 1994).
  *Extraordinary chronicle of active worship of Isis today, edited by
  Jackie Onassis (out of print).*

The Gospel of Mary Magdalene, by Jean-Yves Leloup (Inner Tradi-
  tions/Bear & Company, 2002).
  *First English language version of the little-known Gospel of
  Mary.*

My Name Is Mary: The Story of The Mother of Jesus, by Denise
  Sawyer (Still Waters Publishers, 2002).
  Interesting interpretation of Mary's story.

The Goddess of Fifth Avenue, by Carol Simone (Dayden Books, 2001).
A modern woman's experience with Kuan Yin.

The Goddess Path: Myths, Invocations and Rituals, by Patricia Monaghan (Llewellyn 1999).
Primer on stepping onto the path.

Conversations With Goddesses: Revealing the Divine Power Within You, by Agapi Stassinopoulos (Stewart, Tabori & Chang).
Greek Goddess in everyday life.

Ritual Work and the Art of Gathering With Others:

The Joy of Everyday Ritual, by Barbara Biziou (Golden Books/St. Martin's Press, 1999).
Best ritual book on the market for people of all faiths, paths and level of experience.

The Art of Ritual: Guide To Creating/Performing Your Own Ceremonies for Growth/Change, by Renee Beck and Sydney Barbara Metrick (Celestial Arts, 1990).

Calling The Circle: The First and Future Culture, by Christina Baldwin (Bantam Books, 1994).

The Spiral Dance: A Rebirth of the Ancient Religion of The Goddess, by Starhawk (HarperCollins, 20th anniversary edition, 1999).
A great primer on the religious worship of the goddess.

Women's Spirituality:

Sacred Circles: A Guide to Creating Your Own Women's Spirituality Group, by Robin Deen Carnes and Sally Craig (HarperSanFrancisco, 1998).
Best book on the market to support the spiritual gathering of women in many contacts outside of religion.

The Feminine Face of God: The Unfolding of the Sacred in Women, by Sherry Ruth Anderson and Patricia Hopkins (Bantam Trade, 1991).

A compelling look at how women evolve their spiritual lives and needs.

Sacred Voices, by Mary Ford-Grabowsky (HarperSan Francisco, March 2002).
A fabulous roundup of prayers and sacred readings by and for women.

The Witch in Every Woman: Reawakening the Magical Nature of the Feminine to Heal, Create, Empower, by Laurie Cabot, with Jean Mill (Delta Trade Paperbacks, a division of Bantam Doubleday Dell Publishing, 1997).
Modern insights, practical expressions of ancient earth religions.

Special Tools To Help You Learn More:

The Goddess Oracle: A Way to Wholeness Through the Goddess and Ritual, by Amy Sophia Marashinsky, illustrated by Hrana Janto (Element Books, 1997).
A wonderfully colorful, informative and fun divination deck of cards with beautiful art and accompanying book on goddesses of all traditions and how they can empower you and help in your life.

Resource for Nondenominational Priestess Training:
The Crossroads Lyceum
Crossroads Lyceum is a home-study center and modern-day mystery school within the Fellowship of Isis. They offer a complete range of correspondence courses for personal and spiritual growth and Priesthood training. As the Fellowship of Isis honors the *Goddess of Ten-Thousand Names,* this Lyceum honors all pantheons and goddesses equally.
P.O. Box 19152
Tucson, AZ 85731
E-mail: CRLyceum@aol.com

Resource for simple teachings in Wicca:
A retired High Priestess teaches the tenets of WICCA and the history of the goddess. *An affordable eight-week course.*
Rhiannon
208 11 D. Bear Valley Road, Suite 148
Apple Valley, CA 92308

INDEX